Essays on Kant's
Critique of Pure Reason

Essays on Kant's Critique of Pure Reason

Edited by
J. N. Mohanty and Robert W. Shahan

The King's Library

University of Oklahoma Press • Norman

Also edited by Robert W. Shahan

(With Francis J. Kovach) *Bonaventure and Aquinas: Enduring Philosophers* (Norman, 1976)
(With Kenneth R. Merrill) *American Philosophy: From Edwards to Quine* (Norman, 1977)
(With J. I. Biro) *Spinoza: New Perspectives* (Norman, 1978)
(With Chris Swoyer) *Essays on the Philosophy of W. V. Quine* (Norman, 1979)
(With J. I. Biro) *Mind, Brain, and Function: Essays in the Philosophy of Mind* (Norman, 1982)
(With J. N. Mohanty) *Essays on Kant's* Critique of Pure Reason (Norman, 1982)

Library of Congress Cataloging in Publication Data

Main entry under title:

Essays on Kant's Critique of pure reason.

Papers reprinted from Philosophical topics, v. 12, no. 2.
Includes bibliographical references and index.
1. Kant, Immanuel, 1724–1804. Kritik der reinen Vernunft—Addresses, essays, lectures. 2. Knowledge, Theory of—Addresses, essays, lectures. 3. Causation—Addresses, essays, lectures. 4. Reason—Addresses, essays, lectures. I. Mohanty, Jitendranath, 1928–   . II. Shahan, Robert W., 1935–   .
B2779.E64   1982   121'.092'4   81–40295

Contents

Preface 7

1. *Intentional Objects and Kantian Appearances*
   Richard E. Aquila 9

2. *Reduction-Realization: A Key to the Structure
   of Kant's Thought*
   Gerd Buchdahl 39

3. *Kant's Notion of Transcendental Presupposition
   in the First* Critique
   A. C. Genova 99

4. *What Kant Really Did to Idealism*
   Moltke S. Gram 127

5. *Kant's Tactics in the Transcendental Deduction*
   Paul Guyer 157

6. *Kant's Theory of Mathematics Revisited*
   Jaakko Hintikka 201

7. *How Kant Almost Wrote "Two Dogmas of Empiricism"*
   Philip Kitcher 217

8. *Two Kinds of Transcendental Objectivity:
   Their Differentiation*
   Charles M. Sherover 251

Notes on Contributors 279

Index 281

Preface

These essays on Kant's *Critique of Pure Reason* have been put together during the bicentenary of the publication of that epoch-making work. Since 1781, when the first *Critique* appeared, western philosophy has never recovered from its influence. It inaugurated a new mode of philosophizing, a new style of argumentation, a new way of relating philosophy to the sciences, and a new understanding of the nature and limits of human reason. In our own century, both the logical positivists and the phenomenologists —the former in their anti–metaphysical crusades and the latter in their concern for the world–constituting role of the human subjectivity—have returned to the *Critique* for their inspiration. Between these two extremes a whole gamut of philosophical positions—intuitionism in philosophy of mathematics, Heideggerean *Daseins–Analytik*, the Copenhagen interpretation of quantum mechanics, the concern with the role of conceptual frameworks in human knowledge, voluntaristic psychologies (through the lineage of Fichte and Schopenhauer), and Hegelian dialectic (as also its Materialist transformation)—all trace their insights to some text or other in the *Critique*.

But what has, all along, proved both irresistible and intractable are the Kantian texts themselves. While there are Kant interpretations galore, most—in fact, all of them—founder on the Kantian texts themselves. If one discerning reader said that reading the *Critique* is like entering a well–illuminated room, others have found in Kantian texts inpenetrable darkness or the hazards of crossing the great Arabian desert.

By and large, the essays in this volume get down to the task of exegesis of Kant's texts. The concepts of 'intuition', 'appearance' and 'transcendental object' come in for detailed scrutiny, and in some cases a new way of understanding those concepts emerges. This is especially true of the intriguing notion of 'transcendental object'. Charles Sherover's long textual analysis and Gerd Buchdahl's large interpretive framework throw new light on a concept whose ambiguities and difficulties have baffled generations of Kant scholars. Anthony Genova ably handles a more recent interest, that in 'transcendental *arguments*', while Moltke Gram (who, in several earlier papers, argued that there are no specifically transcendental modes of argument) identifies the stages through which Kant's refutation of idealism developed. After showing where Kant and Quine agree and disagree on the problem of a priori knowledge, Philip Kitcher proceeds to sketch an account of Kant's theory of mathematical *knowledge*. Citing both the appropriate texts and Kant's historical background, Jaakko Hintikka defends his well–known interpretation of the Kantian theory of mathematical method against critics of that interpretation. At least three of the essays (those by Sherover, Buchdahl, and Aquila) underscore the relevance of certain notions in phenomenology for the understanding of Kant. Sherover exploits the contrast between intentional object and real object, while Buchdahl uses the strategy of reduction and realization. Aquila presents a carefully analytic study of the place of intentionality in Kant's theory of perception. In Aquila's view, the Kantian 'appearance' is best understood as a Brentanian 'intentional object'. Paul Guyer undertakes a detailed analysis of Kant's arguments in the Transcendental Deduction. After carefully isolating Kant's various strategies, Guyer tries to show why at most one of the strategies has any prospect of success.

The editors hope that these essays will stimulate Kantian studies and thereby help contemporary philosophy to trace its "origins" to the first *Critique*.

Intentional Objects and Kantian Appearances

RICHARD E. AQUILA
University of Tennessee

I

Fairly obviously, Kant's epistemology raises questions concerning the intentionality, or the "object-directed" character, of perception. It is, as one might therefore expect, fruitful to consider Kant's views in comparison with some of those of Franz Brentano. This, it turns out, is no mere exegetical device, for it is not unreasonable to suggest that precisely the originality of Kant's approach to perceptual awareness lies in his anticipation of a point of view characteristic of the later thinker.

Brentano's thesis, for the purpose of this discussion, does not involve his claim that all psychological states are intrinsically object-directed.[1] Kant in fact appears to reject that claim, for he appears to share with Husserl the view that mere "sensations" constitute an exception to it.[2] The relevant Brentanian thesis may be stated by restricting our attention to those sensory states which, in the opinion of all parties, *are* object-directed, namely, ordinary perceptions, or Kantian (empirical) intuitions (as opposed to the mere "sensations" ingredient in those intuitions). The thesis concerns a particular *sense* in which each such state is, in its intrinsic character, an object-directed state. Each, namely, is object-directed in a way that is logically independent of the ascription of ontological *status* to any object of that state.[3]

The "intentionality," in other words, to which Brentano directs our attention is not simply the property of psychological object-directedness; it is a certain *sort* of psychological object-directedness. It is Brentano's claim that this sort is a precondition for all others. These other sorts of object-directedness would be those which are sometimes said to involve psychological attitudes *"de re"*—as, for example, when, of some really existing thing, I am said to obtain a perception of *it*, or to have some desire regarding *it*. Judgments concerning these sorts of states involve, on Brentano's view, some sort of "identification" of the thing in question with the object of an intentional "relation" which is not of the *de re* sort at all (and which thus, indeed, is not really a relation). They involve identifying a real entity with some thought-about entity.[4] That, of course, implies that the real entity is also a thought-about one, but insofar as my judgment identifies the real entity with some thought-about one that *might not have been* a real one, then I must also be considering some "thought-about entity" not already supposed to be real. In all this, of course, we are not speaking of what we ordinarily think of as "identity." We are not, for example, considering a case in which one entity is identified as satisfying two distinct descriptions. Rather, we are considering a case in which an intentional object (which, so far considered, is not an entity at all) is identified with (or as) some entity.[5]

On Brentano's view, then, it is only the kind of psychological reference that is neutral with respect to the possibility of regarding its object as real that is the "intentionality" characteristic of psychological phenomena. And the relevant thesis, with respect to perception at least, is, then, that all instances of perceptual object-directedness presuppose that the states in question are, intrinsically considered, intentional in this sense.

Now what is important, with respect to this thesis, is that its formulation requires recognition of the following point. It is a point that Brentano himself took pains to emphasize. It is also a point, I would suggest, recognition of which constituted one of Kant's own achievements in the theory of perception. Consider a case in which someone is thinking about some flowers (whether *de re* or not). Brentano points out, then, that the relevant "state" of psychological activity in this case is not the relational (or apparently relational) *state of affairs* of thinking about flowers on this occasion. It is, rather, something of which "being about flowers" is merely one of the *properties*:

> When we said that the relation to something as object is the most characteristic property of psychological activity, this should not be so interpreted as if precisely the same thing is to be understood by "psychological activity" and "reference to something as object."[6]

The reason he gives is that one and the same psychological activity might possess more than one *sort* of object-directedness. Thus (although this is not Brentano's example) the same state which is, intrinsically, an "intentional" state might also be, in virtue of certain extrinsic relations, a state of psychological directedness *de re*, and any state of the latter sort must, in any case, be of the former as well.

In perception, for example, a necessary condition for a perception's being, *de re*, a perception of some particular thing, is that this very perception also be, considered quite *apart* from any *res* beside itself, an object-directed state.

It may in fact be the case that the tendency of some critics to give too metaphysically literal an interpretation to Brentano's claims about intentional "inexistence"[7] stems precisely from neglecting this point. If, one might ask, "the" object of a *de re* attitude is something real, then what is "inexisting" about it? It could not, one might argue, be that the object in question *might have failed* to be real, without any prejudice to the identity of the state in question. For the object of *that* sort of state could not possibly fail to be real. So the object must "inexist," one might conclude, in some metaphysical realm of peculiarly mental being, over and above that of its real being. Brentano's distinction, however, allows one to maintain that *the very same state*, intrinsically considered, might indeed retain its identity, despite the loss of the extrinsic context essential to its constituting an awareness *de re*. So considered, then, its object may be said to be an "inexisting" one simply in the metaphysically harmless sense that occurrence of this instance of directedness *to* that object is neutral with respect to the latter's ontological status. It might or might not be something that there is (in anything more than the sense that there is *awareness* of it).

Another preliminary point: Suppose someone grants that one might "see" a bunch of flowers on an occasion, even if there really are no flowers that one sees. This is still compatible with denying Brentano's thesis. Suppose that a necessary condition for seeing a bunch of flowers is the apprehension of a "sense datum" of some sort and, further, that a condition of the latter is that the sense datum in question really *exists*. Then while the apprehension of the flowers is indeed independent of the being of any *flowers*, still the total state of flower apprehension is nonetheless directed in an essential way to certain objects, from the being of which that state is *not* independent. Brentano's thesis is presumably intended to rule this out.

This point, it should also be clear, is independent of any willingness of the sense-datum philosopher to grant that sense data are real only while actually *apprehended* and hence are not real beings "independent" of consciousness. What one thereby fails to maintain is that a sense datum, while it is the object of consciousness, is real only *in the sense that* it is apprehended by consciousness. Were the latter claim in question, then one could not

11

regard the apprehension of a sense datum as any sort of relation between a mental state and some object that *is* in fact a sense datum.

This comment should help us see why, for example, Berkeley denies Brentano's thesis, though he does not regard the immediate objects of perception as anything other than mentally "inexisting" *ideas*. On the other hand, Berkeley does seem to lack a certain consistency:

> . . . when I speak of objects as existing in the mind or imprinted on the senses, I would not be understood in the gross literal sense, as when bodies are said to exist in a place, or a seal to make an impression upon wax. My *meaning* is only that the mind comprehends or perceives them; and that it is affected from without, or by some being distinct from itself.[8]

Now one might ask what other sense there *could* possibly be in which, e.g., shapes and colors might exist "in the mind" yet *without* the mind literally containing shape or color. There is, it seems to me, only one such sense available to Berkeley, short of denying that "ideas" are real beings altogether. Perceptual states, namely, are precisely what Brentano denied they are. They are certain sorts of relational *states of affairs*.[9] The expression "in the mind" is, in other words, an ambiguous one. It might mean what is literally contained in mental "substance," and then Berkeley is simply saying that ideas are not in the mind. Or it might mean what is literally contained in mental *states*, and in this sense it seems that ideas are in the mind (assuming, that is, the legitimacy of describing the constituents of a state of afairs as "contained" in that state of affairs).

It is not unreasonable, I think, to suggest that Kant was virtually alone in refusing to choose between the following two alternatives: Either a sensory state is not, intrinsically, object-directed at all (like Kantian "sensations"), or else it is merely a relational state of affairs of some sort, one of whose *terms* is the "proper" or "immediate" object of the state in question. Rather, a sensory state, insofar as it is an object-directed state, is more like a *particular* of some sort, where one of that particular's properties is simply that of directedness to the object in question. This view, unlike the other, leaves room for the possibility that the object in question has no existence at all (apart, that is, from its existing in the sense that there is an apprehension *of* it).

One way to bring out the force of Kant's insight is to contrast his conception with some standard empiricist conceptions of the "receptive" nature of sense perception. Locke, Berkeley, and

Hume, one might say, regard sense perception as the reception of some perceptual *object*. Sense perception is receptive because it is the means whereby we "receive" into our perceptual faculties the objects of immediate sensory awareness. Of course, one could not literally receive physical objects into one's perceptual faculties, but then it is only sensory *qualities* (i.e., "ideas" or "impressions") that are the immediate objects of perception for these thinkers. In addition, as we have seen, reception of sensory qualities into the faculties of the perceiver need not in any case imply literal *containment* of those qualities in the perceiver. It might only imply, as in Berkeley's case, their containment as constituents of the "state" (or, *pace* Berkeley, the "act") of perception itself. In the case of Hume, on the other hand, for whom the mind is indeed but a "bundle" among whose constituents are numbered all the qualities that one apprehends by sense, containment of a sensory quality within a perceptual state is *tantamount* to its containment within the perceiving "mind" itself.

For Kant, by contrast, sense perception is "receptive" only in a purely *causal* sense. Apprehension (*de re*) of some material object is dependent upon a causal relation in which we stand to that object: the object needs to place the perceiver in an "internal state" of the appropriate sort. That state, we might say, is one that the perceiver has "received" from outside. This would be to speak loosely, however. In any case, no perceptual *object* is thereby regarded as received. What is "received" is simply the internal state. Whether any perceptual object is in question, and how indeed that object may be described (at least phenomenologically), is a matter of the intrinsic *nature* of the state thereby "received." Unless that state, in its intrinsic nature, is of a certain sort (or possesses the appropriate "form"), then no object at all will be in question, from a phenomenological point of view; and unless an object is in question from a phenomenological point of view, no perceptual object *at all* will be in question. We will be dealing with at most a causal, not a properly perceptual, relation.

Kant's situation with respect to his rationalistic predecessors is not, of course, quite the same as that to the empiricists. In the case at least of Leibniz and Spinoza, however, one point remains unaltered. Sensory awareness is an inherently *relational* state of affairs, and one term of the relation in question is precisely the perceptual object itself. This is assured by Spinoza's insistence that a sensory "idea" is indeed in some sense *identical* with its material object.[10] It is also assured by Leibniz's tendency to regard the infinitely complex manifold of causal relations in which we stand to other entities (or rather the complex of quasi-relational "mirroring" situations corresponding to our somewhat confused judgments *concerning* such relations) as an infinitely complex *perceptual state.*[11] For Kant, by contrast, a manifold of causal relations is never as such constitutive of a perceptual state; what is crucial is the intrinsic "form" of the internal state *generated* by those relations. This, I suggest, is the insight embodied in the following statement:

> . . . for the various things in an object which affect the senses to coalesce into some representational whole there is needed some internal principle in the mind by which those various things may be clothed with a certain *species* in accordance with stable and innate laws.[12]

Or by this: "While the matter of all appearance is given to us *a posteriori* only, its form must lie ready for them *a priori* in the mind" (A20/B34).[13] These assertions, combined with Kant's equation of the "forms" of intuition with the forms of spatiotemporal representation, have appeared to some to imply the absurd doctrine that variations in sensory stimulation might affect, for example, the colors that one sees on some occasion, but not the visual shape or size of the object; variations in the latter indicate not the effect of an object on a perceiver but some element added *by* the perceiver *to* that effect. There is no reason to attribute this absurd doctrine to Kant. It is more reasonable to suppose Kant's view simply to be this: that a "sensation" (i.e., sensory stimulation) by itself never amounts as such to the occurrence of a perceptual state. What is essential, rather, is the intrinsic nature of the state thereby produced within the perceiver. It is a matter of the intrinsic nature or "form" of the latter whether anything at all is perceived (and also *what*, phenomenologically, is in fact perceived). There is no absurdity, of course, in supposing that the representation of spatiotemporal forms is essential in this regard and that the representation of any further specific "sensory qualities" is merely a contingent matter of fact concerning the *way* in which we happen to have evolved to apprehend such forms.

With respect to Descartes, finally, one might simply note an ambiguity in his own thinking. On the one hand, he appears inclined to regard the "reception" of sensations as the reception into the mind of certain perceptual *objects* (colors, odors, etc.).[14] On the other hand, he denies that sensation as such involves the "objective" (i.e., intentional) presence of any object at all. The latter requires the presence of judgment and corresponding *intellectual* ideas.[15] In fact, Descartes's view is perhaps a combination of these two points. In virtue of a (generally "confused") judgment *accompanying*, and in some way causally stimulated by, nonreferential sensations, we come to be in a total state that *is* referential, and part of the *object* of which is precisely those sensations. Here more than one anti-Kantian point emerges. First, the apprehension of sensory quality is by its intrinsic nature the apprehension of an ontological constituent *of* that very apprehension, namely a sensation. Second, any properly referential or intentional aspect ingredient in perception must be a matter of some thought or judgment merely *accompanying*, and at most causally stimulated by, the internal states that one happens to "receive" *via* physical stimulation. On Kant's view, as I have suggested, it is rather a matter of the internal form *of* the very state in question (together, as I shall suggest in section III, with additional conceptual "enrichment" of that form).

II

What we need to focus on now is Kant's view that the objects of sensory awareness (i.e., of empirical "intuitions" in the primary sense of the term) are, as such, mere "appearances." The interpretation which would, of course, assimilate Kant's to Brentano's view would regard appearances as merely "intentional objects." One thing, at least, that this would mean is that assigning such objects to intuitions does not, of itself, carry any ontological *commitment* with respect to such objects. One alternative to this would be the "sense-datum" approach: Appearances are entities in their own right, distinct both from the apprehension of them (though perhaps, nonetheless, in some sense "subjective") and from whatever realities might be appearing *through* them (awareness of ordinary material objects would then, of course, be, in accordance with Kant's Transcendental Idealism, the product of some sort of *synthesis* of the items in question). A second alternative (which we might call the "double-aspect" approach) regards the notion of an "appearance" as a misleadingly substantival device for talking about the fact that a thing appears to us in various *ways*. This thing, presumably, may also be considered to be something "in itself," apart from the ways in which it appears to us. In any case, the thing does not (perhaps, indeed, by definition) appear to us *as* it is "in itself." It appears as an "appearance." Furthermore, on the approach in question, the only legitimate notion of

15

"object-directedness" in perception is the notion of perceptual directedness precisely *to* such objects.

The issue is complicated by the fact that Kant himself speaks of *Erscheinungen* in at least two different ways. In one sense the term applies to real material objects and hence neither to sense data nor to merely *intentional* (e.g., merely imagined or hallucinated) material objects. Let us call these "objective" appearances. Thus this piece of paper would be an objective appearance. In another sense, however, Kant seems to regard the concept of a real material object as explicable in terms of that of the synthesis of a certain *manifold* of appearances. Here "appearances" could not, of course, be such things as pieces of paper, or at least they could not be such things considered as "objectively real." In addition, Kant regards mere imagination, and even hallucination, as instances of empirical intuition.[16] The "appearances" that are the *objects* of such states are presumably not, as such, material realities. They might, of course, be sense data. Or they might be Brentanian intentional objects. Or they too might even be the ways in which "things in themselves" *appear* to us (in that case the piece of paper, which may be a way in which "things" appear to us, would itself be a synthesis of a whole *manifold* of ways in which things appear to us). Whatever they are, let us call them "phenomenological" appearances. One point to be made, then, is this. It is perfectly compatible with maintaining that objective appearances are, essentially, the ways in which certain things appear to us, to hold in addition that *phenomenological* appearances are either sense data or merely intentional objects (or perhaps something to be treated in a third way altogether).

Apparently those who have recently defended the double-aspect approach to Kant as opposed to the sense-datum approach, or at least have distinguished the two, have meant so to regard the former that it is *incompatible* with the sense-datum approach to phenomenological appearances.[17] These writers rest their case for the double-aspect reading on those passages in which Kant describes appearances as the ways in which things (which are also something "in themselves") *appear* to us, or as indeed *being* those very things, as they appear to us (e.g., Bxxvi–xxvii, B69, A251–252). Unfortunately, none of the passages seems to contain any evidence that Kant is speaking of appearances *simpliciter*, and not just of objective appearances, and it seems perfectly reasonable to suppose that he is in fact speaking only of the latter.

It might, of course, be thought that if objective appearances are indeed mere "ways in which" certain things appear to us, and are in addition somehow "synthesized" out of merely phenomenological appearances, then the latter could not possibly be construed as "sense data." For a sense datum, presumably, is an entity of some sort, not merely a way in which something appears to us. At most, it is an entity that stands in a causal *relation* with things that appear to us, i.e., with those things that appear *through* them. How then could the whole be viewed as a "way in which" something appears, when none of its parts is? At least in a somewhat loose sense, however, sense data might, of course, be described as the ways in which something appears, even if they are, strictly speaking, merely causal *effects* of the thing in question. By the same token they might even be said to *be* that thing *as* it appears. What then might be considered a reasonable basis for denying the sense-datum approach to phenomenological appearances is not in fact such. On the other hand, once having distinguished the sense-datum from the *intentional-object* approach, at least one of the primary motivations on behalf of the former does in fact disappear. This motivation derives from Kant's preference in a number of passages for what has been called (following Ayer) the "language of appearances" versus the "language of appearing."[18] In these passages Kant does not treat phenomenological appearances merely as ways in which objects appear to us. Rather he treats them as being objects of sensory awareness in their own right. This preference, however, no more points to the sense-datum approach than it does to an intentional-object approach.[19]

There is a second reason that might be offered for favoring the sense-datum approach. This concerns a number of passages in which Kant appears to regard phenomenological appearances as merely a manifold of our own *sensations* structured by (at least in outer appearances) spatial form. The apparent force of at least some of these passages is, as it turns out, an artifact of translation.[20] Apart from doubts concerning translation, however, Kant's tendency to speak of *Empfindung* as an aspect of perceptual objects, and not just of our perceptions *of* them, may be explained without attributing a form of the sense-datum theory to him. First of all, we should note, Kant uses the general term 'representation' (*Vorstellung*) in a twofold way. In its primary use it stands for those of our psychological states, or aspects of them, by means of which we become aware of and form judgments regarding objects (A320/B376–77). In a secondary sense, however, the term may be used precisely with respect to the *objects* in question. At least part of the point of using the term in this way is of course that such objects are to be considered precisely *as* objects or referents of *Vorstellungen* in the primary sense. Thus, in this secondary usage, Kant describes nature itself as a system of "representations" (A114). Similarly, with respect to *Anschauung*, Kant uses the term in question both for a certain mode of awareness (e.g., for our awareness, empirically, of bodies and of spatial forms in perception as well as, in "pure" intuition, for our awareness of the space and time in which we locate such objects) and also with respect to space and time themselves as *objects* of awareness (A24/B39). This latter, presumably, is a secondary use of the term. Similarly, we might then suppose, Kant uses the term 'sensation' (which is also a form of "representation": A320/B376) in a twofold way. In one usage it stands for an ingredient in perceptual states. In a secondary sense, however, it signifies some aspect of perceptual objects corresponding *to* that ingredient, namely, that aspect whose representation is a function of the presence of that ingredient *in* a perceptual state.

It might be argued, of course, that, while phenomenological appearances are not indeed sensations, in the primary sense, spatially organized, nevertheless they are still similar to what some philosophers have called "sense data," i.e., entities immediately apprehended in sense perception. There can be no internal motivation for such an interpretation, however, for the only reasons for regarding phenomenological appearances as *entities* are (1) Kant's sometime preference for the "language of appearances" and (2) his apparent description of them as "sensations" spatially organized. I have already responded to (1). With respect to (2) we simply need observe that it could constitute a ground for regarding phenomenological appearances as genuine entities only in case we are considering sensations in the primary sense of that term. It is only in that sense that there is reason to suppose that sensations are *themselves* genuine entities. With respect to the use of that term in its secondary sense, on the other hand, no reason has been offered why we should not suppose "sensations" to be merely intentional objects or aspects of such.[21]

Now it may or may not be reasonable, as I have already suggested, for a philosopher to describe such entities as sense data, which are strictly distinct from the objects that appear through them, as nonetheless *being* those objects (*as* they appear through them). It is not at all unreasonable, I think, so to describe appearances when they are regarded as merely intentional objects. Suppose that Kant in fact regarded phenomenological appearances (at least in those instances in which they are part of the manifold constituting some objective appearance) as the effect of certain things in themselves that are said to appear through them. That is, to speak a little more strictly, suppose he regarded the instances of *apprehending* those appearances as standing in the causal relation in question (the appearances themselves, after all, *qua* merely "subjective," would not be genuine entities, and hence they could neither stand nor fail to stand in some real causal relation). In that case, then, it would not be unreasonable for Kant to describe such appearances as *being* the very thing that appears through them (*as that thing appears*). Certainly, at least, we would no longer be prey, in this case, to the compunction against so speaking that we might have had on the sense-datum approach. For the misgiving in the latter case seems to rest on the fact that appearances are literally different *entities* from the things that appear through them. In the present case, however, they would not be entities at all. Kant's choice of terminology may in fact reflect precisely his desire to emphasize this point. In *some* sense, certainly, phenomenological appearances would still be the "ways in which" things appear to us, and the step from here to describing them not simply as the *ways* in which things appear but as those things *as* they appear would seem a perfectly natural one, given Kant's desire precisely to avoid suggesting that the ways in which entities appear to us are *themselves* entities that need to be countenanced in our ontology. As we have already seen, Brentano himself did not hesitate to speak of the "identification" of a merely intentional object *qua* intentional, which is not as such an "entity" at all, with some entity existing in itself.

III

So far, then:

1. Kant's descriptions of the objects of intuition as the way things that are also something "in themselves" appear (or as those things *as* they appear) is compatible with an intentional-object approach to perception. Kant, so speaking, would simply be expressing his conviction that the apprehension of appearances is somehow grounded in the existence of entities that are also something, perhaps inconceivable to us, "in themselves." This conviction is, of course, compatible with holding that, *intrinsically considered*, the apprehension in question is intentional in the primary Brentanian sense. That is, my "identification" of the appearance that is its object with something that appears *through* it involves the "identification" with such a thing of a merely *intentional* object.

2. Contrary to what is often supposed, a sense-datum approach is also compatible with the description in question, but it is, from a textual point of view if none other, considerably less plausible than an intentional-object approach.

There is one alternative that we have not yet taken into account. I shall call it the "comparative" approach. Consider the seeing of a red spot, considered merely phenomenologically (considered, that is, so as to remain neutral with respect to the real existence of anything that one might in fact be seeing). The comparative approach does not regard the classification of that occurrence in question as introducing a relationship between the occurrence and some peculiar object. Rather, it introduces a mere *comparison* of some sort. It introduces a comparison between that occurrence and instances that *would* involve a relationship, were such to occur, with ordinary material objects. Thus one form of the comparative approach would regard the classification in question as a case in which we simply regard the classified occurrence as bearing certain *similarity* relations to standard cases in which a red, roughly circular surface is apprehended. On this approach, in other words, the "intentionality" of phenomenological apprehension is derivative from that of "objective" apprehension.

One might also note that the comparative approach fits nicely with the double-aspect approach to appearances and "things in themselves." On the comparative view, talk about phenomenological appearances is neither talk about peculiar entities such as sense data or externalized sensations nor talk about perceptual states that are, intrinsically considered, "object-directed" in Brentano's sense. Perhaps, indeed, neither can we say that such appearances are always the "ways in which" certain things appear to us, for that might fail to allow for some kinds of hallucinations. Nonetheless, phenomenological appearances might be regarded as the ways in which certain things appear to us in the sense that their "apprehension" would be defined as nothing other than our coming to be in states that are *comparable* to those that we would find ourselves in were we *not*, e.g., hallucinating but instead apprehending some objectively real thing. To speak of the "appearances" involved in the apprehension of some real table or chair could only be, on the view in question, to acknowledge that the table or chair is *appearing* to us in a certain way. If any question remains, then, concerning "things in themselves," it would seem most natural for the proponent of the comparative approach to suppose that this signifies only Kant's desire to indicate a distinction between tables or chairs as they appear to us and whatever such entities might be in complete (and hence to us perhaps inconceivable) abstraction from the ways in which they appear to us (I leave out of consideration here any things that might be something "in themselves" yet do not appear at all). On the comparative approach, in other words, both "phenomenological" and "objective" appearances might naturally be viewed as the "ways in which" things appear to us, that they might also be considered as something *apart* from those ways. The only difference would be that the "apprehension" of the former would be wholly defined by comparison with instances of the apprehension of objective appearances, whereas the notion of apprehending the latter is not itself to be defined by means of any further comparison. That it is not to be defined in further comparative terms is, of course, perfectly compatible with supposing that what is thereby apprehended is also something possessing an identity "in itself."

Now one might suppose that, on the comparative approach, phenomenological appearances are in fact being regarded precisely as Brentanian intentional objects. Certainly, at least, they are not being identified with any *actual* objects. I think it is clear, however, that Brentano himself would have disagreed with the supposition in question. Clearly, when we *classify* a psychological occurrence as similar, in certain respects, to the merely hypothetical apprehension of a certain sort of object, then *that* object might be regarded as a merely intentional object. The question, of course, remains whether the subject who is *experiencing* the state (but without in fact classifying it) could be described as experiencing a state that is intentional in Brentano's sense. There is no doubt, I think, that Brentano himself would insist that the latter description is applicable to that subject only when we have already specified that the respect in which the present occurrence is "similar" to certain standard cases is that, *like* them, it involves (for example) phenomenological apprehension of a red spot. But that, presumably, is just what the comparative approach is trying to avoid, for considered *intrinsically*, on that approach, a sensory state cannot be regarded as "object-directed" at all.

Two things Brentano says indicate that this would indeed be his response. According to Brentano, first, an awareness of the intentional directedness of a psychological occurrence is *in every instance included* as part of the intrinsic character of that occurrence. This, on Brentano's view, is part of the self-referential nature of any psychological occurrence.[22] But there is no reason at all, of course, why the self-directedness of an occurrence should be expected to include an apprehension of its merely external relations. Second, *the very same state* to which one ascribes at least phenomenological intentionality in this case (and to which the comparative view ascribes at least a kind of *comparative* "intentionality") might also (and indeed *must*, on Brentano's view), include an intentionality of a *judgmental* sort.[23] Yet the very reason that the comparative approach ascribes a merely *comparative* "intentionality" to the states in question is presumably that they are thought be, intrinsically, states of too primitive a sort to be possessed of any *other* sort of intentionality (as opposed, e.g., to conceptual states). Brentano clearly regards the states in question as more sophisticated than that, and so, I would suggest, does Kant.

Now, to be sure, the comparative approach might also acknowledge the existence of a *complex* sort of phenomenological apprehension that is not merely comparative. This would be a complex consisting partly of the more unsophisticated sort of occurrence and partly of thoughts, beliefs, or judgments (perhaps in some causal connection with the former). The latter would presumably possess an intentionality of a noncomparative sort. They, however, unlike the former, would not be intrinsically *sensory* states. The complex generated out of their conjunction would be, of course, "intrinsically" sensory. On the comparative approach, then, intrinsically sensory states are either intentional in a merely comparative way or intentional in virtue of the presence in them of states that are *not* intrinsically sensory. It is difficult to avoid concluding, I think, that the sorts of unsophisticated states that we are now talking about are what Kant called mere *sensations*. He was apparently prepared to regard them (in virtue of their status as part of the manifold of "inner sense") as within the domain of psychology. It is not clear whether Brentano would deny the existence of such states or, conceding their existence, simply exclude them from the realm of the psychological.

The comparative approach to Kant, then, would regard sensations as aspects of, or as entering into, states that are intrinsically intentional only in virtue of their connection with *distinct* states that are intrinsically intentional and properly conceptual in nature. I would suggest, on the other hand, that it was precisely one of Kant's achievements to have seen that, without lapsing into a sense-datum approach, intrinsically sensory states might, and indeed *must*, be regarded as capable of an object-directedness that is not merely a borrowing from states externally attached to them. Sensory states, so regarded, are just "sensible intuitions." The minimal condition for so regarding them is, of course, on Kant's view, the presence in them of "forms of intuition."

It is important to be clear that, on this approach, the notion of a "formal" element in intuition takes on an ambiguity paralleling some others that I have already noted. Thus in one sense the formal element is the counterpart of the *sensations* which (taken in the primary sense) constitute the material aspect of a perceptual state. In this context, "sensation" is that aspect of a perceptual state in virtue of which it is not merely directed toward an object so-and-so describable but directed precisely in a *sensory manner*. The corresponding formal element would be whatever aspect of the state in question accounts for the specific sort of *object*-directedness it has (apart from the fact, of course, that it is a *sensory* sort, and also, on Kant's view, from whatever judgments might contribute to the *identification* of the object in question). In another sense, the formal element in an intuition is simply whatever spatiotemporal form is apprehended in the *object* of an intuition. The material counterpart of form in this sense is, of course, sensation not in the primary sense but only in the secondary sense introduced earlier. (Kant's view is that the same aspect of an intuitive state as accounts for the fact that it is a *sensory* state is also what, when combined with the appropriate formal element, accounts for the fact that the apprehended object involves a specifically appearing sort of material aspect, e.g., is a red rather than a green expanse. Kant's reason for this identification involves the possibility of "pure" intuitions wherein reference obtains to an at least imaginary[24] expanse of a certain form, yet where the expanse in question is *not* apprehended as "filled" with color. Since the conditions for reference to an intentional object still obtain in this case, while those for that reference's being of the *sensory* sort are absent, one is led to identify the latter conditions with those whose presence would also provide the missing material "filling.")[25] Kant does, undeniably, also speak of a formal element in intuition as an aspect whose counterpart is sensation in the *primary* sense and whose role is precisely that of directionality to an object.[26] The only alternative, then, to conceding that the notion of a "formal element" is ambiguous in the way I have suggested would be to embrace the view, previously rejected, that the objects of intuition are *themselves* just sensations, in the primary sense, spatially formed.

Now an objection to this might be drawn from the very first sentences of the Transcendental Aesthetic. There Kant seems to identify the object of intuition with the real *cause* of sensations. This suggests either a double-aspect reading, or at least some sort of *de re* approach to intuition (a non–"double-aspect" *de re* approach would presumably regard the objects in question as ordinary material objects yet not regard material objects as also being something "in themselves"). On the other hand, it does seem clear that Kant regards *forms of intuition* (i.e., some aspect of subjectivity itself) as accounting for the apprehension of appearances through what might otherwise be merely nonintentional sensations. Yet how could a purely subjective and internal element of a perceptual state (its "form") constitute reference of a *de re* sort for that state?

What seems most reasonable, however, is the following reading. Consider a case in which some state of a perceiver is generated by an entity in a manner standard for perceptual situations. Kant now asks, what conditions need to be added to our description of the situation so far, in order that it describes the occurrence of an *intuition* of that entity (at least as it appears)? The answer is that "forms" of intuition need to be present, i.e., that the generated state must be of a certain *sort*. But this, clearly, is compatible with the view that, quite apart from the causal aspects of the situation in question, the presence of such forms in whatever "material" is thereby involved would *still* generate the intuitive apprehension of some object. In this case, though, the object could at most be an intentional object.

In fact, it would seem that nothing other could be Kant's view. How could the presence of just those forms succeed in the first place in generating the objective (*de re*) reference in question if it would *not* have constituted a state that was at least phenomenologically intentional quite independently of the causal factors involved? Thus the role that Kant assigns to the forms of intuition *precludes* the possibility of adopting a merely comparative approach to the intentionality of intuitions, phenomenologically considered. It appears precisely to require that any intuition of objective appearances must, intrinsically considered, also be an intuition of phenomenological appearances. (The only way to escape this conclusion would be to regard the forms of intuition as merely *comparative* features of an intuition. What could be the standard for the comparison in question? Clearly, only objective intuitions. Yet the concept of an objective intuition, according to the Transcendental Analytic, *presupposes* that of a "manifold of intuitions" in the first place. Hence, presumably, it presupposes the concept of an intuition that might or might not *turn out* to be a genuinely objective intuition, depending on whether or not it fits in fact into the manifold anticipated by application of the concept in question.)[27]

Let me conclude this section by returning to the question, broached earlier, concerning the relation between sensory and conceptual elements in perception. On the present approach, forms of intuition determine the reference to some (possible) region of space (or time). The sensory "material" involved in that reference accounts for *the way* this region appears (as red, e.g., or as green). So far, however, no concepts have been introduced of, say, redness or greeness *as qualities of material objects* (in fact, Kant's claim in the Aesthetic is that no concepts *whatsoever* need yet have been introduced). Thus if one were to specify the objects of intuition at this point, one might regard them as similar to "sense data" in some ways, but with two exceptions. First, their status as objects does not depend on their possessing any sort of *ontological* status (over and above that of their being apprehended, of course). Second, the very spatial expanse that is thereby apprehended, as "filled" with sensory material, might ultimately turn out to *be* a spatial region filled by the material composing an ordinary material object. Thus the object of the intuition in question is, one might say, a *possible* material object (which, in case that intuition should in fact be of some object *de re*, would also be an *actual* one).

This suggests a comparison between Kantian phenomenological appearances and what Roderick Firth has called "ostensible physical objects."[28] Of course, we might balk at this too, if we give much weight to Kant's suggestion that no material-object *concepts* need be involved at this point. In that case the subject would not yet be conceptualizing what he sees *as* a material object, not even as a possible one. One might, nevertheless, so describe the object, even if material concepts were not being employed. Indeed, one might even specify a sense in which what the subject is now apprehending is "the same" object as what he only later in fact comes to conceptualize as a material object. The sense would be this: The present intuition is the very same *state* (or appropriately *connected* to some state) which only later becomes enriched by the introduction of the appropriate conceptual elements. In virtue of that enrichment, we might say, the (possible) region of space in question is *then* finally apprehended as a (possible or actual) material object. This would be impossible on the sense-datum approach. On that approach, it would always be a *mistake* to conceptualize what is given in intuition as a material object. At most it could be part of a certain manifold, reference to a *synthesis* of which constitutes reference to a material object (it would also be impossible on the double-aspect approach to conceptualize what is given in phenomenological intuition as a material object, for *nothing* is given in phenomenological intuition; i.e., there is no "object-directedness" except in *objective* intuition, i.e., intuition *de re*).

It is essential to note, furthermore, the compatibility of all this with the claim that the conceptual enrichment of an intuition, of the sort that we have been considering, is not simply a matter of the attachment of external thoughts, beliefs, or judgments *to* the original intuition. The "formal" aspect of an intuition is, indeed, as we have seen, a certain aspect of it. It is not something merely externally related to it. It is, one might, therefore, say, a certain *property* of that intuition.[29] In precisely the same way, then, the addition of conceptual elements might be regarded as the addition of *further* properties, of a special sort, instantiated by the state in question (in actual fact, most instances of perception no doubt involve *both* internally and merely externally "attached" conceptual content).

It is precisely this point, I think, that allows Kant to avoid what would otherwise be an insuperable difficulty. Suppose that the conceptualization of the object of a given intuition did consist merely in some external relation between that intuition and certain thoughts or judgments. Then what could in fact account for those thoughts or judgments constituting a conceptualization of precisely *that* object? There would, presumably, have to be something in the thought or judgment that constituted a *reference* to that particular object. How could this be? Any description of the object in question would at best be an extremely *general* one, for the intuition, as such, would at most be presenting its object as such-and-such a shaped spatial expanse "filled" with such-and-such (apparent) material. That would hardly distinguish the object from innumerable other possible objects. Alternatively, one might attempt to refer to the object simply as the object of *this intuition*, but that, of course, simply duplicates the problem, or at least it does so unless we have access to something other than purely descriptive means for referring to the intuition in question. The only other means available is by intuition itself (in this case, presumably, the further intuition being an *inner* one, with the original intuition providing its object). Hence there is, after all, no escaping the need for some sort of conceptualized intuitions, the conceptual aspects of which are indeed *aspects* of those intuitions and not merely externally attached states. We might as well then simply concede that the conceptualization of some intuited region of space as a material object (possible or actual) involves the introduction of conceptual elements that are just as much internal aspects of the intuition in question as the "forms of intuition" that constituted it as an apprehension of a region of space in the first place. This does, after all, correspond to the phenomenological fact that we do not simply judge what we see to be material objects; we *see* them as material objects.

It is important to see, finally, that this approach requires precisely the Brentanian point considered in the first section above. Were a Kantian intuition merely a kind of relation (or relational property) involving a perceiver and an object of some sort (whether a sense datum, for example, or a thing that happens to be appearing in a certain manner), we could make no sense of the idea of a conceptual *enrichment* of that intuition *except* in terms of the attachment to it of distinct referential states. For Kant, however, an intuitive state at most involves as one of *its* properties the property of directedness to an object. It is not itself, therefore, the relation of object-directedness (or a corresponding relational property). Hence it makes sense to suppose that *other* intentional properties, besides those constituting it as a minimally describable intuition in the first place, might be shared by that very same state.

Thus two crucial points come together in Kant's account of intuition. The first is that an intuition is not a relational state of affairs at all but simply an internal state of a perceiver, one of the descriptive *properties* of which is directedness to an object of some sort. The second is that, apart from the obvious exception of *de re* contexts, *what* sort of object is thereby apprehended is simply a fact *about that state itself* and not a fact about some entity to which it is related. The "object," in other words is, so far considered, a purely "intentional object."

IV

I have been defending, so far, a view of "phenomenological appearances" as intentional objects (namely, possible *material* objects). Now in one obvious sense an "intentional-object" approach could not be adopted with respect to the objects of intuition when the latter is considered to be intuition *de re*. In one sense, that is, "objective" appearances could not possibly be merely intentional objects, for they are, by supposition, *real* objects. Nonetheless, I still propose to consider the possibility of regarding the apprehension even of *objective* appearances as the apprehension of merely intentional objects.

Although the textual evidence is perhaps inconclusive, there is some direct evidence that Kant adopted a "phenomenalistic" view with respect to the existence of objective appearances. Kant does explicitly hold that for such objects to be "real" (as opposed to merely hallucinated, for example) is just for perceptions of a certain sort to be obtainable; i.e., they *would* be obtained under the appropriate circumstances.[30] (Of course, a Kantian phenomenalism would have to differ from some other views that have gone under that title. For example, the minimal description of each of the perceptions in question would not involve any sort of commitment to sense data.) If this is indeed Kant's view, then there is also a certain sense in which objective appearances are merely intentional objects. They exist not "in themselves" but merely as objects of possible (i.e., hypothetically *necessary*)[31] intuitions.

One way to bring out the force of this point is to compare it with Kant's approach to the debate between the absolutists and the relationalists concerning space. The absolutists regarded space as an object existing in its own right. The relationalists did not regard the awareness of space as the awareness of any sort of object at all. What we *call* our awareness of space (or of regions of space) is at most our awareness of the possibility (or actuality) of the existence of objects with spatial forms and standing in spatial relations. Kant rejected the idea of space (or even of a particular region of space) as an object existing in itself. Yet at the same time he appears to have rejected any attempt to regard what we call our awareness "of space" as the awareness of some different sort of object altogether. The upshot seems to involve a separation of two heretofore conflated issues. First, what are we aware of when we are aware of regions of space? Second, what sort of *ontological status* is in question? Kant appeared to agree with the relationalists that space exists not as an object in its own right but as an object (indeed, a necessary object) of possible intuitions only. On the other hand, Kant rejected the relational view concerning *what* it is that one is aware of when one is said to be aware "of space." It is just *space* that one is aware of (or at least specific regions of space) as a particular (or particulars) given as intentional object(s) to consciousness. The same sort of strategy, one might suggest, governed Kant's approach to material objects. He agreed that such objects exist not as things "in themselves" but only as objects of possible intuition; yet he disagreed with the attempts of idealists such as Berkeley, who would substitute for our *awareness* of material objects the awareness of something altogether different (e.g., mere "ideas" or mental entities of some sort).

It is clear, of course, that on Kant's view even the most "objectively real" perceptual objects are not things as they are "in themselves." Furthermore, space and time have no *applicability* to things as they are "in themselves." There is, however, more than one interpretation of these claims. The most minimal one would simply take them as Kant's way of saying that, while things necessarily appear to us in a context of space and time, these things are also known only *as* they so appear to us. Yet it is difficult to see why Kant would have put such a view by saying that space and time are *merely* forms of appearances and why he would say that they do not pertain to things as they are *apart* from the ways in which they appear to us (e.g., A42/B59). Furthermore, the interpretation sheds no light on the *relation* that is supposed to obtain between appearances and things as they are in themselves. So far as it is concerned, appearances might be constructs out of manifolds of sense data or of merely intentional objects, or they might be diverse "ways in which" certain things happen to appear to us, yet without any introduction of sense data or intentional objects.

Another minimal interpretation of the claim that things are not spatial or temporal "in themselves" takes Kant to be making a claim about our spatial and temporal *concepts*. He is claiming, namely, that all such concepts contain a reference to possible *activities* in relation to the things they characterize.[32] Thus the concept of a rectangular surface represents the possibility of *circumscribing* a surface in accordance with a certain set of rules. Kant himself argues that one reason for maintaining the "ideality" of spatial forms is that our intuitive representation of regions of space "contains nothing but mere relations, namely, of locations in an intuition (extension), of change of location (motion), and of laws according to which this change is determined (moving forces)" (B66–67). In the first place, however, the very fact that this claim arises from reflection on intuition, antecedent to any questions concerning our attempts to *conceptualize* intuition, shows that Kant's point could not be the one that has been suggested. In addition, Kant says nothing in the passage in question concerning the relation of an object of intuition to possible intelligent beings and their activities. Rather, he speaks only of relations *among locations*. The most reasonable interpretation, I think, is simply that, apart from conceptualization, we could only be said (though of course not by ourselves) to be apprehending, in various orders, various regions of space. Certainly, the primary contrast that Kant draws in B66–67 is between what intuition presents independently of conceptualization and what conceptualization adds to it: "Now that which, as representation, can be antecedent to any and every act of thinking is intuition; and if it contains nothing but relations, it is the form of intuition" (B67).

The point then is, I think, that only in virtue of the presence of concepts in an (outer) intuition can that intuition be said to be an awareness of some object that *occupies* a region of space. Apart from such conceptualization, the intuition in question would at most amount to the sensory awareness of a region of space, and our total perceptual state would at most amount to a *succession* (possibly a law-governed one) of sensory awarness of regions of space. Now how does this constitute an argument for "idealism"? My suggestion is simply this: If *what* a person is conscious of is something that can be determined by the presence or absence of certain *concepts* within his perceptual state, then it is reasonable to conclude that, so far considered at least, the "objects" of the consciousness in question must be regarded as merely *intentional* objects. Of course, this may appear at most to establish that "phenomenological appearances" are merely intentional objects. Soon, however, I shall propose an explanation of Kant's move from the conclusion that phenomenological appearances are merely intentional objects to the further conclusion that *objective* appearances are so as well (in the special sense indicated above, of course, which regards the existence of objective appearances in terms of a *synthesis* of phenomenological appearances).

A third approach is more radical than either of these two. On such an approach one takes Kant's claim to be just what it initially seems to be. It is the claim that anything (other than a phenomenological appearance) that might be regarded as spatial could be so regarded only in the sense that it presents phenomenological *appearances* of a spatial sort. Unfortunately, this approach will allow of just as many versions as there will be various ways in which we take the notion of an "appearance" in the first place. Thus on one account the claim is that the objects of immediate apprehension are sense data spatial in form, and nothing *other* than such entities would be said to be spatial except in the sense that those entities could be regarded precisely as appearances *of* such a thing. On a second account the claim will be that the objects of immediate apprehension are merely intentional objects, and nothing other than such an object will be characterizable in spatial terms except in the sense that such objects are regarded as appearances of it. Finally, one might regard appearances merely as various "ways in which" something might be said to appear to us, yet deny that the notion of either a sense datum or a merely intentional object might serve to explicate such "ways."

I have argued for a view of phenomenological appearances as intentional objects. Awareness of such appearances, in other words, is awareness of something that might or might not turn out to be a really existing object. It might or might not turn out to be, that is (at least in the case of "outer" intuition), a really existing *material* object: the objects of (outer) intuition, considered merely phenomenologically, are possible material objects. I have also suggested the following view with respect to *actual* material objects. An actual material object is to be defined in terms of syntheses of (the apprehension of) possible ones. Thus, on this account, the claim that some object of intuition is not a *merely* possible material object but a fully actual one is simply to be defined in terms of certain necessary connections *between* the apprehension of that object, phenomenologically considered, and the apprehension of various other phenomenological appearances. The latter, of course, will be just those whose apprehension our concept of the *sort* of object that is in question tells us we should be *able* to connect with the initially given one. Things as they exist "in themselves," finally, will be whatever exist in some sense that it is impossible to define, but which is connected with the "form" of the existential judgment, when such a judgment is not taken merely phenomenalistically (cf. A601/B629). That there is such a sense will not, of course, be denied by anyone except the most extreme of phenomenalists. The only sort of phenomenalism that I have attributed to Kant is a phenomenalism with respect to the existence of objects of intuition.[33]

Now with respect at least to the relation between phenomenological and objective appearances, finally, we may consider what I think is a good reason *why* Kant might in fact have been led to the view that I attribute to him. It is, I would suggest, a logical consequence of his view concerning phenomenological appearances, or at least it is a consequence of that view when combined with a certain empiricist thesis that we know Kant to have held. This is the thesis that the only objects of human cognition are those which, at least in principle, are *directly perceivable*. It is not unreasonable, then, to suppose that Kant would have reasoned as follows: The thesis in question implies that, at least in some cases, the phenomenological appearances that I apprehend must *be* the objects to which, *qua* objects of presumed cognition, I ascribe reality (and Kant does, of course, take the pains to produce a "Refutation of Idealism" which has, as its consequence, that spatiotemporal reality is actually *presented* to us, and not merely the object of inferential *judgments*). Hence, Kant may have inferred, at least in some cases phenomenological appearances must be objective also. Yet what sense could it make to say that an appearance, which is an intentional object, is identical with something that exists in itself? To consider phenomenological appearances as intentional objects is, strictly, just to say something about the *awareness* of them. The awareness of them, namely, is such that its occurrence is neutral with respect to the reality of its object (even with respect to the objective "phenomenal" reality of such an object). So it would seem to be a "category mistake" (in the Rylean, not the Kantian, sense) to attempt to regard a phenomenological appearance as literally identical with some thing in itself. Of course, as we have already seen, Kant might, regard an intentional object as, loosely speaking, "identical" with a thing existing in itself. He could, however, regard it as "identical" with such a thing, it would seem, only in the sense that the latter stands in the right sort of *causal relation* with the apprehension of the object in question. But in that case, we can suppose Kant to conclude, the alleged objects of human cognition would be merely *hypothesized* entities, merely the "objects" of causal *inference*, and not really "presented" as objects of intuition at all.

Thus perhaps it is not surprising that Kant should conclude that, if appearances *are* ever "identical" with some objectively "real" object that is immediately presented to us, then that object must itself exist in a merely intentional sense. It must exist, that is, simply in the sense that perceptions of it obtain or are obtainable, for only in that case would both sides of the "identity sign" refer to something in the same ontological *category* (again in the Rylean, not the Kantian sense). Hence only in that case would both sides refer to objects that are genuinely *objects* of possible perception. That a merely intentional object *could*, at the same time, be an empirically real one (as opposed, e.g., to a merely imagined or hallucinated one) Kant might in fact have regarded as one of his own most fundamental discoveries. And he would have been right, at least, in suggesting that Berkeley, among others, missed the notion entirely. That

Brentano, on the other hand, did not follow Kant's path may simply reflect his own tolerance of a much weaker empiricist thesis. Brentano, after all, did not hesitate to define natural science itself as a body of knowledge about the *hypothesized causes* of the psychological states whereby "physical phenomena," i.e., subjective appearances, are apprehended.[34] In any case, as we have seen, it is Brentano himself who defends the notion of judgments that "identify" an intentional object with some really existing one. On Kant's view, as I have argued, this notion becomes that of a judgment that identifies a phenomenological appearance as also something *more* than that, i.e., as an objectively real material object.

Finally, we might even attempt to use the notion of "identifying" some phenomenological appearance with an objectively real material object *of* which it is an appearance to explain what might otherwise seem inexplicable on my view. This is Kant's claim that it is an *absurdity* of some sort to deny that appearances are appearances of some entity that appears through them yet also is an entity "in itself" *apart* from its appearing through them (Bxxvi, A251–52, B306). Kant in fact seems to suggest that it is a logical contradiction to deny such a claim. Now the view that this position appears most naturally to suggest is some form of the "double-aspect" view. If appearances are, by definition, simply the various "ways in which" some entity appears to us, then the inference in question would appear to be perfectly in order. I have conceded, of course, that much of Kant's language in fact suggests the double-aspect view. It is important to remember, however, that the double-aspect view is one that denies the legitimacy of the introduction either of sense data or of intentional objects as part of an attempt to explicate the notion of a "way in which" something might be appearing to us. On the other hand, as I also argued, none of the passages appearing to support the double-aspect view are in fact incompatible with such attempts. If, of course, the "ways in which" something is supposed to appear to us were understood in terms of the apprehension of either sense data or intentional objects supposed to be stimulated within us *by* the thing thereby appearing, then there would be no absurdity at all in supposing appearances to be apprehended apart from such a thing. There is no absurdity in the supposition that sense data or intentional objects might be apprehended apart from something that stimulates that apprehension, or at least apart from something *of* which those objects must thereby be regarded as appearances.

What I suggest is that Kant was guilty of a certain confusion. This, of course, is by no means an approach foreign to commentators on the particular claim in question. There is, I think, an interesting way to explain Kant's confusion. First of all, let us suppose that Kant is restricting his attention, in the contexts in question, to instances in which objective appearances are in question. Let us call such an object, for example, this piece of paper, O. In addition, let us designate as O_1 the present phenomenological appearance that I happen to be apprehending, in the course of apprehending O. Given, then, that we are dealing with a case of objective, and not merely phenomenological apprehension (though, of course, we are also dealing with the latter), the following propositions will obtain:

1. O_1 is the appearance of something that appears *through* it, i.e., a "way in which" something is appearing on this occasion.
2. O_1 is "identical" with O, a piece of paper in front of me.

From these two propositions, one might suppose, Kant was led to conclude that O, being "identical" with O_1, must be, like O_1, the appearance of something that appears through it. That is, an ordinary piece of paper is really itself a "way in which" something appears to us. This something, of course, could only be a thing that exists "in itself." Whatever confusions this argument might harbor, we should at least recognize that it issues from fundamental insights foreign to Kant's predecessors, concerning the intentionality of perception.

NOTES

1. Franz Brentano, *Psychologie vom empirischen Standpunkt*, ed. Oskar Karus (Hamburg: Felix Meiner, 1924), vol. 1, p. 124. Reprinted in English translation by D. B. Terrell in Roderick Chisholm, ed., *Realism and the Background of Phenomenology* (Glencoe, Ill.: Free Press, 1960), p. 50.

2. Edmund Husserl, *Logische Untersuchungen* (Tübingen: Max Niemeyer Verlag, 1913); English translation, *Logical Investigations*, by J. N. Findlay (New York: Humanities Press, 1970), Inv. 5, sec. 15(*b*). Kant says that sensation "relates solely to the subject as the modification of its state" and that, unlike intuition, it is not an "objective" representation of anything (A320/B376). He even says, at one point, that sensations are not really "representations" *at all*, but only the "material" thereto. *Reflexionen zur Anthropologie*, ed. Erich Adickes (in vol. 15 of *Akademie-Ausgabe*), refl. 177. This contradicts the passage at A320, among others. Elsewhere he does say that sensations have objects (B210), but he also says (refl. 238) that it is intuition which *gives* sensation that object. The view to which Kant subscribes, I believe, is that the object of intuition involves a "material" aspect whose presentation is a function of the sensations which that intuition involves but whose presentation is nonetheless accomplished by the intuition (perception) as a whole, and not by the sensations considered on their own. In the *Critique* sensations sometimes seem to be "states" of the perceiver, albeit not themselves *perceptual* states. If so, it would seem at least

("logically") possible for sensations to occur apart from intuitions (though the sense in which we could then be said to be *aware* of them becomes problematic). At other times the sense in which sensations are regarded as mere "aspects" of empirical intuition seems to be taken more strictly; cf. *Anthropologie, Ak.-Ausg.*, vol. 7, pp. 153 ff. (references to the *Critique of Pure Reason* appear with the standard A and B pagination; Kemp Smith's translation unless otherwise noted).

3. Brentano's formulations sometimes suggest a peculiar *sort* of ontological status, known as "mental inexistence" (cf. Brentano, *Psychologie*), but he later denied that he meant this. Cf. *Wahrheit und Evidenz*, ed. Oskar Kraus (Leipzig: Felix Meiner, 1930); English translation, *The True and the Evident*, ed. Roderick Chisholm (New York: Humanities Press, 1966), p. 78: "I allowed myself the term 'immanent object,' in order to say, not that the object exists, but that it *is* an object whether or not there is anything that corresponds to it. Its *being* an object, however, is merely the linguistic correlate of the person experiencing *having* it as object, i.e., his thinking of it in his experience." That Brentano does not here misrepresent his own earlier stance seems indicated by the footnote to the *Psychologie* passage cited earlier, in which he contrasts his view of "mental inexistence" with Anselm's.

4. Brentano, *Psychologie*, vol. 2, suppl. essay 4, p. 147.

5. That this is not a case of what we might call "literal" identity—wherein an entity might be said to be identical with itself, or wherein a single entity is identifiable as the same entity under two distinct *descriptions*—seems clear from Brentano's concession that at least certain related sorts of "identifications" (which he calls "attributive") involve identifying "the most diverse objects with one another," e.g., a round object (*qua* intentional object) with a red object (*qua* intentional), when we judge that some round thing we see also *is* a red one; supp. essay 4, p. 146. For an interesting and detailed discussion of the concept of identity along what seem to be the same lines, see Panayot Butchvarov, *Being Qua Being* (Bloomington: Indiana University Press, 1979), esp. Chaps. 1 and 2.

6. Brentano, *Psychologie*, suppl. essay 2, p. 138.

7. Compare Chisholm's distinction between a "psychological" and an "ontological" aspect of Brentano's thesis: "Brentano on Descriptive Psychology and the Intentional," in *Phenomenology and Existentialism*, ed. Edward N. Lee and Maurice Mandelbaum (Baltimore, Md.: Johns Hopkins University Press, 1967).

8. Berkeley, *Third Dialogue*, in *Works*, ed. A. A. Luce and T. E. Jessop (Edinburgh: Nelson and Sons, 1948–57), vol. 2, p. 250.

9. This suggestion parallels one that I have also made about Hume in *Intentionality: A Study of Mental Acts* (University Park: Pennsylvania State University Press, 1977), pp. 2–5.

10. Strictly, I would suggest, an "ideational state of affairs" for Spinoza is a state of affairs whose only constituent is its own *object*. If this is so, then one might question the point of describing it as a relational state of affairs. The point does not effect my claims here. For a discussion see my "The Identity of Thought and Object in Spinoza," *Journal of the History of Philosophy*, vol. 16 (July, 1978), pp. 271–88.

11. Cf. "Correspondence with Arnauld," October 9, 1687, trans. Leroy E. Loemaker, in *Gottfried Wilhelm Leibniz: Philosophical Papers and Letters* (New York: Humanities Press, 1970), p. 339.

12. Immanuel Kant, "Inaugural Dissertation," trans. G. B. Kerferd, in G. B. Kerferd and D. E. Walford, eds., *Kant: Selected Pre-Critical Writings* (New York: Barnes & Noble, 1968), sec. 4 (translation slightly modified).

13. Kemp Smith's translation modified.

14. Cf. *Principles of Philosophy*, part L, LXVI–LXXI, trans. Elizabeth S. Haldane and G. R. T. Ross, in *The Philosophical Works of Descartes* (Cambridge: Cambridge University Press, 1931), vol. 1, pp. 247–50.

15. Cf. "Replies to Objections IV," idid., vol. 2, pp. 105–107.

16. Compare B151, 277n., 278. That even dreams, illusions, and the most bizarre of hallucinations are included within the realm of "imagination" is clear, for example, from A278 and 376 and from *Anthropologie* secs. 24 and 28.

17. Stephen F. Barker, "Appearing and Appearances in Kant," *Monist*, vol. 51 (July, 1967), pp. 426–41; Robert Howell, "A Problem for Kant," *Essays in Honour of Jaakko Hintikka*, ed. E. Saarinen, et al. (Dordrecht: D. Reidel, 1979), p. 344. Cf. also Gerold Prauss, *Kant und das Problem der Dinge an sich* (Bonn: Bouvier, 1974), esp. pp. 12–23, for a statement of a "double-aspect" view. Prauss, however, seems to regard Kantian appearances somewhat as I do, namely, as "intentional objects." Cf. also his contribution to the 5. *Internationales Kant-Kongress* (Bonn: Bouvier, 1981), pp. 763–71. This leaves me unclear in what way we might then consider one and the same thing both as appearance and "in itself." For a discussion of Prauss, see my "Things in Themselves and Appearances," *Archiv für Geschichte der Philosophie*, vol. 61 (1979), pp. 293–308.

18. A. J. Ayer, *The Foundations of Empirical Knowledge* (London: Macmillan, 1940), pp. 19ff. For typical passages see the Axioms of Intuition and Anticipations of Perception (A162/B202ff.). Here Kant is dealing, as he tells us (A160/B200, A178/B220), with appearances without regard to the possibility of attributing *existence* to them, i.e., without regard to the question whether they are objective or merely phenomenological appearances.

19. Howell, in "A Problem for Kant," dismisses *both* the sense-datum and the intentional-object approaches (n. 22) by appeal to passages of the sort in question. As I argue shortly, such a dismissal seems even *less* warranted in the latter case than in the former.

20. At A29/B45, e.g., Kemp Smith has Kant say that we ought to "guard anyone from supposing that the ideality of space as here asserted can be illustrated by examples so altogether insufficient as colours, taste, etc. For these cannot rightly be regarded as properties of things, but only as changes in the subject." The original passage, however, consists of a single sentence, the second half of which seems present not as Kant's own view but as the sort of consideration to be offered by those whose suppositions he is attempting to guard against in the first place. I presented a detailed discussion of other passages in a paper at the meeting of the APA, Eastern Division, in December, 1980, forthcoming in a volume edited by M. S. Gram.

21. Howell "A Problem for Kant," p. 344 also presents a telling objection to the sense-datum account which is independent of the "alternative-language" issue: it requires regarding a sense datum as *itself* a sort of thing existing in itself. Here, presumably, existence-in-itself is simply anything more than a merely *intentional* existence, and the point is, then, the same as the one I raised earlier with respect to Berkeley. Oddly, however, this line of approach would seem to suggest precisely a view about *phenomenal* existence that Howell rejects: that phenomena exist merely intentionally. In any case, the problem remains, with respect to Howell's approach to a sense-datum reading of Kant, of contending with the possibility that Kant's views are simply contradictory. That they are is, in fact, the point of his paper. I am, of course, attempting to avoid the attribution of contradictory positions to Kant. (An additional reason for accepting the sense-datum account might be supposed found in passages in which Kant speaks of appearances as existing only "in us," e.g., A42/B59.

Such passages, however, I would suggest, at most imply that appearances exist only in the sense that they are, or might be, *perceived*, i.e., are merely intentional objects.)

22. Brentano, *Psychologie*, vol. 1, pp. 179ff.

23. Ibid., vol. 2, suppl. essay 2, p. 139.

24. That "pure" intuition is a kind of "imagination" is clear, e.g., from A713/B741 and from *Anthropologie*, sec. 15, p. 153.

25. This seems to be the move between the third and fourth paragraphs of the Aesthetic.

26. A23/B38: " . . . in order that certain sensations be referred to something outside of me." B41: " . . . the formal character of the subject, in virtue of which, in being affected by objects, it obtains *immediate representation* of them." With regard to A20/B34, see my "Two Lines of Argument in Kant's Transcendental Aesthetic," *International Studies in Philosophy*, vol. 10 (1978), pp. 85–100.

27. This, one should note, is compatible with the Kantian claim that the *ability to ascribe* even phenomenological intuitions to oneself requires an ability to ascribe *objective* intuitions to oneself, or that possession of the *concept* of phenomenological intuition requires that of objective intuition as well. Both of these claims are compatible, it seems to me, with the view that the concept of an intuition, phenomenologically considered, as possessing the sort of "directionality" connected with the forms of intuition, is the concept of an intrinsic and not merely a comparative feature of an intuition.

28. Roderick Firth, "Sense-Data and the Percept Theory," *Mind*, vols. 58 and 59 (1949 and 1950), reprinted in Robert J. Swartz, ed., *Perceiving, Sensing, and Knowing* (Garden City, N.Y: Doubleday, 1965), esp. pp. 250ff.

29. This, one might note, is compatible with the view, introduced, for example, at A20/B34, that the formal aspect of an intuition involves relations and ordering among a manifold of elements. That the formal element is an intrinsic property of an intuition is compatible with its involving some relation or relations among a manifold of distinct sensations which are *ingredient* in that intuition. Variations in such relations presumably would then be what carries the quasi-semantical function of representing intuited regions or expanses as variously shaped, variations in the intrinsic "quality" of the related sensations corresponding to variation in, e.g., the color of what is thereby represented *in* the regions in question.

30. "For the appearances, as mere representations, are in themselves real only in perception. . . . To call an appearance a real thing prior to our perceiving it, either means that in the advance of experience we must meet with such a perception, or it means nothing at all." A493/B21–522; cf. A225/B272, A601/B629.

31. As has been forcefully argued by, e.g., Bella K. Milmed, what Kant usually means by "possible" intuitions is intuitions which *would* (necessarily) occur were the appropriate conditions satisfied. See Milmed's " 'Possible Experience' and Recent Interpretations of Kant," *Monist*, vol. 51 (July, 1967), pp. 442ff.

32. Cf. Arthur Melnick, *Kant's Analogies of Experience* (Chicago: University of Chicago Press, 1973), pp. 151ff.

33. For an elaboration of some of these points, see my paper referred to in note 17 above. I also give brief attention there to the objection that the view I suggest cannot account for the "double-aspect" conception essential to Kant's pronouncements concerning human agency.

34. Brentano, *Psychologie*, vol. 1, p. 138; Chisholm, ed., *Realism and the Background of Phenomenology*, p. 59.

Reduction-Realization: a Key to the Structure of Kant's Thought

GERD BUCHDAHL
Cambridge University

This essay is an attempt to look afresh at the whole structure of Kant's transcendental approaches, as developed in the first *Critique of Pure Reason (CPR)*; in particular, it constitutes an attempt to view the Kantian structure by modeling it on a quasi-dynamical process which I shall label the reduction-and-realization process (*RRP*), a process which we shall find to involve a kind of 'movement' (or 'dynamic') between the nodal points of this structure: the world of 'objects,' understood in the many different senses distinguished by Kant in *CPR*, senses that will be defined in terms of this process, for instance, as the "object in the transcendental sense,"* as the "empirical object" and as "appearance," as "noumenon" (in its various senses), and as "thing in itself." Kant himself never furnished a systematic presentation of the deepest layers of his philosophical method; to lay these bare (the object of this essay) will provide a key for, a guiding thread through, some of the knottiest passages that have perplexed generations of students of Kant since the first publication of the *Critique*.

I. *Phenomenological and Ontological Levels of Discourse*

We will begin with a distinction that needs to be observed in connection with any discourse concerning Kant's world of objects and the changes (observational and theoretical) which these may undergo. The distinction is between what I will label 'phenomenologically' and 'ontologically' oriented discourse.[1] 'Phenomenological', here used in its literal sense, simply denotes 'the account of the phenomena'—such an account involving both the observational and lawlike and the systems presentation met with in the various sciences. One might think of this as a kind of Husserlian "*Lebenswelt*," but without making Husserl's somewhat 'instrumentalist' distinction between scientifico-theoretical and

---

* Throughout this article double quotation marks are used to enclose Kant's and other authors' specific terminology. Otherwise, single quotation marks are used.

prescientific language,[2] instead assuming a Quinean ocean of naturalistically conceived objectivity (I shall term this φ-level discourse, for short).

By contrast, ontological discourse, in the sense of 'ontology' here adopted, is best explained through the objectives of classical and modern philosophy, when engaged on reflections about the φ-level of the world. Examples are here better than definitions. Ontological claims centrally involve assertions about what things or objects 'really are.' Thus for Berkeley objects (in the φ-level sense) are 'really ideas' (i.e., in the o-level sense); for Hume they reduce to impressions of sensation; Leibniz interprets them as 'phenomena' that are ultimately 'grounded' in a world of intelligibles or monads. For Kant the objects making up what he calls "the sensory world" (A538/B566)[3]—a φ-level expression!—may have variously the status either of "appearance" or of something "intelligible" (A538/B566), expressions which I shall understand as operating at the 'ontological' level (o-level) of discourse. Historically speaking, such ontological characterizations usually involve reference to some source or principle which 'activates' (as we might say) the mode of being of the objects of the world, when taken in the φ-level sense. Thus for Berkeley, Hume, and in a way for Kant also it is mind or self which is the activating source; for Plato it was the Form of the Good; for Leibniz and the *early* Kant the principle is modeled on the "divine understanding."

Clearly, o-level discourse is concerned not with the actual existence of things and their causation (questions that belong to φ-level discourse) but with the question of what 'makes things possible,' *as* things, or, to give the epistemic version of this question, what makes any cognitive grasp ('knowledge') of such things possible. Thus for Berkeley knowledge of things is possible only *qua* 'ideas'; for Kant, *qua* "the appearance" of such things. By contrast Leibniz and the *early* Kant wrestle with the nonepistemic version: things (*simpliciter*) are possible (not just 'logically possible' but 'really possible') by virtue of a principle of sufficient reason, which reason is "grounded" in a "necessary substance . . . which is called God" (Leibniz, *Monadology*, sec. 38; cf. also Kant, *Nova Dilucidatio* [1755], sec. ii).[4]

The motivation for such questions must itself lie in some basic assumption or assumptions. In the instance last mentioned, we have the puzzle how anything can get off from a position which starts with "nothing," the sort of Leibniz-Heideggerian question, 'Why should there be something rather than nothing?' For Leibniz

40

the difference is formulated in terms of an infinite number of logically possible worlds, by contrast with the one actual world, concerning which Leibniz remarks that it is as though God has placed into the universe

> an exigency in possible things towards existence . . . a pre-tension to exist . . . or that all possible things tend towards existence . . . in proportion to the degree of perfection which they involve.[5]

The concept of perfection here referred to is part of the general 'framework' in terms of which the existence of things is evaluated; it is a kind of 'descriptive metaphysics.' Heidegger's wealth of elucidations of the ontology of things in *Being and Time* operates in just such a way—albeit with an apparatus of much greater complexity. Wittgenstein's concept of "language games" is in the same line of business. All these constitute ways of attempting to lay bare interesting 'presuppositional' *frameworks*; cf. Heidegger's "being-in-the-world" (to cite just one) or the conditions of communication, explained in detail in some of Habermas's writings. The danger here is that one may simply be 'telling how it really is'; instead of ferreting out a descriptive *metaphysics*, one ends up with a descriptive *physics* (this was indeed the case in pre-Socratic Greek philosophy: creation myths, etc., there conflate phenomenological and ontological discourses). One of the great values of Kant's transcendental justifications consists in picking out effectively some rather 'hidden' variables buried in ordinary experience, as when he claims that the enabling concept involved in our perception of a contingent empirical sequence of events is the concept of causation (for this see below, sec. IV.1).

Leibniz's and Heidegger's metaphysical positions are occasioned by the most radical puzzle, that of 'nothingness', but for the most part problems of 'real possibility' are confined to more specific and limited positions or assumptions. For instance, in the *Dissertation* (1770),[6] Kant broaches the question, How is it possible to discourse significantly about "wholes" which themselves consist of independent individual parts? The assumption underlying this question is that the parts as such are predetermined "substances," possessing the character of "monads," seemingly all that makes up the 'ultimately real', clearly a characterization of the ontological status of things and an assumption which produces his problem in the first place. Now common experience somehow *unites* the parts when it sees them as 'a whole'; but that which thus unites, the "coordinating bond," seems something additional, something which at first sight (says Kant) seems to have its foundation in nothing more than our "minds."

Let us note, in brackets, the particular formulation in which Kant couches his question; it is a question which, he says, concerns not "*actual*" connections but merely

> some principle by which it may be *possible* that the states of several things whose subsistence as such is independent each from the other, should be related to one another as mutually grounded.[7]

By thus framing his question in terms of 'possibility', Kant makes clear that it concerns the purely 'ontological' side of things, his chief aim being that of finding a way to interpret the relations involved (in turn supposed to generate the notion of a whole) to possess a 'realist' status and not, as in Leibniz, the idealism of a preestablished harmony.

In the earlier *Nova Dilucidatio* the "common principle" which holds the substances together is explicitly "the divine intellect," acting by means of the concept of interaction,[8] foreshadowing the treatment in the *Critique*, twenty-six years later, in the Third Analogy, albeit with the "substances" replaced by "perceptions" and the problem of coexistence (*simpliciter*) replaced by that of the possibility of our obtaining *cognitive grasp* (Erkenntnis) of this coexistence.[9] Moreover, since it is again taken for granted that we *actually cognize* coexistence, it is this fact which, in the *Critique*, will now generate the "objective validity" of the category of interaction, necessarily *presupposed* in (Kant's construal of) the notion of the *possibility* of our *assumedly actual* cognition of coexistence. In this way Kant converts the earlier "dogmatic" into the later "critical" position; by making coexistence 'internal' to cognition (experience), we need no longer anchor interaction in a merely hypostatized divine source.

Although with these last remarks I have tried to summarize some characteristics of Kant's argumentation in the *Critique* (the nature of "transcendental deductions"), what is most noteworthy here is that the basic imagery underlying *both* positions (precritical and critical) is much the same, the activating principle in each case having something to do with 'mind', or 'ideality', the only difference being that in the precritical position the center of gravity is something metaphysical, located in the *divine* understanding, by way of sheer postulation, whereas in the critical teaching the category is instead justified or 'deduced' as a condition of the possibility of objective cognition, i.e., of experience, itself involving the *human* understanding, as the new (transcendental) center of gravity (I shall presently use such similarities and continuities for a diagrammatic representation of the sequence of precritical and critical positions in the history of philosophy; cf. fig. 1).

Ontology, as here defined, pertains thus to questions of real possibility, in the form indicated by these examples, the term 'ontological' being more or less in line with Kant's own occasional usage.[10] Kant's main objective may thus be described as that of providing ontologies, in the sense explained, at three different levels of the enterprise: "nature in general," "material (or physical) nature," and nature as an "ordered" system of objects and of the empirical laws that govern their behavior. Correspondingly we may thus distinguish among a 'general', a 'special', and a 'systems' ontology. The last named is concerned with the problem of the validation of the methodological maxims and ideas of natural science, supposedly yielding a "projected" system of empirical laws, constituting a description of the "unity" or "order of nature."[11]

'Special ontology' (Kant calls it "special metaphysics") investigates the possibility, and thus intelligibility, of the basic concepts and laws of Newtonian science. For instance, it seeks to show that gravitational action-at-a-distance is a real possibility and a legitimate hypothesis, the problem here arising from an explication of the concept of matter which belonged to a previous scheme of physics, and which thus seemed to make such action *im*possible.[12] In this article I shall confine myself to the level of general ontology, which deals with the problem of the real possibility of objective cognition, or experience in general. (An Appendix will briefly deal with 'systems ontology'.)

II. *Reduction*[13]

Consider now some object O_w, understood as part of ϕ-level discourse. First, I shall symbolize the distinction between the phenomenology and the ontology of O_w by writing O_w^ϕ and O_w^o, respectively. O_w^o will thus represent the ontology of O_w, the account of 'possibility' of O_w, in the sense of the previous section. For my next step I want to fall back on some hints from Husserl, especially as formulated in one of his earlier writings on phenomenology, *The Idea of Phenomenology* (1907).[14] The problem of 'possibility' is there formulated in terms of the problem of "transcendence," of how to formulate the existence of an object which purports to be 'apart from' the cognition of objects, *as we say*. The details do not concern us here, merely Husserl's general philosophical methodology. As just seen, we certainly *assume* ourselves *actually* to stand in relation to an external world, 'apart' from the cognitive setting. Yet, Husserl remarks, in a way we are not really entitled to *state* this until we have shown *how* transcendence is *possible*. What is required is an account that would show *how*, and even *whether*, transcendence is a genuine part of cognition.[15]

Now clearly this 'whether' does not really belong in phenomenological discourse (in my sense of the term) but makes reference to a problem in ontology. But we may use Husserl's remark as a hint, to formulate the final step in his argument somewhat more clearly than he perhaps does himself. We shall simply translate the 'doubt' involved in the question of 'whether' (and, of course, 'how') into something more radical, by pretending that no ontological account of O_w is so far available. To express this in Husserlian terms, without necessarily adopting Husserl's exact arguments and intentions, we shall subject O_w^o to a "reduction," equivalent to the assignment of a 'zero value' to O_w^o constituting a generalization of the Leibniz-Heideggerian position of starting with 'nothing'. Using Husserl's graphical locution, we may describe this as "assigning" to the ontology of O_w "the index of indifference, of epistemological nullity."[16] Notice that this does not at all imply that a zero value has been assigned to O_w^ϕ; the latter must be deemed to remain completely insulated from the ontological reduction, "suspended" in a kind of Husserlian "epoché," a fact which expresses very clearly the separation of the ontological from the phenomenological domains (Husserl's question about the "whether" would then become, in an ontological context, something like, '*In what sense* may we suppose ourselves to have knowledge of a transcendent world?').

We can now use these concepts to develop a proper insight into the Kantian structure, though noting in passing that the idea of 'reduction', when applied to the Kantian procedure, turns out to be more radical than is the case in Husserl's philosophy, where "reduction" is accompanied by a step which positions the "phenomenon" ("reduced" object) simultaneously relative to a cognitive (or transcendental) subject.[17] In the language of what is to follow, we may say that Husserlian reduction converts the object to the status of Kantian 'intuitions,' whereas Kant's reduction ends up with the object as something with a genuine zero value, as an "object in the transcendental sense."

Let us write the result of a reduction of O_w^o, i.e., $O_w^o \rightarrow$ zero, as O_r. Any philosophical interpretation of O_r will depend on the particular metaphysical positions taken by various philosophers (as already implied, in Leibniz's philosophy, for instance, O_r will be construed as a purely 'logical' entity; let us label this O_l). In general, O_r represents the object in a state where no ontological account is (or is as yet) provided, or where such an account is only implicit, or unacknowledged.

III. Realization

We will now turn to a process which moves, as it were, in the opposite direction and which we will term "realization," corresponding to the provision of a certain ontology. We have already noted one or two instances of this process, e.g., the Leibnizian nisus from logical to real possibility (and with this, actuality) by virtue of divine mediation. Similarly, as we saw, in Kant's *Nova Dilucidatio* it is the divine understanding which provides the source of activation in accordance with the concept of interaction. Realization is thus meant to provide, literally, an account of 'real possibility.' In Kant's precritical period realization refers to the "possibility of the object"; in the *Critique* (as already noted) this becomes "possibility of cognition of the object." In the latter case Kant employs this term, indeed, in precisely such a sense when he concludes the chapter on Schematism by saying that "sensibility . . . realizes the understanding" and its categories, in order to convert the merely logical status of the latter into something with "objective meaning," i.e., into the corresponding schemata (A147/B187).

What I wish to emphasize is the sense of 'a dynamic' that becomes a prominent feature in the account of ontology here outlined: the movement from $O_w^o \rightarrow O_r$; and from O_r (under a certain construal of this) to some given realization, e.g., a realization of the object as "appearance," or, more properly, as a thing that appears (T_a). More of this presently, in terms of a generalization of certain Kantian key notions. For the moment I want to remain with the different construals of O_r that parallel the various types of realizations that may be distinguished.

1. Metaphysical Realization

The Leibniz–early Kant type of realization, whose main outlines have already been sketched, corresponds to a process that may be symbolized as $O_r = O_l$; $O_l \rightarrow T_m$, where T_m stands for "substances," by Leibniz called "monads"; one of the referents of Kant's umbrella term "thing in itself" (cf. A270/B326) to be symbolized as T_s^* when the reference is to Kant's use of this term for a characterization of a precritical position whereas, for a 'critical' construal of this term I shall use the symbol T_s. Naturally, the later Kant will disallow this type of realization—still utilized, as we have seen in his *Nova Dilucidatio*, as involving divine "intellectual intuition"[18]—which is not available to man (cf. B72); T_s^* then becomes T_s, in the counterfactual or "negative sense" of a mere thought object, or "noumenon" (T_n^-) (B307).

2. *Ideational Realization*

In this form realization takes place by virtue of a 'percipere' (or, in the case of Descartes, a *'concipere'* or *'cogitare'*), which mediates the thing as 'idea', with 'as' denoting more or less identity (compare *'esse = percipi'*). It is not clear what interpretation to accord here to O_r. Berkeley refers to 'archetypal ideas' in God's mind, which determine perhaps the kind of realization effected; thus, according to Berkeley, the "ideas of sensation" are due to God's activity. Kant's own picture of Berkeley is different, bearing a closer resemblance to Hume's scheme: i.e., by virtue of *percipere*, things, *qua* "ideas" (let us symbolize this as T_i) simply come to be, or to be perceived, either actually or hypothetically; hence Kant's choice of the term "material idealism" to characterize this position (B274, B519n.), one reason being that realization here fails to yield a distinct 'formal' characteristic as such; for instance, it fails to generate an independent foundation for the phenomenology of space and time, which latter (as in Leibniz) are viewed as only 'confused' accompaniments or derivatives of the 'material' content of the idea. In Kant 'formal' and 'material' aspects are accorded a place of equal importance, if, indeed, priority is not given to 'form' (cf. A267/B323).

3. *Transcendental Realization*

This replaces the near-psychological approaches of Berkeley and Hume by a transcendentalization of the notions of 'mind' and 'understanding', involving thereby also a fresh construal of O_r, in addition to a near-Leibnizian notion of the object (O_l) in a "purely logical" sense (remember the transition $O_l \rightarrow T_m$); interpreting O_r

now also as something entirely novel, viz., as the "object in a transcendental sense," or "transcendental object" for short (O_t).

It will be seen that Kant's transcendentalism, and its corresponding realizational approach, is formulated, like that of the preceding 'ideational' type, in epistemological terms, with the emphasis on the 'knowledge-orientated' notions of the understanding, and of sensibility. This is, of course, only one of many possible alternatives, such as the more praxiological approach of Heidegger, or the action-orientated transcendentalism of more recent years, as illustrated in the writings of Habermas. One of the aims of the present study is to clarify the nature of any transcendental philosophy by reference to the special version first initiated by Kant.

To make a start, I want, as foreshadowed, to place the Kantian position schematically within its full historical context, partly to create some clarity about the way Kant sees his own scheme as a response to intellectual pressures arising out of the thought of his predecessors, and as an attempt to reinterpret certain key notions, to be found there in a way that would remove some well-known difficulties arising therefrom.

It is a commonplace that Kant sought to effect a reconciliation between, and a synthesis of, the rationalist (noetic idealist) and the "empirical" or "sensualist" idealist doctrines of his predecessors (cf. A369; A271/B327 for these expressions). In figure 1, I have sought to give a visual representation of the basic outlines of these doctrines, more or less as interpreted by Kant himself. Positions 2 and 3 Kant labels "material idealism" (B274). One of his motives for the choice of this term has just been noted: the inability of this position to account ontologically for the 'forms' of space and time in any independent way. A more important reason, however, is that this form of idealism "doubts or denies the existence of outer things themselves" (B519n.).[19] This objection may at first sight seem puzzling to those who have a somewhat Humean impression of Kant's philosophy, and we shall not be able to explain the full depth of Kant's appraisal of "material idealism" until we have fully elucidated his account of the "transcendental object." For the moment, we may briefly put this as follows: (1) as is well known, Kant's "transcendental idealism" has another side to it, viz., "empirical realism" (especially of space and time), a doctrine meant to furnish an ontological foundation for the ϕ-level locution of objects (*qua* "appearances" only, of course) as "outer things"; (2) Kant, as we shall show, has a double interpretation of 'the given'

Fig. 1. Four Ontologies of the Subject-Object Relation: Descartes to Kant (Approximately as interpreted by Kant)

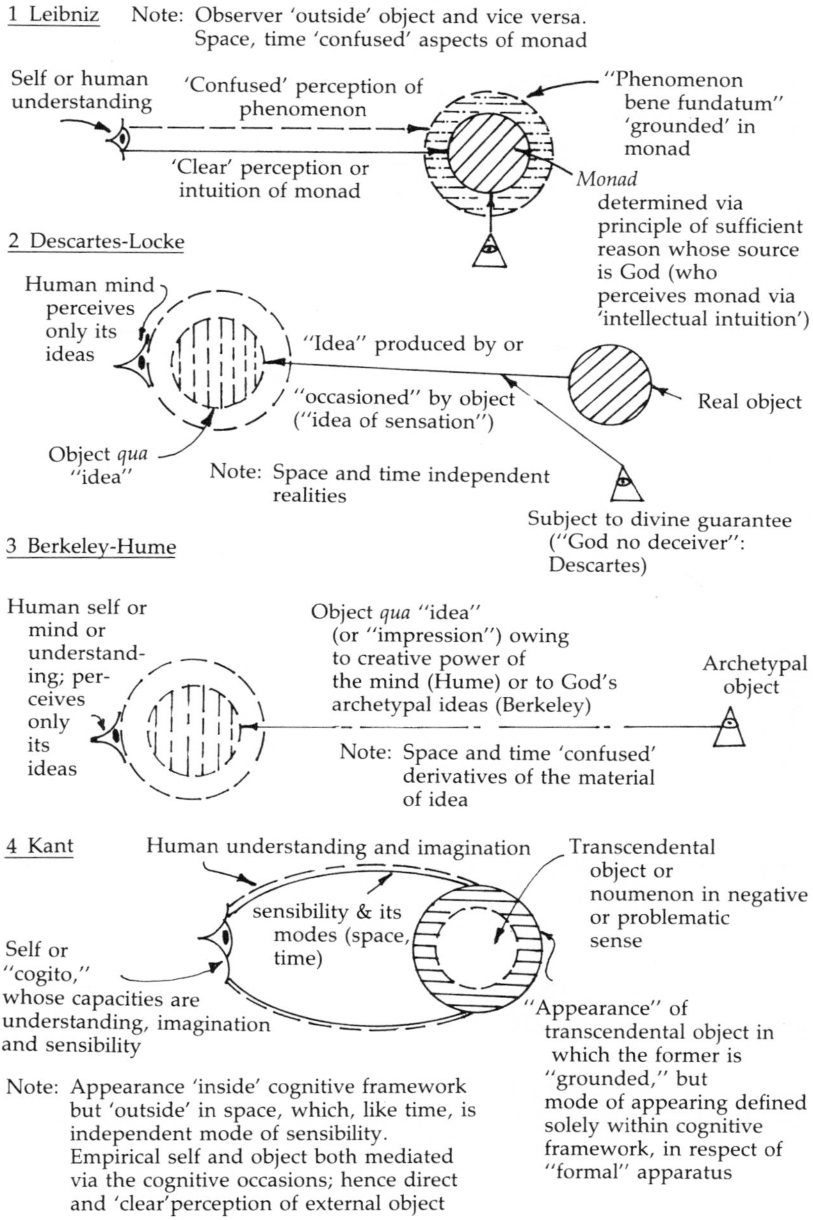

1 Leibniz   Note: Observer 'outside' object and vice versa. Space, time 'confused' aspects of monad

Self or human understanding

'Confused' perception of phenomenon

'Clear' perception or intuition of monad

"Phenomenon bene fundatum" 'grounded' in monad

Monad determined via principle of sufficient reason whose source is God (who perceives monad via 'intellectual intuition')

2 Descartes-Locke

Human mind perceives only its ideas

"Idea" produced by or "occasioned" by object ("idea of sensation")

Object *qua* "idea"

Real object

Note: Space and time independent realities

Subject to divine guarantee ("God no deceiver": Descartes)

3 Berkeley-Hume

Human self or mind or understand-ing; per-ceives only its ideas

Object *qua* "idea" (or "impression") owing to creative power of the mind (Hume) or to God's archetypal ideas (Berkeley)

Archetypal object

Note: Space and time 'confused' derivatives of the material of idea

4 Kant   Human understanding and imagination

sensibility & its modes (space, time)

Self or "cogito," whose capacities are understanding, imagination and sensibility

Transcendental object or noumenon in negative or problematic sense

"Appearance" of transcendental object in which the former is "grounded," but mode of appearing defined solely within cognitive framework, in respect of "formal" apparatus

Note: Appearance 'inside' cognitive framework but 'outside' in space, which, like time, is independent mode of sensibility. Empirical self and object both mediated via the cognitive occasions; hence direct and 'clear' perception of external object

(labeled in the sequel as m_i and m_t, respectively), such that there is *a* sense in which the given is not (or not only) 'in' the mind, not just 'in' sensibility, but also 'apart' from, and in this different sense: 'outside' the context of cognition, 'outside', that is to say, in the "transcendental sense." By contrast, in a philosophy like Hume's—at least on Kant's interpretation—the real or "material" element of experience, the "impressions of sensation," is simply occasioned by "the creative power of the mind" (*Treatise*, I.iii.5), to which alone it is confined.[20]

Kant's response to these difficulties, as per position 4, will become intelligible only as we proceed.[21] As a preliminary, we note that it posits a basic subject-object complex, while at the same time placing these supposedly 'separate' entities—'ego pole' and 'object pole'—inside a unifying 'cognitive shell.' It seeks to achieve these seemingly contradictory demands (separateness and unity) by a fresh interpretation of both components, each activated by the elements of the cognitive shell, regarded as possessing transcendental status, another way of describing the already mentioned move from accounts of the possibility of the world to accounts of the possibility of experience of such a world, the notion of 'world', *simpliciter*, disappearing below the ontological horizon.[22]

I proceed to an explanation of the Kantian reinterpretation of the items shown in position 4, by the use of the reduction-realization technique. Kant (in one of his *Reflexionen*)[23] alludes to a "method of reduction," by reference to a process of "abstraction," or "suspension" of the dimensions of space and time, a process, he says, which alone will make possible the advance from the domain of "appearance" to that of the noumenon. It will be seen that 'reduction' in this case moves, not from O_w^o to O_r, but from T_a ("appearance") to O_r (itself under a given interpretation, here "noumenon").

Let us apply this use of 'reduction' to position 4. The object then ceases to function as "appearance," as does the subject, since reduction now involves the "abstracting" of sensibility *and* understanding, and, indeed, the 'activating' capacities of the self through which these functions are defined.[24] Both self and object are turned, in the first place, into merely logical entities, into "things in general" (cf. A242), very much like the O_l of Leibniz's 'logical world', as per position 1. In Kant, and confining ourselves to the case of the 'object', we find that the "matter of intuition,"[25] as a character of T_a, under reduction becomes a purely logical notion, variously defined by Kant as "the determinable," "the given," "the

49

real," "the constituent elements" (A266/B322)—all to be taken, so far, in a purely logical sense. The "forms of intuition" under reduction disappear altogether, while the noetic aspect of form is defined as "determination" [*Bestimmung*], "relation," or again, as "copula" (A266/B322).

Now all the above "logical" aspects of O_l, on Kant's reading, must be retained in any account of realization, understood as a process operating in a direction opposite to that of reduction. The 'vectorial' aspect of *RRP* is central for an understanding of the term "transcendental" (especially as occurring in the expression "transcendental object"), when used to designate the status of a concept which (1) is (as something purely logical) not so far engaged in a process of realization but which (2) is *intended* in due course to function as part of such a process (call this the 't_o' sense of transcendental). Indeed, Kant's very definition of "transcendental logic," as distinct from mere "general logic," is that, in addition to the *purely* logical dimension of the latter, it involves "a reference to the origin of our cognitions of objects" (A55/B80). Thus concepts like "matter" and "form" have a "transcendental $_o$" status if (1) under reduction we abstract from the specific cognitive *modes* in which 'the given' can be said to 'manifest' itself *as* given, or again (in respect of "form"), if we abstract from the specific cognitive modes in which form is taken to "determine" the matter; (2) if, what is so abstracted (reduced) is viewed as something subsequently capable of entering into a realizational process ([1] is explained in this way at A266/B322; [2], as noted, at A55/B80).

I shall now say that these concepts of "matter and form (in the transcendental sense)" (A266/B322) make up the fundamental character of the *logical* object (O_l) which, when viewed in accordance with the just-explained reduction-realization dynamic, becomes Kant's, frequently felt so puzzling, "*transcendental* object": "the completely indeterminate thought of *something* in general [*etwas überhaupt*]" (A253), (label O_t (f, m), or O_t for short, a second construal of O_r in addition to O_l). From what has been shown, O_t can always be viewed as the starting point for a realization procedure. Here realization might be viewed perhaps on the model of giving an '*interpretation*' to a formal calculus in some system of logic; or one might think of the 'giving of a value to a variable', in either a mathematical or a logical context. In the Kantian case the procedure of realization or interpretation will involve attention to both the material and the formal aspects of O_t (label m_t, f_t), as candidates for realization. Since O_t is the concept of the object prior to, or apart from, any cognitive context, it will obviously be expected to function as one of the referents of Kant's umbrella term "thing in itself" (as we shall see, there are more than half a dozen such referents, a fact which has somewhat confused Kant scholars during the last two hundred years).

It is absolutely essential always to remember that O_t is a concept standing for something that has yet to be subjected to a realization and thus to acquire what Kant calls a "constitution." To ask, therefore, what the constitution of O_t itself may be would be an empty question—as Kant himself points out:

> Although to the question, what is the constitution of a transcendental object, no answer can be given stating *what it is*, we can yet reply that the *question* itself is *nothing*, for the reason that no object is *given* [in the context of] such a question. . . . A question as to the constitution of that something [*Etwas*] which cannot be thought through any determinate predicate—inasmuch as it is posited completely outside the sphere of those objects which can be *given* to us—is entirely null and void. [A470/B507n.; some italics mine]

We can now understand Kant's constant insistence (which has so puzzled many scholars) on the fact that objects, as "appearances," must be "grounded in a transcendental object" (A538/B506), must have a "transcendental ground" (A563/B591) . To this it should not be objected that Kant seems here to be grounding phenomena in a sphere of nothingness, or pure logic. If 'nothingness' is interpreted as a reference to a lack of constitution, then we must remember Kant's response, just cited, that O_t neither possesses nor lacks a constitution. It is not this sort of entity—and he regarded this indeed as an account which supplied a sense to the puzzling features of the Leibnizian monad and its relationship to the phenomena 'grounded' in it.

Kant's insistence on a "transcendental ground" simply means the following: Any empirical object O_w, when interpreted as "appearance" (T_a), is to be viewed as having gone through the transition $O_t \rightarrow T_a$; i.e., it must be viewed as "something in general" (O_t), whose logical characters, m_t and f_t, require certain enabling conditions for their realization. Thus Kant, on one occasion, describes such a process when he says that we may "ascribe to the transcendental object" a formal characteristic, viz., "causality," as a "property by virtue of which it appears" (A538/B566–67), i.e., through which O_t is converted into T_a, so that the object, at first taken in a purely transcendental sense, is thereby transformed into the state of appearing,[26] i.e., acquiring some degree of epistemic and hence ontological significance.

All this shows at once that O_t is clearly not to be viewed as a 'second object,' a thing in itself, apart from the empirical object, *qua* appearance; nor is it an 'empty sphere of nothingness' hiding beneath the phenomenal surface (a mere vacuous shadow of its former Leibnizian self); rather it is simply Kant's way of characterizing the logical status of the object *qua* appearance (T_a) which has emerged from a previous stage, O_t, thus involving a dynamic best visualized through the analytical methodology of *RRP*.

The whole process, in respect of its 'formal' side—i.e., of the function of the categories as explained in the Analytic—is described with great clarity by Kant in the following passage:

> The categories represent no special object, given to the understanding alone, but only serve to determine the transcendental object (the concept of something in general [*etwas überhaupt*]) through that which is given in sensibility, in order thereby to cognize appearances empirically under concepts of objects. [A251]

That O_t is the central notion with which to begin is stated equally firmly in the following:

> The supreme concept with which . . . to begin a transcendental philosophy . . . is the concept of an object in general [*Gegenstand überhaupt*], taken problematically, it being undetermined whether it be something or nothing. [A290/B346]

With these remarks let me proceed to the central aspects of Kant's transcendental type of realization.

IV. *Realizational Levels of Analysis*

In what has preceded, I have referred to O_t (m), or m_t for short, as the element of the 'given' at the level t_o. The thought arises naturally that this must mean that O_t gives or donates something to the mind and the objects which it fashions as appearances; since Kant himself, indeed, speaks of our (or perhaps our sensibility) being "affected" by objects, thus producing "sensation" (A19/B33), itself a condition of 'realizing' any object *qua* appearance. This Kantian formulation has occasioned endless problems—Vaihinger alone devotes twenty-three pages of his magisterial commentary to this sentence, while Adickes wrote a whole book trying to solve 'the puzzle of affection.' Now it is obvious that we cannot be said to be affected by objects qua T_a if affection is a condition of the ontology of T_a in the first place. So naturally people hit on the solution that Kant must mean objects qua things in themselves, particularly since at A358 we are said to be "affected by certain (to us otherwise unknown) objects," to be viewed as "noumenon (or better, as transcendental object)." "But," people exclaim, "Kant doesn't believe in the reality of things in themselves, and even if he did, how can he endow them with causally efficacious powers; what right has he to a hypothesis whose legitimacy the whole *Critique* is meant to put in doubt?" and so forth.

Per contra, others are confused by Kant's use of the term 'thing in itself' in its precritical interpretation of T_s^*—for instance, as T_m, a version of Leibnizian monad, standing for something with metaphysical realist status, a tempting entity to which to assign the agency of affection, standing in a putatively causal relationship with the cognitive subject. It is unlikely that this solution adequately describes Kant's position since the, for him counterfactual, supposition of a "positive sense" of T_m, i.e., T_n^+ (noumenon) surely rules this out. Adickes's doctrine of "double affection"[27] is a marvelous conflation of imaginary actions on the part of T_s^*, T_s, and T_a on the perceptual subject. A greater confusion of levels it would be hard to imagine. Prauss, in his *Kant und das Problem der Dinge an sich*, envisaging affection in terms of such causal or quasi-causal transactions between the variety of putative noumenal and phenomenal agencies and the self, rightly dismisses all such 'solutions' as untenable, though unfortunately not offering any positive interpretation of Kant's real intentions as such.[28]

Finally, there is perhaps little need to refer also to the occasional 'vulgar' supposition of a source of affection that is viewed as the empirical object exerting its influence on the perceptual apparatus of the subject through physical action. This reading is exceedingly tempting since it is not only probable but absolutely certain (on excellent scientific grounds) that physical bodies act on the sensory organism of the observer. But this was not the problem, and the supposed solution here given simply amounts to an impermissible mixing up of o-level and φ-level discourses, involving a confusion which the whole approach of this essay is designed to obviate. We are after all—as was indicated at the start—concerned here with *how* the 'real possibility' of the world, i.e., its ontology, is to be construed. Nor is it just a matter of the problem of the relation between the physical world and the mind of the lone, Robinson Crusoe–type subject—an image sometimes attributed to Kant. We are concerned solely with the nature of Kant's *realizational* approach, an approach that models the world through the transcendental functions of sensibility, imagination, and understanding. So the problem is how to characterize that element in the cognitional process which corresponds to the 'object of knowledge,' and in particular that aspect of the object which corresponds to the *a posteriori* component of knowledge and which, as a 'foreign contribution' triggers off, so to speak, such information as we can gain about our world.

But to return to the core of our problem, and to an advance toward a solution. And here the reader will perhaps already have become convinced that for Kant there simply are not several lots of objects but only one, itself rendered under a variety of descriptions.

Kant's choice of the term "transcendental object" (in the passage mentioned earlier) gives us perhaps a small hint. Of course, at first sight it seems to make matters worse if we think of O_t as an empty shell, or as a merely logical entity. How can logic bear on empirical reality, or real possibility? I think myself that the solution to this problem is as simple as it is unambiguous, but it does involve the full deployment of the resources of the *RRP* technique, including a clear appreciation of the need for keeping sharply distinct the large variety of levels involved in the analysis, and especially keeping separate the ϕ-level from the varieties of o-level discourse which I shall now try to explain in more detail, by reference to the general structure of Kant's deductions, analyzed in figure 2. (It seems to me of the utmost importance to present Kant's arguments in such summary fashion, to avoid getting lost in the usual style of endless distinctions heaped upon distinctions, interrupted by continual censorial exhorations of Kant, telling him that what he says is not clear and that he ought to be clearer and less misleading than he represents himself to be, a most ungenerous denigration of a great philosophical genius.)

Turning to figure 2, we see that the ontological account of O_w is divided into three sublevels, t_o, t_i and r. Spelling out the Kantian structure in table form has the subsidiary function of presenting graphically the vast number of 'correlates' and 'correspondences' alluded to throughout the *Critique*, terms which represent some of the trickiest and yet most profound relationships in Kant's writing. Going through the *RP* at length, even with the help of this figurative representation, would make this essay of inordinate length; the whole thing seems clear enough, for the most part, to speak for itself. I will therefore confine my comments to some of the more general, and more difficult, aspects of this representation of the *RRP*.

Column 2 involves, as can be seen, a sense of "transcendental," which Kant terms "immanent" (A308/B365; A327/B383), symbol t_i. Categories have an "immanent" or "empirical" employment, given a context provided by sensibility (*S*), i.e., "sensation," and the "modes" of sensibility, corresponding, at the ϕ-level, to space and time. Apart from such a context, the concept may be pictured as 'idling', the case represented by t_o in column 1, the level at which we operate with O_t, i.e., with the object at the transcendental level[29] (see above, page 50). Thus at A247/B304, Kant remarks that, if the mediation of sensibility is not available, "the object is merely transcendental, and the concept of the understanding has only transcendental [both times in the t_o sense] employment," which (he adds on the next page) is "really no employment at all," for which reason the "pure categories" may at best be said "to have only transcendental [t_o] meaning," all of which seemingly contradictory pronouncements become perfectly intelligible in the light of our structural distinctions.

But let us consider the *RP*, represented by the transition $O_t \rightarrow T_a$ (T_a being the "appearance" interpretation of O_w^o). As will be seen, this proceeds through several stages and substages, the sequential presentation being—as Kant remarks at B160a—purely for convenience. To these stages there correspond the different 'descriptions' given of the concept of the object, e.g., as "transcendental," as "indeterminate," and as "determinate." Viewing each of these as stages in the whole process of realization will prevent the usual agonizing over how Kant could have referred to the precategorized variety as 'object', or how he could have spoken of 'judgments of perception,' when judgment 'proper' presupposes similar categorization, etc., etc. Seeing all this through the eyes of *RRP* gives us the means for a special application of the 'principle of charity,' allowing Kant to speak of the 'object' in multivalent senses. In the two subsections that follow, I will give some small illustrations of the application of *RRP*.

Before we turn to details, it may be useful to summarize the basic components of the Kantian account in the *Critique* itself, albeit in the light of our process of 'transcendental realization,' in order to

Fig. 2.

← REDUCTION　　　REALIZATION →

1	2	3	4
t_o-level Transcendental framework 'idling'	Stages 1 to 3: The ontology of O_w t_i level: Transcendental framework 'engaged' or "immanent" Stages of Mediation by Sensibility, Understanding, Imagination (S, U, I) (viewed as ego-functions, the 'ego' with t_i status only)	r-level 'Realized' object interpreted as "appearance" (T_a)	ϕ-level Phenomenology of O_w "Sensory world"
Transcendental object (O_t): m_t (Transcendental matter) determinable, the given, real, constituent elements	Aesthetic I. First Stage of Realization: Mediation by S (a) Affection or Determination or Modification of Sensibility = Sensation s ⌢ matter of intuition m_i (when "reference is to subject merely") (when "reference is to object") f_i Intuitional manifold, empirical intuition; m_i, f_i → if s → O: pure intuition (b) Modes of Sensibility ⌢ forms of intuition (Forms of inner sense and outer sense) (Note: $m_i = m_{is} + m_{it}$)	T_a^i "the thing in the appearance"; "the indeterminate object of intuition," with its "matter" and "form" $(m_a\, f_a)$	Secondary qualities: "Indeterminate" space and time "Indeterminate object" "Judgment of perception" "Subjective cognition"

56

f_t (transcendental form) determination, relation, copula	Analytic		
	II. Second Stage of Realization: Mediation by U, I (a) Mediation via U (coming from the side of "thought") Concept (logical category) now 'attached' to U, operating as the "unity" of a synthesis ("Unity of Apperception")—a formal, or "intellectual," synthesis, the unity expressed through the purely logical content of the categorial concepts, f_c ("Determination of the intuitional manifold"). (b) Mediation via I (coming from the side of "sense") I effects "synthesis" of the intuitional manifold ("figurative synthesis"), the aspect of 'unity' of this synthesis being defined under (a), but via the schematization of the categories, interpreting them as being "time-determined under a rule," f_{rs} (the rule comes from the logic of [a], the time from the "sense" [S] of [b], so yielding the required "homogeneity" of "sense" and "thought"). "Formal intuition."	T_a^t appearance qua "determinate object of intuition plus thought"; "phaenomenon"	"Determinate" space and time "Objective cognition" "Judgment of experience" "Objective experience" or "Experience of object" or "Empirical Object"

Note:

1. The determinateness of $S \sim$ the contribution from the object $\sim m_t$ (thing-in-itself qua O_t).
2. An intuitive understanding would yield T_n^+ at this stage 3, without assuming O_t at stage 1 (but this is counterfactual: since we only have T_o^-).
3. "Correspondences": $O_t \sim S$, and to U; $m_t \sim s \sim m_t \sim m_a$
Modes of sensibility $\sim$ forms of intuition $\sim$ space and time.

57

explicate the transition from O_t to T_a (see also the more detailed layout of fig. 2).[30]

O_t will be said to be 'realized' (or 'receive a T_a-type interpretation') by way of the following stages: (1) it comes to be interpreted as "empirical intuition," the equivalent of "appearance" when viewed in an 'object-side' mode, the 'subject-side' mode of which is an "affection of sensibility" ("sensation"), resulting in the representation of the appearance of the object as an "indeterminate" entity; formally: $m_t \rightarrow m_i \ f_i \ (= T_a^i)$; (2) this is followed by a "determination" of the intuitional manifold, via the various syntheses (of imagination and understanding) whose "unity" is defined by the different categories, to yield to an "appearance" of the object as a "determinate" entity; formally: $m_i, \ f_i, \ \rightarrow m_i, \ f_i, \ f_{cs} \ (= T_a^d)$.

1. The Second Analogy of Experience[31]

Our general task will again be that of providing an ontology capable of representing the relevant phenomenology, as rendered by the appropriate form of discourse. In terms of our schema, this will have to be done by way of a realization of O_t, i.e., by 'activating' the m_t and f_t aspects of the object considered as having been subjected to a previous reduction. Only in this way can we be a priori certain that "objects conform to our concepts"; i.e.; T_a is construed via the t_i structure, itself a priori because "we can have a priori cognition only of that in things which we ourselves put into them" (Bxviif.), albeit, as just noted, the ontology of the object (T_a) thus generated will have to reproduce as far as possible the desired features of ϕ-level discourse. The 'activation' of m_t and f_t will, as usual, have to proceed via the mediating functions of sensibility, imagination, and understanding.[32]

The world will thus be reconstructed as a function of experience in general, that is, of the forms of some suitable ϕ-level discourse, itself, however, now viewed as grounded in the required t_i-level structure. The 'world', as it were, first 'gets off the ground' only via such a discourse. We must thus construct a framework of the world for which our speech forms will be adequate, and we can do this only if simultaneously we construct speech forms adequate to the world thereby constructed. This, after all, is the teaching of the Critique. In the Second Analogy this general approach is applied to the notion or speech form of objective temporal sequence.

Very briefly, stage 1 (cf. fig. 2) yields an indeterminate series of "perceptions" with a temporal and spatial dimension ($m_i, \ f_i$);

formally: $p(P) \ldots q(Q)$, the perceptual occasions of events P, Q, with the status of T_a^i; also $P \ldots Q$, for short. This stage does not, so far, yield the locution whereby "things may be said to be necessarily somewhere" and somewhen (in the words of the *Dissertation*, sec. 16). *A forteriori*, neither does it yield a locution whereby we could say that—or even question whether—things are located in an objective time sequence, $P \to Q$, for this requires that $p(P)$ and $q(Q)$ should first be relatable in principle, and the aspect of relation is (according to Kant's position) never contained in the domain of receptivity (sensibility). Stage 2 of the t_i-level apparatus will thus be called upon to supply a model that will provide a *meaningful* notion of 'relating,' Kant's model for this being an "empirical" and "subjective" act of combination or synthesis. Naturally, as a t_i-level component, this "empirical" synthesis will simultaneously have (as an *"actus* of spontaneity" [B130]) a transcendental function: as a condition *sine qua non* of yielding at least a starting point for the definition of the objective time relation, with "empirical realist" import.

So far, however, the relation is construed on the model of an act by the subject, clearly insufficient to ground a speech form which says that P and Q not only are related by the subject but are related "objectively in time" (B219). It is as though we had to demand that the plurality which "the mind had forced into an ideal unity" (*Dissertation*, sec. 2; cf. above, sec. I) would also—in order to prevent it from representing just an "accidental" combination—have to be such that the mind itself was *being determined* to produce an order or "unity" which simulated objectivity. We have hence to represent the combination as something which is tied down in a definite way, which is expressed when we say, for instance, that P precedes Q rather than vice versa. But this necessary determination, whereby we say that, given P, it is Q which is then also given "necessarily," rather than the reverse, is the concept of cause ($= C$). (In terms of our schema this step represents, of course, the activating mediation by the understanding of f_t as the schematized category f_{cs}.) Symbolically: $[p(P) \ldots q(Q)] + C_1 = P \to Q$. Notice that $P \to Q$ is 'causal' only in the Pickwickean sense shown. To represent the non-Pickwickean sense, i.e., $P \to Q$, itself as an instance of an empirical causal law, we would (given suitable empirical evidence) have to formulate this by writing $[P \to Q] + C_2 = P \overset{\Rightarrow}{\to} Q$, the double arrow indicating an 'empirical' causal relation.

This gives us, incidentally, a second sense of 'analogy', in the expression "analogy of experience." Just as at the *empirical* level we feed the causal relation into a temporal sequence $P \to Q$ in order to obtain $P \nrightarrow Q$, so at the *transcendental* (t_i) level we feed the causal relation into an indeterminate time relation, $P \ldots Q$, in order to obtain $P \rightarrow Q$ (Kant's own explanation of the choice of the term "analogy" is that the time relation $P \rightarrow Q$ is modeled in an analogous way on that of the causal relation, $x \nrightarrow y$). The similarity of the two cases has given rise to much misunderstanding (and Kant's examples in *Prolegomena*, secs. 20, 22, have done nothing to lessen it!). The confusion is due to the fact that both $P \ldots Q$ and $P \rightarrow Q$ are described as "accidental" sequences (in German 'accidental' and 'contingent' are in particular used as synonymous terms). But once again 'accidental' in the first case relates to a preexperiential stage 1, $[m_i, f_i]$, whereas in the second case it relates to the postexperiential T_a^d stage.

Innumerable authorities have argued that Kant is here rather confused, claiming either too much or too little, and in any case that he is sliding from the transcendental to the empirical case. If, however, we keep in mind Kant's theory of science, especially as formulated in the official introduction to the *Critique of Judgment* (*CJ*), it will be clear to anyone who cares to read that Kant was perfectly aware that the 'strong' (C_2) case of causality required independent foundation. For instance, in section vi of the introduction he expressly distinguishes the fact that C_1 is a use of the concept, such as to "*prescribe*" causality to nature in general, whereas C_2 is a use where the concept is "*ascribed*" to the order of nature and is justified only via the systematization of suitable empirical laws. Or again: in *CPR* he distinguishes between the C_1 case, which enters as a regulative principle of the *understanding*, whereas in the scientific case, C_2 is said to enter as a "regulative principle of *reason*" (A561/B590).

The perceptive reader will thus see that a fine-structure account can yield a veritable mountain of insights into such problematics as 'Kant's answer to Hume.'

2. *The Notion of Affection*

As hinted before, perhaps the most puzzling feature of Kant's construction is his doctrine of affection, involving as it does also the problem of the relation between things in themselves and the appearances—already itself a thoroughly misleading locution, if we remember that there is only *one* sort of object, albeit under a variety of descriptions corresponding to the various levels indicated in figure 2. Part of the solution to our problem does indeed consist in this awareness that we are dealing with only one object, and the different descriptions, especially in columns 1 and 2, must be regarded as logically independent characterizations of the sequential—and, above all, corresponding—stages of the *RRP*.

Consider stage 1 of column 2: sensation, and the corresponding intuition, is conditional upon an "affection of sensibility" (A253/B309; Kant also speaks of the "determination of sensibility" [A140/B179]; and on the previous page, of the "modification of sensibility"; cf. also A494/B522, where sensibility is said to be "affected in a certain manner with representations").[33] Now there is, as already noted, a strong temptation to look for a 'cause of this affection.' And there is good reason for this, not only by virtue of the Kantian locution, "affection by the object," already referred to, but also because Kant on occasion implies that the "origin of our cognition of objects" involves aspects that must by "attributed to [these] objects" (A56/B80).

To deal with this, I shall attempt the following hermeneutic formulation. Considering the situation at the t_i–level, the description of the origin of our cognitions as involving an "affection" or "determination" of sensibility is, at that level, an 'ultimate'; we simply *describe ourselves* via sensibility being "determined" (*bestimmt*, i.e., specified) in such and such respects, this manifesting itself by way of our obtaining such and such an empirical intuition (m_i, f_i in fig. 2), equivalent to some spatiotemporally and qualitatively specified object (T_a^i). This is much in the way in which Hume's doctrine is usually interpreted: the mind just finds itself with such and such impressions, which are not due to any 'external causes' but are simply mediated by the mind. That 'there is such an object (T_a^i) before me, *says* that there is a *corresponding* "affection of sensibility." Moreover, the empirical content, m_i, f_i, and in particular, m_i, has, as shown in the figure, two components. The first of these implies that the qualitative character of our intuitions is, like space and time—though not 'universally the same' for all men, as is the latter—connected with the "subjective constitution of our manner of sensibility" (A29/B44), such that we perceive the world via, say, the modes of "colors, sounds, and heat," or again, of "impenetrability [and] hardness" (A29/B44; A20/B35). There is, however, yet another element, part of m_i, which is *not* a function of the cognitive apparatus, an element which Kant treats via the notion of the "receptivity" of sensibility (call this element m_{it}) and which likewise characterizes the object *qua* T_a^i, all of which simply expresses the fact that sensibility is determined in a way that is not a function of its "manner" of being affected and which expresses no more than the ultimacy of the fact *that* it is affected, so as to provide a grounding for the notion of the *a posteriori* element in the intuitional part of cognition.

But now, since this element expresses an aspect of intuition that is independent of the "manner of sensibility" (and of its "modes," the groundings of space and time), it will remain behind after reduction, meaning that m_i (here m_{it}), itself "corresponding to sensation" (A20/B34), will, at the t_o level, come out as m_t. In sum: our analysis of the concept of the object involves an ultimate and contingent element, 'the given,' to be regarded as the 'contribution by the object to the cognitive occasion' (cf. A56/B80), which, in the interpretation of the object as "appearance" (T_a), is isolatable as m_{it} and which, under reduction, corresponds to m_t. This is precisely what Kant in fact says when he writes:

> That which corresponds, in objects *qua* appearances, to sensation, is the transcendental matter of all objects [sc. O_t] *qua* things in themselves (matter-of-factness [*Sachheit*], reality [*Realität*]). [A143/B182]

I think no better support for my general reading in terms of *RRP* could be demanded. Note well the use of the term "corresponds": $O_t(m)$, or m_t, does not 'cause' or 'produce' the "affection of sensibility"; it simply *corresponds* (at the t_o-level) to the affection, and hence to m_i, and thus, m_i, f_i, at the t_i-level of the process of realization. This, and nothing else, is the significance of the Kantian locution of "affection by the [transcendental] object" (A358).

In all this it is once more vital to remember, as Kant again and again also emphasized in *Opus postumum*, that throughout these accounts there is reference only to *one* object, and not to many. Thus, for instance, it is important to understand that "intuition" is only the term through which we "refer" to the 'object aspect' of T_a. There is no intuition whereby we *contemplate* a *separate* object; for, as Kant says, "Intuition is that through which [a cognition] relates itself [or refers: *sich bezieht*] immediately to objects" (A19/B33), where the intuitional mode of representation corresponds to "sensation" (cf. Erdmann, *Nachträge*, 12: "intuition is to be taken in respect of [*bezieht sich auf*] the object, sensation merely of the subject").

In sum, Kant's doctrine needs expressing in the 'formal mode of speech' (rather than in his own, more frequent 'material mode'), due note being taken of the different 'correspondences' involved in the presentation of figure 2; m_t then becomes the precognitional rendering of m_i, which latter expresses (at a corresponding ϕ level) the 'empirical' aspect of any cognitive grasp of an empirical object (or matter of fact), involving a reference to the unanticipatable element of the real in sensation, m_{it}. Thus it is not the case that sensibility is 'affected' by m_{it}, still less by m_t, but rather *that* m_{it} obtains (at the t_i level) *says*, simultaneously, that there is an affection of sensibility, as an ultimate fact of the matter, corresponding to the ϕ-level notion of empirical cognition, equivalent to the o-level sense of 'being apprised of a something (an x) in the mode of appearing.' It is this state of affairs, and this only, which is expressed, in a somewhat misleadingly conflated manner, by the Kantian locution of our being affected by an object. This, one may hope, will dissolve the 'riddle of affection.'

This doctrine, in any case, could never have borne the interpretation put on it by many commentators, viz., the idea of a 'causal influence on the part of an external thing in itself on the cognitive subject,' since Kant, at A372, expressly rejects such a doctrine in these terms when he censures the skeptical consequences which flow from position 2, figure 1, in terms of the mistaken idea of regarding "outer appearances as representations produced in us by their objects, these objects being things existing in themselves [*sic!*] outside us." Confusion results only if we fail to distinguish between the thing in itself *qua* O_t and (as here) *qua* T_s^*, the Descartes-Locke (or even Leibniz) 'real object' of positions 1 and 2. Indeed, in the same place, Kant expressly seeks to distinguish the T_s^* doctrine from his own, since by contrast with the former "we may indeed admit that something [O_t], which (in the transcendental sense) may be outside us, is the cause of our outer intuitions (A372)"; but it is then vital to remember that, in the context of O_t, Kant explicitly lays it down that "the word *cause* of course, . . . only signifies the *ground* which determines . . . things" (*Critique of Judgment*, where the O_t is usually referred to as "the supersensible," and cf. B429 for the same point), "ground" expressing something like logical determination, an analogy for which might also be the way in which a scientific law determines the behavior of things, thereby also functioning a bit like a 'ground'.

It was not, therefore, nodding senility which provoked Kant, in his dispute with Eberhard, to insist that, contrary to what had been claimed to be Kant's opposition to things in themselves, the latter were absolutely unavoidable in the scheme of the *Critique*. For:

> The *Critique* places the ground of the matter of sensible representations not . . . in things as objects of the senses, but in

something super-sensible, which *grounds* the sensible representations, and of which we can have no cognitive grasp. It says: the objects quâ things in themselves *give* the matter to empirical intuition ([i.e.,] they contain the ground of the determination of the faculty of representation in accordance with its sensibility), but they *are not* the matter of these intuitions.[34]

In this passage we should note in particular the interpretation of the (actually precritical) notion of "giving" (cf. "producing") by that of "the determination of sensibility." A very similar contention occurs at A496/B524, where, after throwing in a suggestion that O_t may usefully be employed where needed, to render the logical myth of a world existing apart from the context of cognition, and (*per impossible*) with the same phenomenal character as T_a, Kant ends up by characterizing the nonmythical aspect of O_t thus:

The cause [ground, i.e., O_t], of the empirical conditions of this advance [of perceptions], that is to say, [what determines] what members I shall meet with, or also how far I can meet with any such in my regress, is transcendental [in sense t_o], and hence necessarily unknown to me.

Wherever such passages occur, there has been a tendency to overlook their implication or to attribute them to an earlier period of Kant's thinking (on the lines of Kemp Smith's *Commentary*). And it is interesting to note that Graham Bird, when discussing the transcendental object in the context of this passage, interprets the fact that the concept O_t is here *used* to represent a logical myth, implying that this is indeed its true status overall.[35] If the general meaning of *RRP* is accepted, nothing could be further from the truth.

It is, however, very tempting to grasp the nettle by way of the version of O_t as a 'logical myth,' since—as commentators soon discover to their astonishment and confusion—one moment the *transcendental object* is said to "correspond to sensibility as a receptivity" (A494/B522), while earlier on it is the "thing in itself" which is said to be "the true correlate of sensibility," though it "is not known, and cannot be known, through these representations" (A30/B45). Yet the next moment it is the transcendental object which is suddenly declared to be the "correlate of the unity of apperception" (A250), clearly harking back to the *CPR*, first edition, A109, treatment of the transcendental deduction, where the transcendental object is said to be "what alone can confer upon all our empirical concepts in general relation to an object, that is, objective reality" (read 'provided it has advanced to a stage of realization, involving a schematism of the categories, viewed as concepts of the understanding,' etc.). However, the moment one takes the function of O_t (m, f) seriously, Kant's meaning becomes obvious. He is simply making the old point that, in O_t (m, f), m_t *corresponds* to an affection of sensibility, which in turn is the equivalent of m_i; while f_t (the apparatus of the categories) when employed in the context of the understanding represents the set of those functions (the schemata) which expresses the unity of the synthesis involved in stage 2 of the realization procedure (cf. fig. 2 for the details). What is true is that in all this Kant failed to outline the general approach implied to give a clear statement of the fact that the expression "transcendental object" signifies what I have symbolized as O_t (m, f).

For a convenient summary, we may perhaps formulate the affection doctrine in the following way. As represented in figure 1, diagram 4, the ontology of O_w must be interpreted entirely by reference to items that are part of or situated within the boundary given by sensibility, imagination, and understanding. Ontology is not concerned with anything outside that boundary. Expressions such as sensibility's being affected *by objects* thus need to be rendered in a way that keeps them within the boundary. This phrase must therefore be taken in the sense of sensibility's being affected *by way of object*-type representations, as being "determined" in this way (cf. the Eberhard passage rendering cited above), indeed, being "affected *with*" such representations, as per the rendering of A494/B522.

With respect to the ontological account, there is thus no breaking out of the t_o-t_i-r levels of correspondences of figure 2. As one of Kant's correspondents tried to explain this to himself in a letter to Kant:

> The central thesis of the *Critique*, of which one must not lose sight, is this: a regression to discover the nature and conditions of our cognitive faculty is not a search for anything outside that faculty. . . . One can only become aware of them [receptivity and spontaneity] and make them evident to oneself.[36]

Furthermore, affection involves sensation, and the corresponding intuition (m_i, f_i), one of whose components, we saw, m_{it} expresses the fact *that* we are affected in the particular determinate way we are. If we refer to this fact by means of a symbol which indicates its 'existence' in abstraction from the context of sensibility (i.e., under reduction), we obtain m_t, a 'fact' which we have seen Kant to render by the very *terms* "factuality, reality" (A143/B182). The slide from the speech form 'affected in or by the T_a-type way, whose reductive form is $O_t(m)$' to 'affected by $O_t(m)$' is then as tempting as it can be misleading. What is correct is that there is a sense in which T_a is "grounded" in O_t, the sense which is equivalent to defining the ontology of any object in terms of its 'realization,' or, at least, *some* process of realization or other (it need not be on Kantian lines). It is an appreciation of this fact that will remove much of the paradoxical air from the locution which 'grounds' a 'real object' in a foundation of 'mere logic': in Tieftrunk's words, the "ultimate ground [which] is, for our understanding, nothing more than a thought with negative meaning, though, as a mere thought, it is permissible and even necessary."[37] It is the explanation of this 'necessity', in terms of *RRP*, that has hitherto been missing.

In other words, given that O_t has no 'positive' T_n *realization*, it can express no more than the *logical* (transcendental) fact that a T_a realization is 'determined' not only by the a priori framework of space, time, and the categories but also by an element which in its epistemic aspect is wholly *a posteriori*. To view this element as something 'external', with 'causal' import, is to confuse relations *between different objects at the φ level* with relations *between different interpretations of 'the object' at the o level*. There is only one world, O_w, of which we seek to give an ontological account, here in transcendental terms. Both subject and object here come to be located inside the boundary represented in figure 1, diagram 4, and t_i-level happenings can hence be characterized only with respect to that boundary. But this characterization, in terms of the realization procedure, requires the logical anchorage of O_t in which to 'ground' this whole process, a fact which Kant pictures graphically by his misleading reference to the 'external, real, object' which precedes the context of cognition (*Prolegomena*, sec. 13 [2]). At any rate, once a Heraclitean attitude is taken, in terms of *RRP*, rather than the more usual Parmenidean, the center of gravity being placed in the *process* and its governing rules, rather than the entities which it governs, most of Kant's puzzles disappear. And it is then easy to see that no 'external' causal factors are available to make the notion of 'determination of sensibility' anything other than an 'ultimate' fact, part of the analysis of realization, Kant's "matter in the transcendental sense." If this is not an 'external cause', neither should it on any account be described as standing for the 'affection of the self *by the self* '[38]—the disastrous Fichtean direction of post-Kantian idealism. The self does not "posit" itself as an entity affecting itself; rather, it is our analysis of realization which posits the self (sensibility) as affected or determined, a concept intended to render nothing more than the aspect of 'the given' in the object of that analysis.

In concluding this section, I perhaps need not add that Kant's constant insistence that the "transcendental object is entirely unknown to us" is not an empirical, or ϕ-level, characterization of some hidden component or of some mysterious substance or what have you, and for that reason entirely hypothetical, not to say meaningless or redundant, but is once again an expression (albeit formulated in a 'material mode' of speech) of the status of O_t, as a prerealizational entity.

3. *The Doctrine of 'Alternative Realizations'*

As is well known, Kant's transcendental approach has as one of its principal objectives to "contrive" the logical possibility of a method that would allow us to "view the same objects from two different points of view" (Bxviiin.), viz., the object as appearance and as thing in itself, respectively.[39] To bring this about, Kant—in terms of RRP—must represent this as

$$O_t \begin{array}{c} \nearrow T_a \\ \searrow T_n \end{array}$$

where T_n stands for one of the referents of the 'thing in itself,' the 'unstarred' T_s this time being the version of T_s that does not "fill" the whole of "space" but "leaves open a space," unlike T_m and T_i (cf. A287/B343f). Furthermore, O_t, to do its job of transforming into T_a under realization, will—as involving m_f—have to be described as "real object" (albeit, in the "transcendental sense" only, as explained at length above, and on the lines defended in *Prolegomena* sec. 13 [2]). In all this, precritical philosophy of course, in Kant's view, had failed. Thus Leibniz, or the Leibnizian version of *Nova Dilucidatio*, effected realization via the mediation of the divine understanding, via the mode of "intellectual intuition," which can thus generate only *one* type of 'reality,' the purely 'intellectualist' "noogony" of A271/B327. And the same goes for the "sensualized" versions of Berkeley and Hume.[40] On Kant's scheme, we start with O_t (m, f), which "precedes" T_a and T_n (cf. B72); unlike the case of his opponents, where "the representation is . . . itself the cause of the object" (*Nachträge*, xi). We can then invoke *two* mediating functions, understanding *as well as* sensibility, pointing in the direction of two alternative realizations, one of which employs the joint action of sensibility and understanding, generating T_a, the other employing the understanding alone (T_n).

Now we have seen that a realization of an object *qua* T_n, taking place via the understanding alone, is possible only by virtue of "intellectual intuition." But according to Kant's *critical* position (as distinct from the precritical), this type of intuition is a counterfactual assumption, at least with respect to humans. It does not represent a cognitive possibility. However, Kant claims, one can give a "positive sense" to T_n (T_n^+), if the context is not a "theoretical" but a "practical" one, viz., the domain of "pure practical reason." For the domain of 'what ought to be' does not require the sensory constraints which in the field of theoretical reason are alone capable of bestowing "empirical meaning" on objects. Hence the domain of practical reason yields a field in which a realization is effected by the understanding (the pure category of causality) through a determination of the will in accordance with law.

The passage where Kant explains this (the Third Antinomy) is interesting in implying also an almost visionary rendering of the logic of the situation when seen through the eyes of *RRP*. It goes as follows: Empirical objects have to be interpreted *qua* T_a; this implies their being "grounded in a transcendental object," which in turn gives at once a double realization possibility,

$$O_t \mathrel{\substack{\nearrow T_a \\ \searrow T_n}}$$

There is nothing to prevent us from ascribing to this transcendental object, besides the property through which it appears [e.g., causality, as required by the Second Analogy], a causality which is not appearance. . . . On the above supposition, we should, therefore, in a subject belonging to the sensory world have, first, *an empirical character* . . . in accordance with unvarying laws of nature. . . . Secondly, we should also have to allow the subject an *intelligible character*, . . . which is not itself appearance. We might entitle the former the character of such a thing in the appearance, and the latter the character of this thing in itself. [A539/B567]

This passage makes again very clear that our 'triadic' diagram represents not 'three objects' but one and the same object under different descriptions: O_w^o, reduced to O_t. And under no circumstances should O_t be confused here with T_s^*.

Still more interesting, in the *Critique of Practical Reason* there is a passage in which Kant characterizes what I have labeled the transition from O_t to T_n^+ by employing the terminology of realization explicitly:

> I hold open a vacant place for speculative reason, viz. the intelligible, in order to place the unconditioned therein. But I could not realize this thought [*konnte diesen Gedanken nicht realisieren*], i.e. I could not convert it into the cognition of a being that acts, even in respect of its mere possibility. This vacant place practical reason now fills, by way of a specific law of causality in an intelligible world (causality by way of freedom), viz. the moral law. [Beck edition, p. 50. I have modified the translation; for "realize this thought" Beck has "give content to this supposition"!]

How such an argument could be made comprehensible without the use of the transcendental object, and the associated *RRP*, I do not know; yet the number of writers are legion who, since the time of the publication of *CPR* have either denied its cogency or simply forgotten to mention it; alternatively, they have treated it as a first-edition synonym for 'thing in itself,' to be dropped in the second edition. But this too will not do, since O_t is not a synonym for T_s, let alone T_s^*, nor for T_n, since O_t as well as T_n are interpretations of the all-purpose term 'thing in itself,' which itself has, as we have noted, a precritical(T_s^*)and a critical use: (1) precritical, to stand for all the objects, 'real' or 'ideal' (T_m, T_i) occurring in positions 1 to 3 of figure 1; (2) 'critical', to stand, alternatively, for the noumenon in the three senses in which Kant defines the latter: (a) T_n^+, a "positive sense," which attaches to T_n in a "practical" context alone; (b) T_n^-, a "negative sense," which signifies the denial of the possibility of intellectual intuition and which hence amounts to a case of a 'failed realization' of O_t, with T_n collapsing back into the latter: $T_n \rightarrow O_t$; and (c) T_n^o, in a "problematic sense" (A254/310f.), denoting the "problem" constituted by the task of effecting a realization in the absence of the context of sensibility, evidently a 'halfway stage' between O_t and T_n^+, or between O_t and T_n^- (a final interpretation, T_n^b, will be deferred to a later section). Taken with our three versions of T_s^*, the expression 'thing in itself' thus has at least eight uses: O_t, T_n^+, T_n^-, T_n^o, T_n^b, and the three versions of T_s^*, each of which Kant claims to function as a 'thing in itself', for a variety of reasons.

It is thus no wonder that confusion has reigned since the days of the appearance of the first *Critique*. The use of the term 'object', in the expression "transcendental object," when coupled with a lack of appreciation of the multivalent employment by Kant of the term "thing in itself," casts its baneful spell over most Kantian commentaries. One of the most brilliant of these, by P. Strawson, is no exception.[41] In his discussion of the thing in itself, by which we are said "to be affected" (*The Bounds of Sense*, p. 253), he comes to the conclusion that we cannot make the distinction between the thing in itself and as it appears because distinctions in general "must, if they are to be significantly employed, find an empirical use, have empirical criteria for their application" (p. 255). Now to start with, the reference, on the same page, to the A30/B45 passage—I have already alluded to it above—to the "true correlate of sensibility" as "the thing in itself," without further explanation, betrays at once Strawson's ignoring of the distinction between O_t and T_s, whether regarded as T_n^+ or T_n^-. For, as we have seen, only O_t can legitimately be used for a characterization of the doctrine of affection; moreover, we have noted that at A494/B522 it is indeed O_t which is expressly stated to "correspond to sensibility viewed as receptivity."

But now to the main point. Strawson notes quite correctly that realization (I am using my term, for short), in the sense admitted by the *Critique*, yields only cognition of objects, not the objects themselves, unlike "intuitive understanding" (or "intellectual intuition"), which can achieve such an aim, albeit counterfactually, as already noted. But Strawson now uses this fact for quite a different purpose. Not being able to make sense of the contrast between transcendental object and empirical object, he thinks that Kant wants to *create* a sense by formulating a contrast between the empirical object and the object of intellectual intuition (corresponding to our T_a, as contrasted with T_m). Since Kant in the *Critique* no longer allows the latter any empirical meaning, Strawson concludes that Kant's attempt to give *any* meaning to nonsensory objects is doomed to failure: "Identity of reference . . . is impossible of performance." Worse still, Kant seems to insist—incomprehensibly, Strawson thinks (I have myself, of course, already sought to give this a legitimate sense)—that the object of cognition *preexists* (cf. B72, and *Prolegomena*, sec. 13 [2]). Against this, since we cannot give any empirical meaning to this object, Strawson concludes, we have nothing to compare; so "Kant fails" (p. 254); he cannot legitimately speak of 'pre-existing'.

I have selected this version from among the multitude of

objections that have been made against Kant since the *Critique* first appeared in print because it presents with particular clarity what confusions result—despite brilliance of exposition—if we do not first make clear to ourselves the elementary distinctions involved in the various uses of T_s, together with the whole conception of *RRP* which this implies. Without this, Strawson's critical apparatus is far too thin; the emphasis on 'empirical meaning,' which in turn entails the complaint of the lack of 'identity of reference' between T_a and T_s, has lost sight entirely of Kant's methodological concept of "transcendental meaning," itself in turn requiring interpretation in terms of the *RRP* method. Strawson's complaint is like a complaint one might urge against the notion of the "interpretation" of an uninterpreted calculus, on the grounds that the two lacked identity of reference. Yet O_l is related to T_a formally in just some such way. In short, Strawson's conclusion turns out to be not so much a rejection of any intelligibility claim concerning the thing in itself as a rejection of the whole method of transcendental argumentation, on the cogency of which as a whole I have, of course, no comments.

V. *Transcendental Reflection and the Image of the Sphere of Reason*

Two images stand out in what has preceded: the logical sphere which represents in some way the place where 'the object is brought to a state of appearing' and the image of the 'boundary' which confines things *qua* appearances to a finite region of logical space. Now Kant himself introduced here a very appropriate model, the model of the "sphere of reason," which occurs in the section of *CPR* entitled "Transcendental Methodology."[42] The simile occurs at A762/B790, where "reason" is compared not to an "indefinitely extended plane" but to a

> sphere, the diameter of which can be obtained from the curvature of the arc of its surface—that is to say, from the nature of synthetic a priori propositions—and whereby we can likewise specify with certainty its volume and its limits. Outside this sphere (the field of experience) there is nothing that can be an object for reason; nay, the very questions in regard to such supposed objects relate only to the subjective principle of a complete determination of those relations which can occur under the concepts of the understanding to be found within this sphere.
>
> We are actually in possession of such a priori synthetic cognitions, as is indicated by the principles of understanding which anticipate experience.

Fig. 3. Ideogram

Kant's Sphere of Experience
(As seen in transcendental reflection)
(Solid lines denote effective realizations)

Diagram 1

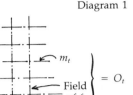

t_o level: Transcendental object:
f_t Defines the vertical, or logical (formal), coordinates of this space
m_t Defines the horizontal or 'material' coordinates.

Diagram 2

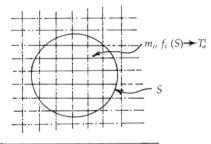

t_i level: Stage 1
Introduction of condition of sensibility into t_o- space: m_t thereby converts into m_i, under the condition of the modes of sensibility, thus yielding f_i; $m_i, f_i \rightarrow T_a^i$, corresponding to *the undetermined object.*

Diagram 3

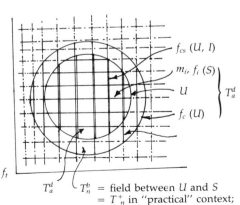

T_a^d T_n^b = field between U and S
= T_n^+ in "practical" context; otherwise O_1

t_1 level: Stage 2
The f_t coordinates here are pictured as 'curling round' the domain of sensibility, through the mediation of the understanding and imagination.* Note that only part of the 'space' created by f_c is filled by the domain of sensibility, inside which the categories f_c are schematized to f_{cs}. The space between the S domain and the total U domain is "empty" of intuition, thus yielding a place that may be filled in some other, e.g., the "practical" context: the domain of the noumenon; whilst $m_i, f_i, f_{cs} \rightarrow T_a^d$, the determined object of intuition.

* This 'curling round' pictures Kant's "empirical employment of the categories."

I want to use this image in order to give a more diagrammatic representation of the *RRP* approach (see fig. 3), partly also because I believe, as before, that images can provide important schematizations of abstract arguments, and in particular of Kant's formal presentations. (The individual diagrams in this figure represent the various stages of realization through which O_t goes on its way to achieving T_a status, represented by the sphere in the bottom diagram of position 4 shown in figure 1.)

To facilitate access to the significance of these figures, we may avail ourselves of a concept (suitably generalized) which Kant calls "transcendental reflection" (A261/B317f.; A269/B325) and the allied notion of "transcendental cognition" (A56/B80). In terms of figure 2 the latter is simply our account ("cognition") of the t_i-level apparatus, considered as conditions of the "possibility of cognition" of empirical objects. (These are clearly two uses of 'cognition', of the t_i-level framework and of the ϕ-level object, respectively.) Transcendental reflection itself relates to the boundaries of the sphere of experience. "We resort," so Kant explains, "to transcendental reflection, in order to determine for which cognitive faculty [certain concepts, e.g., space and time] are to be objects" (A269/B325), for instance, whether space and time are ultimately 'grounded' in sensibility or—as in Leibniz—in the understanding. A little later in our passage Kant says, "Let me call the place which we assign to a concept, either in sensibility or in pure understanding, its *transcendental location*" (A268/B324). Transcendental locations are not, of course, physical or geometrical locations, just as terms like 'existence' or 'outside', as already shown, have, in addition to any empirical meaning, also a transcendental significance.[43]

To obtain a proper grasp of the notion of "transcendental reflection," we imagine ourselves to have effected a reduction. Let us picture this as the vacating or emptying of a 'space'—again in a transcendental sense, the sort of 'space' implied at A286/B343 or at A289/B345, or at *Prolegomena*, section 57,[44] where Kant speaks of the transcendental "boundary" as the place of "contact of filled space (experience) with empty space (of . . . the noumena)"—the empty space corresponding to our previous notion of the result of reduction leading to an ontology of zero value. The 'objects' in such a space will be what I have defined as O_r. Then, in order to proceed to a process of transcendental realization, O_r will be construed, as before, as O_t (m, f) in the way explained at length above.

In such a space transcendental reflection not only abstracts, of course, from all phenomenological considerations, these having been "bracketed out" (to use Husserl's term), but also starts from a state of "nullity" with respect to the ontology of the object. All we have to begin with is a transcendental basis (or "ground"), in sense t_o, represented by the coordinates of diagram 1 in figure 3,[45] a space which we imagine to be gradually 'filled', via the activating functions of the ego, in the context of actual occurrences of cognition. Transcendental reflection stands thus 'outside' the world which it then proceeds to envisage as 'brought into being' via the various stages of realization. With respect to our diagrams, for convenience shown as two-dimensional structures, though representing, of course, three-dimensional spheres, the onlooker (reader), as the 'center' of transcendental reflection, may thus be pictured as positioned in an additional (here, third) dimension. We have already noted Kant's point that "the transcendental object" is "outside us," an "expression . . . [which] signifies, what, as *thing in itself* [sc. O_t], exists apart from us," in contradistinction from the sort of 'outside' "which belongs solely to outer *appearance*" (A373). Not for nothing, therefore, does Husserl, in section 32 of *Crisis*, describe this as "the possibility of a concealed truth in Kant's transcendental philosophy; the problem of a 'new dimension.' "

The realization type modeled in these diagrams connotes, as mentioned, the "transcendental" case, in particular, the processes taking place at the t_i level of figure 2. That is to say, it effects the possibility of the *cognition* of objects, not of *objects, simpliciter*, the object, apart from the context of experience, having no "empirical" but only "transcendental meaning" (A248/B305; B308). And only in this type of realization (which involves O_t) can we speak of any object as 'preceding' the realization process, represented by diagram 1 in the figure. O_t corresponds somewhat to Wittgenstein's "colorless objects" (*Tractatus*, 2.0232). In reflection, we may imagine the object 'lit up,' acquire 'color', i.e., brought to a state of 'appearing', via the activating functions of the 'self', in the context of actual occasions of objective cognition, the first stage of such an activation being shown in diagram 2, i.e., as a function of the "affection of sensibility". m_i, f_i ($= T_a^i$) is shown as a function of this "affection," equivalent to the mode in which the "indeterminate object" represents itself (cf. again, "The indeterminate object of an empirical intuition is entitled appearance" (A20/B34)). And here the formal aspect of receptivity is, of course, represented by the m_t of diagram 1.

Diagram 3 is the most interesting since it represents graphically much of the situation as described by Kant in the 'transcendental space' sections alluded to a moment ago (A288/B344f.). Note here that the vertical ordinates of diagram 1 signify something like the categories in their purely logical interpretation (f_l); by contrast, the single vertical full lines of diagram 3 represent these categories (labeled f_c) as 'belonging' to the understanding. (Remember, in *Nova Dilucidatio* they were attached to the *divine* understanding, whereas in the 'neutral' or 'idling' case represented by diagram 1—the t_o level of column 1, fig. 1—they are altogether 'unattached', or 'idling', i.e., we do not have to decide at that stage whether the categories represent forms of human thinking or Platonic Forms or divine concepts or *purely* logical concepts, etc.) Finally, inside the sphere bounded by sensibility as well, the vertical lines f_c are shown doubled up (f_{cs}), to represent the schematization of the categories, what we have seen Kant describe as the "realization of the categories by the schemata of sensibility" (A146/B186), "sensibility thus realizing the understanding in the very process of restricting it" (A147/B187).

This last remark is plainly illustrated in diagram 3: here the understanding bounds a larger field than sensibility. According to Kant, the categories acquire "empirical meaning" or "employment" only within the sphere bounded by sensibility; the latter thus "restricts" the space bounded by the understanding. Moreover, the *area between* the circles S and U is the area of the 'intelligible' (the understanding), "left vacant" by sensibility, but for which one can now at last conceive a function; e.g. in the moral context:

> The categories accordingly extend further than sensible intuition, since they think objects in general, without regard to the special mode ([such as] sensibility) in which they may be given. But they do not thereby determine a greater sphere of objects. [B309]

The 'object in general' here mentioned is best interpreted as representing the noumenon *qua* T_n^b, i.e., as the "boundary notion" of A255/B310, already noted before, Kant's intention being, as we have seen, "to ascribe" to f_t, or rather to f_c, a function in a noncognitive, i.e., "practical" context.

VI. *Conclusion*

I have tried to present not an argument but instead a key to the 'critical' structure. Its use, it will by now be appreciated, yields a powerful insight into and grasp of even the trickiest of Kantian pages. Such a key could not have been constructed in previous times, since fresh insights (e.g., from Husserl as well as many others) were needed to translate into more graphical language those strands of the Kantian consciousness which were so close to the action that they were barely perceived consciously by him and hence not expressed in any explicit manner.

I should like, in conclusion, to test our newfound understanding of the structure of Kant's thought, with the aid of our 'glossary' of terms, and the point of view of the processes involved in *RRP*, by reference to two or three 'difficult' passages, in which Kant seeks to explain how we come to conceive mistakenly of the possibility of the existence of noumena—naturally, as the reader will by now appreciate, in the sense of T_n^+. The first passage occurs at A251, where Kant tries to explain why people always feel the need for "adding noumena to the phenomena," instead of being "satisfied with the substrate of sensibility" (clearly O_t). The explanation, he says, is the following. The teaching of the *Critique* clearly implies that "it follows from the concept of appearance" that "something which is not appearance must correspond to it"—note the use of the mysterious 'corresponds'. For the very

> word appearance already indicates a reference to something, the immediate representation of which is, indeed sensible, but which even apart from the constitution of our sensibility (upon which the form of our intuition is grounded), must be something in itself, that is, an object independent of sensibility.[46]

This passage has been thought to contradict much of Kant's 'mature' teaching—as this is often called, e.g., by Kemp Smith. Yet it characterizes the very heart of Kant's doctrine. "Apart from the constitution of our sensibility" indeed: this is the reductionist transition m_i, $f_i \rightarrow m_t$, the latter 'corresponding'—as has been emphasized already—to the m_{it} component of m_t. Naturally, if m_t, and, with this, O_t, is confused with a form of $T_s{}^*$, Kant's account makes no sense at all. Still less will this be the case if one thinks that the passage implies the 'existence' of a realized version of O_t, i.e., T_s in the sense of T_n^+. One will, however, imagine this as the version intended if one remembers that the reference to the 'substrate of sensibility' is to the "ground of the appearance" (A538/B566). For 'How could an appearance be said to rest on the ground of a merely *formal* substrate?' one can imagine a reader to reflect. We have already explained the sense in which, however, this is quite all right;

it just says that there is a correspondence, under realization, between T_a and O_t.

Our reader, however, feels further disconcerted by the next sentence: "There thus results admittedly the concept of a *noumenon*, which however signifies nothing positive, [i.e., not] a determinate cognition of some thing or other, but only the thinking of something in general [*etwas überhaupt*], in respect of which I abstract from all form of sensory intuition." So in response to the imaginary question, Is this T_n in the sense of T_n^+? the answer is, No, the sense is T_n^-, a rhetorical method of sending the reader back to O_t. Now further, however, in the next paragraph Kant expressly declares that "the transcendental object . . . cannot be entitled the noumenon," on the grounds that "we know nothing of what [the former] is in itself," at which point many Kant readers frequently give up in despair, charging Kant with having here reached the very height of incomprehensibility. Yet nothing could be more transparently clear. First, Kant does not mean, of course, that we *do* know what the noumenon is in itself but not what O_t is in itself; instead, his meaning is that (as already explained) O_t is not the sort of thing which as such *has or lacks* a constitution but is always the aspect of the object still awaiting acquisition of such a constitution via a process of realization. Second, though in the previous sentence, quoted, he had implied that under reduction there "results the noumenon"—meaning O_t, the denial in the next sentence that O_t = noumenon, as the context makes perfectly plain, refers to the T_n^+ sense of noumenon, while in the previous passage $O_t = T_n$ in the T_n^- sense of the term. It is thus plain that any understanding of these central sections is once again predicated upon the condition of our reading them in the light of the *RRP* procedure and keeping in mind the distinctions of sense between the various terms involved. My object, however, in focusing on a passage such as the present is precisely to indicate how much in the thought it represents depends on making conscious the underlying *RRP* technique which it incorporates.

As a second test I have already had occasion to allude to the passage at the end of the "Amphiboly of the Concepts of Reflection," where Kant notes that "the concept of an object in general, taken problematically is the supreme concept with which . . . to begin a transcendental philosophy" (A290/B346). And we have seen that in our scheme this concept appears as the transcendental object. Let us see how Kant develops this in the rest of the passage here alluded to, explaining again how we trick ourselves into the mistaken belief in the existence of noumena:

> So we think something in general [*etwas überhaupt: O_t*] and while on the one hand we determine it sensorily [via the mediation of sensibility, to yield T_a], on the other hand we distinguish nevertheless the general object [*Gegenstand*], represented in abstracto [O_t], from this mode of intuiting it; and there remains for us now a mode to determine it [the *Gegenstand*] through mere thinking [i.e., the understanding], which though it is a mere logical form without content, appears to us nevertheless as a mode for the object [*Objekt*] to exist in itself (noumenon) [T_n^+], without having regard to the intuition which is limited to our senses [and which can yield only T_a].

But more remarkably, perhaps, to sharpen the reader's wits, consider a final passage which almost immediately precedes the above:

> Understanding limits sensibility, but does not thereby extend its own sphere. In the process of warning the latter that it must not presume to claim applicability to things in themselves but only to appearances, [the inner circle of diagram 3], it does indeed think for itself an object in itself [*denkt er sich einen Gegenstand an sich selbst*], but only as transcendental object [O_t], which is the cause [ground] of appearance and therefore not itself appearance. . . . We are completely ignorant whether it is to be met within us or outside us, whether it would be at once removed with the cessation of sensibility, or whether in the absence of sensibility it would still remain. [A288/B334]

And Kant concludes by saying that if we wish to call this object noumenon we are free to do so, provided it is remembered that this concept simply marks the boundaries of cognition (experience), T_n^b, leaving "open a space" to be filled in some other way, if that were possible. (Passages such as these, incidentally, explain why Kant after 1781 abandoned the *term* "transcendental object," since the 'noumenon', understood as T_n^b, would do as well, without involving misleading expectations concerning hidden 'objects'.)

But to return to the end of our last passage: What can be meant by saying that O_t might be *removed together with a removal of sensibility*? The answer will now perhaps be obvious: O_t's essential function is here conceived as the starting point of realization procedure which involves, to begin with, sensibility, as well as, subsequently, understanding and imagination. We might put this by saying that O_w is here construed as T_a, where T_a is a notion whose transcendental history *necessarily* involves the 'starting stage' O_t, as an *essential* element. Hence, where the construal of O_w as T_a is abandoned, then O_t disappears as well, unlike the bracketed O_w^ϕ, which is not touched by any such ontological analyses.

This solves the problem of the significance of the first of Kant's two alternatives at the end of the passage. What about the second, which suggests that perhaps the transcendental object might after all "remain behind," despite the cessation of sensibility? This is obvious also: There are after all, as we have seen, a number of possible senses for the term 'noumenon', which sometimes functions synonymously with 'thing in itself', T_s. Thus it might quite well function as T_s^*. In the latter case what Kant would be implying is that an entirely different type of realization procedure is always logically possible, such as the first of the three possibilities described above, the 'metaphysical' type. So Kant may just have doffed his hat, in playful gesture, to the ghost of the Leibnizian monad.

There could be no better instance of Kant's mysterious, sleep-walking ability to conceal the most complex constructions between quasi-rhetorical remarks that at first sight seem to be bereft of almost any significance. In reality, we see that they are profound hints which, as much as some of the most concentrated doctrinal pages at the heart of the *Critique*, involve a series of 'deep-structure' layers which it has been the object of this essay to reveal.

APPENDIX

Kant and the Validity of Scientific Method

I. *Three Ontologies of Science*

In the preceding pages we have concentrated attention on 'general ontology,' which deals with "the transcendental part of the metaphysics of nature [in general]" (*Metaphysical Foundations of Natural Science*, preface, trans., Ellington p. 6), as distinct from "special metaphysics," which deals with the foundations of Newtonian dynamics, and of 'systems ontology,' which confronts the problem of theory construction in science in general. In this appendix I want to deal briefly with the latter—partly to illustrate the clarificatory power afforded by *RRP* in the area of the Transcendental Dialectic (see also note 11 below, especially my chapter in Mellor, ed. [1980]).

To begin with, the significance of 'systems ontology' may best be grasped by considering first Kant's formulation of the criteria for the acceptance of the empirical hypotheses of science, a matter which will involve a comparison of all three kinds of ontology that can be distinguished in Kant's writings on science. (Cf. the appended scheme, fig. 4 "Methodological Components of Scientific Theory [A Kantian Formulation]"). The general formulation is mooted in Kant's lectures on *Logic* (cf. Hartman and Schwarz, trans., pp. 92–93). Kant there distinguishes, first, the inductive "*probability*" of a hypothesis, based on its power to "explain the consequences" that are deducible from the hypothesis, the hypothesis being the "presupposition" of the consequences; second, "the *possibility* of the presupposition itself," which is something that "must be apodeictically certain"; as must likewise be, third, the consequences, in the sense that they must follow with deductive certainty from the hypothesis; finally, the "*unity*" of the hypothesis, by which Kant in this place means the sufficiency of the hypothesis to serve as explanation without additional, e.g., ad hoc, supplementary hypotheses.

This last-named criterion we may expand, in line with the exposition in the "Appendix to the Transcendental Dialectic" (A642/B670ff.), where "unity" is explained as "the systematic unity of the knowledge of the understanding" (A647/B675)—meaning by the latter "the *empirical* acts of the understanding" (A664/B692), it being "the business of reason to render the unity [of these acts] "systematic," acts which bring the phenomena "under empirical

Fig. 4. Methodological Components of Scientific Theory (A Kantian Formulation)

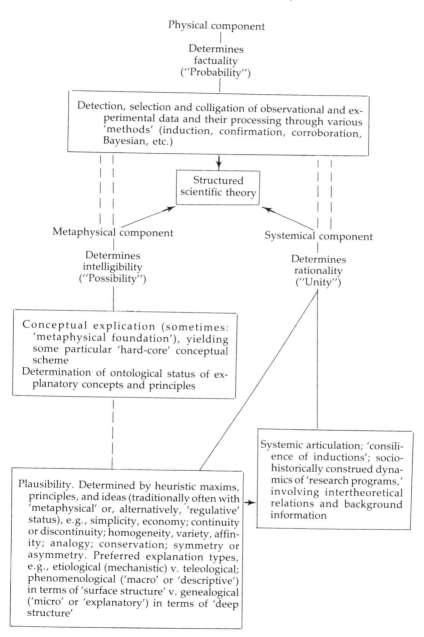

Physical component
|
Determines
factuality
("Probability")
|

Detection, selection and colligation of observational and experimental data and their processing through various 'methods' (induction, confirmation, corroboration, Bayesian, etc.)

Structured
scientific theory

Metaphysical component
|
Determines
intelligibility
("Possibility")

Systemical component
|
Determines
rationality
("Unity")

Conceptual explication (sometimes: 'metaphysical foundation'), yielding some particular 'hard-core' conceptual scheme
Determination of ontological status of explanatory concepts and principles

Systemic articulation; 'consilience of inductions'; socio-historically construed dynamics of 'research programs,' involving intertheoretical relations and background information

Plausibility. Determined by heuristic maxims, principles, and ideas (traditionally often with 'metaphysical' or, alternatively, 'regulative' status), e.g., simplicity, economy; continuity or discontinuity; homogeneity, variety, affinity; analogy; conservation; symmetry or asymmetry. Preferred explanation types, e.g., etiological (mechanistic) v. teleological; phenomenological ('macro' or 'descriptive') in terms of 'surface structure' v. genealogical ('micro' or 'explanatory') in terms of 'deep structure'

81

laws" (A664/B692). So "theoretical reason" brings about the systematization of empirical laws into higher-level scientific *theories*, and one of the criteria here is the logical coherency of the laws—hence the above allusion to "apodeictic certainty" in relation to "unity."

I have used these suggestive remarks of Kant's to construct the triadic scheme of figure 4, incorporating some further methodological ideas that have been developed since Kant's time—though, I hope, in the spirit of the Kantian enterprise. The three components have a peculiar relationship to and relevance for the three types of ontology that we have distinguished, 'general', 'special', and 'systems' ontology. 'General ontology' relates here only indirectly to what I have labeled the 'physical component' which formulates the usual inductive and similar logical processes involved in the formation of hypotheses; it simply defines the 'possibility' of any cognitive relation to empirical fact (Kant's "experience in general"), a subject which does not concern us here any further. Nor does 'special ontology,' which is dealt with in Kant's *Metaphysical Foundations of Natural Science*. "Possibility" there enters explicitly, whereas it enters only *implicitly* into the other two components.

While the metaphysical component treats explicitly of the possibility of the fundamental laws and concepts of Newtonian dynamics, by showing that these incorporate, and are special expressions of, the corresponding categorial principles of the general ontology; in the 'systemical' case the situation is different again. This component (like the 'physical' one) states desirable additional criteria supposedly determining the acceptance of hypotheses involved in the *systematic* account of the phenomena of nature, the choice of any particular criterion (such as shown in fig. 4) being governed by historical, psychological, and other such factual considerations. What is required in addition (on Kant's view at least) is (as in the case of the categories) a "birth certificate" (A66/B129), testifying to the "objective validity" (or its equivalent) of the methods involved in scientific systematics and thus accounting for its "real possibility."

The discussion of this problem is to be found, for instance, at A649/B677f., and in *Critique of Judgment*, second introduction (secs. 5, etc. Bernard trans., pp. 20ff.) The topic of the "real possibility" of systematics, and of the corresponding "order of nature," is discussed in these chapters in terms of "presupposing" certain "transcendental" principles or maxims—"transcendental," of course, just *because* such principles are viewed *as* presuppositional with respect to the possibility of systematics.

To the three branches of figure 4 there thus correspond three questions: How is nature in general possible? How is physical nature possible? and How is an order (or unity) of nature possible? (At A846/B874, Kant refers to the first two of these as, respectively, "ontology" and "rational physiology," in parallel with which we might perhaps label the third "rational systemology").

While these are three separate questions, the fact that they *are* separate has not always been appreciated, far too many Kant commentators thinking that Kant is 'laying the foundations of science' ('special' and 'systems' ontology) when in reality he is concerned only with the concept of 'nature in general' as the object of 'general' ontology. However, the confusion between these different levels which this implies has a source, nowhere made plainer than in Kant's dealing with the problematic of causality.

The reason is as follows. Kant appeals to the relevance of the causal relation at each of the three levels or domains we have distinguished. In the field of general ontology, he seeks to show (as we have seen) that the causal relation is a necessary (transcendental) ingredient in any construal of the notion of the experience in general of objective succession. Thus each evidential instance of a causal law as a contingent empirical sequence of events involves this appeal to the ingredient of causality. But in *Metaphysical Foundations of Natural Science (MFNS)*, Kant employs the 'universal law of causation' (in the form 'Every change has a cause') also at the level of 'special ontology,' as the *general* formulation underlying the law of inertia ('Every change of motion requires the action of a force'), the law resulting from the *interpretation* of 'change' and 'cause' as 'change of motion' and 'force', respectively. This is not, of course—as Kant indeed notes—a transcendental argument; it only *employs* a principle which has transcendental force in the domain of general ontology for the purpose of "application" in the field of special ontology (in Kant's technical characterization of this it is not something "transcendental" but an analysis in "special metaphysics"; cf. *MFNS*, preface, p. 6).

Finally, the *concept* of cause is again required at the level of systems ontology in order to *formulate* empirical uniformities as causal laws, usually by invoking the law of causation as a "regulative principle of *reason*" (not of "understanding," as in the case of general ontology; cf. A561/B589). Now the relationships among these three domains are not deductive. It is simply the case that Kant contends that special and systems ontology, respectively, should be based if possible on the *employment* of the transcendental concept or principle to assure that these two domains involve constructions that are *tied down to* the fundamental structure of general ontology.

Having thus, I hope, clarified the relations and differences among these three domains, let us proceed to the problems involved in the Kantian account of systems ontology.

II. *Reduction-Realization with Reference to Systems Ontology*

In what follows, I shall not, of course, be concerned with the details of the systemic component—of its historical and methodological significance, interesting as this would be in itself (for some details, see my *Metaphysics and Philosophy of Science*, chap. 8, sec. 4(c))—but shall confine myself to the problem of the *validity* of any systems ontology (or 'systemology') as such, corresponding to the question, How is a systematics of nature possible? Not unsurprisingly, perhaps, the way Kant deals with this follows closely (though not identically) the path taken in the case of general ontology, involving the 'injection' of certain "logical" ideas, principles, or maxims which, by 'generating' a systematic account *in the first place*, simultaneously acquire also "transcendental" status.

The 'in the first place' is here, of course, the operative phrase for our characterization of the transcendental approach. As before, we shall formulate its significance in terms of our reduction-realization procedure. Summarily: after reduction, nature will *in principle* present only a concatenation of objects, any systematic order in these objects becoming thereby altogether *undefined* (in Kant's terms, 'undetermined'). Again, as before, we *assume*, of course, that there *is*, as a matter of *actual* fact, an order of nature, symbol O_w^θ. The transcendental question is thus, as usual, concerned solely with the ontology of O_w^θ, with its 'real possibility,' more particularly, with the possibility of the corresponding "*experience*, as an empirical *system*" (*CJ*, first introduction, Haden trans., p. 15; my italics). This differentiates Kant's approach, after all, from the older 'metaphysical' realization procedure. After reduction, 'real possibility' will be defined, as in the 'general' case, in terms of the injection of certain concepts, intended to generate the required mode of systemicity.

At this point one may ask a general question concerning such a transcendental approach: What is the point of this rigmarole of 'depriving' nature of its systemicity or unity, only in order to put it back again? (I call this 'Braithwaite's question,' since it was urged by the latter against Kant about twenty years ago, in criticism of a paper I was then delivering on Kant's philosophy of science.) Actually, our reduction-realization ontology makes an answer to this question particularly clear. It highlights that Kant is not formulating any principles of scientific methodology, still less of science, but instead is concerned only with the question of how we can have "synthetic a priori" cognition of such methodological principles (cf. A663/B691). According to Kant, "We can have a priori cognition only of that in things which we ourselves put into them" (Bxviii); only in this way can we know that the "object" (here the "system" or "unity of nature") will "conform to the concepts" (Bxvii). In other words, the ontology of the order or unity of nature must be so viewed that it 'gets off the ground' only via the usual transcendental injection or realization procedure. And this requires that nature be viewed, in the first place, as having been subjected to a reduction, so that its realization ('transcendental realization') is a function of the autonomous generation of its ontology on the part of the transcendental philosopher, rather than being 'discovered' or 'hypothesized', so to speak, 'from without.' I shall return to the significance of this in the sequel.

For the moment I want to turn to one of the central features of Kant's approach, that of the two alternative ways of viewing objects: as appearances and as things in themselves (cf. Bxviiin.). Where before the contrast drawn was between T_a and T_s, we now find Kant making a similar contrast between the *system* of objects, viewed either at the 'appearance' or at the '*in se*' level; we shall symbolize this as T_a^θ and T_s^θ, respectively; the θ standing for the 'scientific-theory' case (cf. A678/B707f., especially for T_s^θ). In the T_s^θ case, the "unity," instead of being "presupposed," on the lines of the reduction-realization approach, is—says Kant—simply "hypostatized" (A692/B720), so that whatever "systematic unity" there is will be cognizable "merely empirically," instead of being "presupposed a priori," in which case "the unity of nature is really surrendered, as being quite foreign and accidental to the nature of things, and as not capable of being cognized from nature's own universal laws" (A693/B721), the "laws" presumably being the methodological maxims. (Notice here again an interesting point about the characterization of the T_s^θ status: just as at B164 and A129, once again this is nothing 'entirely unknown' but is instead something knowable, albeit "merely empirically," instead of "a priori.") So to make the a priori approach legitimate, we have to convert the status of O_w^θ from that of T_s^θ into that of T_a^θ (the parallelism with the case of the Analytic will be obvious).

It will be seen that the 'reduction' procedure renders this quite plain, for it ensures that for the $O_t^\theta \rightarrow T_a^\theta$ case any ontological account resulting from this realization will not have to 'compete', so to speak, with the character that nature might, *per impossible*, possess 'in itself'; for now there *is* (at least, so far) only the order of nature *qua appearance*, a creature of the regulative process; it is no longer *meaningful* (cf. the long passage quoted below), to ask whether, for instance, nature might perhaps *not* be simple? Whether or not nature is simple is here no longer a question in respect of what it is 'in itself' but concerns only the *suitability* of a certain methodology.

We incidentally see at once that the Kuhnian 'paradigm' approach results from this as a special case. Similarly, Feyerabend's skepticist complaints may now be viewed as due to a misunderstanding, arising from the supposition that any respectable methodology ought (albeit *per impossible*) to mirror nature in itself. Since it cannot do this, Feyerabend reacts 'against method' as such, instead of espousing the more modest program of a 'regulative' approach. One might say that Feyerabend originally dreamed of a metaphysical type of justification associated with a 'constitutive' approach; not allowing for the possibility of a 'regulative' alternative, he throws the baby of methodology out with the constitutive bathwater (all this being by way drawing out the implications that follow from our response to Braithwaite's question).

III. *The Regulative Employment of Reason and the Transcendental Realization of the Unity of Nature*

With these general remarks we may turn briefly to the actual structure of the transcendental-realization account. First, a terminological point, in connection with the maxims given in the left-hand-bottom box of figure 4. At A648/B676ff. these are labeled "logical principles," "logical maxims," etc. Now "logical," in this particular context, means, above all, 'methodological'; thus, at A648/B676, Kant refers to "systematic unity" in this sense as "logical, *qua* method." This means also, however, that so far the application of these maxims will merely yield the logical or methodological form of systematization; it is quite another thing, says Kant, to be "apodeictically certain" that the resulting "systematic unity . . . should be in conformity with nature" (A651/B679; in our language: realization has not as yet got a grip on the process). So far we have merely "postulated this unity a priori, without reference to any interest of reason" (A648/B676; note that this use of the term "interest" is the one blown up in our time into a general philosophical method by Habermas in his *Knowledge and Human Interests*). To effect a full realization, we must therefore "also presuppose a transcendental principle whereby such a systematic unity is a priori assumed to be necessarily inherent in the objects" (A650/B678). All this clearly boils down to our reduction-realization approach as already explained; we need merely add that the "also presuppose" in the last sentence is to be understood as meaning: we must also regard the "logical principle" as capable of functioning, correspondingly, as a "transcendental principle"; there are not two sets of principles but only one, viewed in two ways.

Evidently the whole argument, in parallel with the Transcendental Analytic, would seem to yield a "transcendental deduction" of the maxims, and of the whole "idea" of systemicity or unity. But does it? At A664/B692, Kant says no, but at A671/B699 he says yes; what a field day for the 'Kant constantly contradicts himself' mongerers! As usual, there is no contradiction at all. First, we need to note that for Kant the "unity of nature" is not the sort of thing that is ever "as such given"; it is "only a projected unity" (A647/B675). Systematization *aims* at unity—but this is an 'infinite' process, never coming to an end. "Experience can never give an example of complete systematic unity"; it is nothing "real absolutely and in itself, but is postulated only problematically" (A681/B709). Now remember that the general definition of a "transcendental deduction" is the "explanation" of how certain concepts (here maxims) "necessarily relate a priori to objects" (A85/B117), which objects are thereby 'rendered possible.' But in the present case there is no "cognition of any object itself" but "only a rule . . . for the systematic employment of the [empirical] understanding" (A665/B693), i.e., only a "projected unity," not anything "given." So the methodological maxims, as transcendental, have only a quasi-objective validity (in the first introduction to *CJ*, Kant indeed speaks of them as a "subjectively necessary transcendental presupposition" (Haden, p. 15)); they do not "determine an object" but only "indicate the procedure whereby the empirical and determinate employment of the [empirical] understanding can be brought into complete harmony with itself" (A665/B693).

The "subjectivity" just alluded to is also expressed by Kant as follows: the "transcendental deduction" of the "idea" of unity, and of its defining maxims, is of the type that has no "constitutive" power, since it does not yield any "additional objects" but only "regulative principles of the systematic unity of the manifold of emipirical knowledge in general, whereby this empirical knowledge is more adequately secured" (A671/B699).

All this, incidentally, also yields a more complete definition than is usual of the Kantian use of the term "regulative," in association with "principle": regulative principles are such as (1) lack *constitutive* force, (2) have a *methodological* function, and, finally (3) possess a *transcendental* status. All three characteristics, and not just one or the other, as wrongly implied in many accounts of Kant, define the notion of 'regulativeness'.

To sum up the above, and availing ourselves of the parallel with the structure of 'general ontology,' the process of realization may now be pictured as $O_t^\theta \rightarrow T_a^\theta$; the left-hand side being the equivalent of the transcendental object at the level of theorification. The *locus classicus* for this occurs at A698/B726:

> We presuppose a something [*ein Etwas*], a merely transcendental object, of which, as it is in itself, we have no concept whatsoever. But in order to study nature, we must presuppose it in reference to the systematic and purposive order of the cosmos.

For the purpose of general ontology, O_t was defined as m_t, f_t. For the systemic case, m_t is equivalent to the object *qua* appearance, i.e., T_a, while f_t^θ = the "logical principles" or "maxims" mentioned above; thus: $O_t^\theta(T_a, f_t^\theta)$. Under realization, f_t^θ is converted into "regulative principles," f_r for short, yielding T_a^θ.

At this point it may be advisable to say a few words about Kant's term "idea," where we are particularly interested in the third of Kant's three ideas, the "theological idea"—the other two being the "psychological idea" and the "cosmological idea; cf. A861/B710. Interesting for us also is that Kant here often employs the locution "giving the idea an object" (A661/B709); alternatively he speaks of the "object in the idea" (A697/B725).

The phrase 'giving the idea an object' can once more be interpreted as a reference to 'realization,' particularly in light of the interesting passage at A677/B705, where the "idea" is said to be something that we set ourselves to "realize." We may thus take it that the term "idea" as such must centrally function in a purely transcendental (t_o) context, as when Kant speaks of the transcendental object of the idea (cf. A679/B707 for this locution). (It seems to me that all these locutions have received far too little close analysis in the two hundred years since the *Critique* appeared, scholars hurrying over these last pages of the work more in the manner of literary critics than of critical philosophers.) I shall return to this in the next section. First, however, it may be useful to add a few general remarks on the architectonic of ideas.

For a general definition of "transcendental idea," consult A327/B383f. Ideas are "transcendental" because (1) no objects corresponding to the ideas are given in sense experience, which give them, so far, t_o status; (2) ideas are a "necessary condition" for "the whole [empirical] employment of the understanding"; for instance, they define the notions of the world as a whole, of moral freedom, of the "unity of nature," and so on, which gives them something like a t_i status. In Kant's architectonic, ideas correspond to the categorial concepts, the three ideas already mentioned paralleling the categories substance, cause, and interaction (cf. A323/B379). And just as the *categories* are the special expressions of the *synthetic* unity of the *understanding*, so the *ideas* are expressions of the *systematic* unity of *reason*. While the understanding unifies intuitions, reason systematically unifies objects; cf. the detailed passage at A664/B692 for the parallels.

Take causality: As a category of the understanding, this '*determines*' the sequence of perceptions, to yield an objective sequence in time; as a concept employed by (theoretical) reason (cf. A561/B589), it yields an inference from *ground* to consequence, i.e., from instances of objective sequence to the existence of a causal uniformity or law. Hence Kant defined the understanding also as a capacity that involves concepts and principles, and reason as a capacity for drawing inferences. Similarly, in the domain of pure *practical* reason, causality is viewed as the concept which serves as the "*ground*" of a determination to action (in Kant the notion of "ground" evidently employs a slippery middle between "cause" and "logical premise," probably echoing the Spinozist and Leibnizian "*causa seu ratio*").

IV. *An Alternative Realization: The Substratum of the Order of Nature*

In the pages in question Kant in fact discusses his subject in terms of what we can describe, using our own terminology, as alternative realizations of the idea of systematic unity. Since Kant's treatment is a bit long-winded, I shall summarize it, to start with, by way of a diagram:

$$O_t^\theta \; {\succ\!\!\!\!\!\succ} \; \begin{matrix} T_a^\theta \\ T_s^\theta \end{matrix} \; = \; \text{zero}; \; \sim T_s^{\theta^{\boldsymbol{\cdot}}}$$

fiction of divine ground

First, let us note that "idea," like "thing in itself," is an umbrella term which is given a use in a number of different contexts. For our purpose here, 'idea' may be said to stand for the regulative processing of the empirical laws of nature into theories, as a "regulative principle" of the "systematic unity of the manifold of empirical knowledge in general" (A671/B699). The 'object' of the idea will here simply be this methodological process, a process which is infinite, as never coming to an end. O_t^θ is then "the transcendental object of our idea" (A679/B707), where, if I apply f_t^θ in suitable circumstances (at the t_i level, as f_r), I effect a realization T_a^θ, i.e., obtain a theory proportionate to the projected unity of nature.

We may, however, corresponding to this *infinite* process, also introduce, as an "analogon," "the idea of the [*finite*] maximum in the division and unification of the [empirical] knowledge of the understanding under one principle" (A665/B693); e.g., the harmony which the scientist has always posed only as a problem he may imagine to have reached, as the "ideas of the greatest harmony and unity" (A678/B706). After all, 'in reality,' so we might say, nature is what it is, harmonious or otherwise; it can hardly *be* an infinite process.

Here Kant uses another of his structural notions. Remember the schematization of the categories: since the latter represent only *logical* concepts, they can make contact with reality only by being tied down through the transcendental modes of sensibility, space and time, thus simulating the *individual* nature of experiential occasions. Now Kant employs the same move in the present context: just as intuition supplies a schema for the category and thus "realizes" the latter (A146/B186), so we may imagine the notion of a *maximum* of systematization as the "analogon of such a schema" (A665/B693), albeit providing only a *fictional* realization, only *analogous* to the regulative type of realization, represented by $O_t^\theta \rightarrow T_a^\theta$.

Proceeding with this approach, we may imagine the

90

"maximum," the "greatest harmony" (i.e., the analogon of the infinite process), as actually "given"—but only 'imagine' this; i.e., "*as if*' it were given, as a "substratum" of the greatest possible unity of [systematic] experience" (A678/B706). This '*as it were* being "given," ' would be how the world *is* when given in itself: I would have the "object of my idea according to what it may be in itself" (A678/B706). It is however only an "as if," a *fiction*. Referring back to our diagram, we see that the ontology of T_s^θ = zero. But, on the lines of his precritical position, Kant introduces once again the notion of the thing in itself, and as there, mediated by "self-subsistent reason" (A678/B706), by a "creative reason" (A673/B701), the "author of the world" (A697/B725)—all, of course, nothing more now than a fiction, a "focus imaginarius" (A644/B672), corresponding to *human* reason's systematic employment, with the difference that divine reason yields a *completed* unity while human reason is forever confined to an incompletable one, precisely because of which (I think Kant wants to say) we *necessarily* require the just-mentioned image or analogon of completeness (remember, he had not much idea of the concept of the mathematical limit used in the infinitesimal calculus. And cf. the passage at A675/B703).

Our diagram shows that God is a kind of mirror image of the transcendental object or "intelligible substratum" of the world (the label given to it in *CJ*). To show that this is the correct reading, I will quote a final passage:

> If we ask, *first*, whether there is anything distinct from the world which contains the ground of the order of the world and of its connection in accordance with universal [empirical] laws, the answer is that there *undoubtedly* is. For the world is a sum of appearances; and there must therefore be some transcendental ground of the appearances, that is, a ground which is thinkable only by the pure understanding [viz., O_t^θ]. If, *secondly*, the question be, whether this being is substance, of the greatest reality, necessary etc. [i.e., can we take O_t^θ to be = to God?]*, we reply that *this question is entirely without meaning*. For all such categories through which we can attempt to form a concept of

* In all this it is necessary to remember that there is not really an 'independent God' *as well as* a 'world in itself,' but the latter *is* simply the generated object of intellectual intuition on the part of God, this in turn boiling down to saying that there *is* simply the world in itself, the 'in itself' character being, as I have usually put this, 'mediated by the divine understanding.' For this reason it is never clear in all the passages referred to whether Kant, in phrases like 'the intelligible substratum,' is talking about God or about the world in itself.

such an object, allow only of empirical employment, and have no meaning whatsoever when not applied to objects of possible experience, that is, to the world of sense . . . . If, *thirdly,* the question be, whether we may not at least think this being, which is distinct from the world, on *analogy* with the objects of experience, the answer is: certainly, but only as object in *idea* and not in reality, namely, only as being a substratum, to us unknown, of the systematic unity, order, and purposiveness of the arrangement of the world—an idea which reason is constrained to form as the regulative principle of its investigation of nature. [A696/B724]

In short, you can make a picture for yourself of the unity of nature as something 'given in itself,' as a "reality in itself" (A679/B707) and hence grounded in the divine; and this picture will, so far, be necessary for the completion of your systematic scientific tasks. But its 'cash value' is only what it stands for, viz., $O_t^\theta \to T_a^\theta$. (For Kant, as for most other eighteenth-century thinkers and poets, the 'infinite' was, as he sometimes said, the veritable abyss. Cf. the passage at A622/B650 and the reference to Haller at A613/B641. It had therefore to be constrained via schematization and analogy; Kant's purpose was to prevent this from being given any constitutive strength.)

So we may imagine Kant as saying: To proceed systematically, "if we are to study nature," theoretical reason is "constrained to presuppose the systematic and purposive ordering of the world," and this constraint may be pictured, or "thought *by analogy* with," the ordinances of a "supreme intelligence" (A698/B726). But this is a 'realization' (of the fictional kind) of what is really no more than a "merely transcendental object, of which what it is in itself, we have no concept whatsoever" (A698/B726, quoted above, p. 88), except via the path of analogy, just described. The two points of view expressed by T_a^θ and $T_s^{\theta*}$ (and, equivalently, of O_t^θ and God), are—and here lies Kant's visionary subtlety—*logically equivalent*: "It is a matter of indifference which is asserted" (A699/B727). We *seek* "the greatest possible unity," and we behave as though the world *actually exhibited* this unity (A698/B726).

We are now in a position to summarize the general architectonic of Kant's system in its relationship and correspondences between the understanding and theoretical reason, something that would not be very easy (to put it mildly) without the general symbolism and approach underlying *RRP*:

Concept of the understanding: concept of the object, of nature represented as:

1U: "Unity of the thought of a manifold in general," expressing "the thought of an object in general": "transcendental object" (A247/B304): O_t.

2U: "The formal unity of consciousness in the synthesis of the manifold of intuitions" (A105): T_a.

3U: The thing in itself to which "belongs its conformity to law necessarily also apart from any human understanding" (B164), grounded in the divine understanding (B72): T_s^*.

Level to Theoretical Reason

Idea of reason, of the system of objects, or of the order of nature represented as:

1R: "The systematic unity, order, and purposiveness of the arrangement of the world," but only as a mere "object in the idea and not in reality" (A697/B725), as "a merely transcendental object" (A698/B726): O_t^θ.

2R: "A rule or principle for the systematic unity of all [empirical] employment of the understanding" (A665/B693): $T_a^\theta(T_a, f_r)$.

3R: "Systematic unity" as a "reality in itself" (A679/B707), *fictionally* "grounded" in a divine "intelligence" or "supreme reason" (A678/B706): $T_s^{\theta*}$.

In what has preceded, we have assumed that O_t^θ should be construed as (T_a, f_t^θ). But perhaps we need not have done this. Kant's argument would proceed just as well on *any* construal of O_w^θ, or, rather, $O_w^{\theta o}$—we are concerned only with the *ontology* of the unity of nature. So it might be more accurate to render O_t^θ neutrally as (O_w^o, f_t^θ) and leave it open how the ontology of objects and their aggregate should be construed. It is noteworthy that in his systemology Kant hardly, if at all, refers explicitly to O_w as "appearance." Moreover, this would also accord well with Kant's remark that the Antinomy of Pure Reason "affords [only] *indirect proof* of the transcendental ideality of appearances" (A506/B534; my italics).

Indeed, many of those methodologies of recent times which employ a 'regulative' approach (e.g., H. Margenau) would not necessarily adopt Kant's form of idealism. Similarly, M. S. Gram, in "Kant's First Antinomy" (in L. W. Beck, ed., *Kant Studies Today*), argues that the Antinomy does not unambiguously prove O_w^o to equal T_a. So perhaps the 'solution' of the Antinomies becomes only more elegant and plausible on the assumption of the ideality of the world of sense ($O_w^o = T_a$). *Against* Gram, however, it may be contended that, unless some kind of 'appearance' approach is taken vis-à-vis O_w (i.e., $= T_a$), then the construal of $O_w^{\theta o}$ as T_a^θ, which Kant needs in order to generate the constrast with $T_s^{\theta *}$, would become, to say the least, artificial, and indeed ambiguous.

V. *A Theological Postscript*

In conclusion, it might be noted that, while O_t was completely "*indeterminate*," or undefined (except in a purely 'logical' sense), O_t^θ has, via its analogical *focus imaginarius*, a meaningful function; we have here made—in the words of *CJ*, p. 33,—"the supersensible substrate . . . *determinable* [definable] by means of the intellectual capacity" (viz., scientific, i.e., "*theoretical*" reason). And further, reason in its practical employment fully "*determines*" the supersensible, in "the transition from the domain of the concept of nature to that of the concept of freedom." Thus, while science supplies the concept of God with *meaning*, ethics, which fails in *that* enterprise, supplies it with "objective *reality*" (*CJ*, p. 307). But, finally, "by virtue of the maxim of pure reason, which bids us seek unity of principles, so far as is possible," we are constrained to add together these two aspects, meaning and reality—to "bring" one to the other—and thus to safeguard the foundations of theology and religion. God, though from the theoretical point of view, when reified in the context of systems ontology, is no more than a "transcendental illusion" (A696/B724n.); the latter is a *necessary* one, being an indispensable, albeit fictional, assumption for the business of science; just as in the *Critique of Practical Reason* the "postulate" of God's existence comes up as an expression of the necessity of making morality and nature mutually compatible.

In all these ways, as we have seen throughout, Kant transforms older locutions and arguments, seeking to endow them with fresh significance. Retaining the verbal shell, he seeks to pour new wine into old bottles. Much the same one finds when turning to the field of "special ontology," where Kant seeks once again to tread a middle way between the a priorism of a Descartes and the a posteriorism of the English school of Newton and Locke.

NOTES

1. While in what follows I have sought to provide only just enough contextual background to explain my use of the terms 'ontology' and 'phenomenology', it should be noted that my use differs from that found in writings like those of Husserl and Heidegger, in both of which the significance of these terms seems to merge. Heidegger, in *Being and Time*, trans. J. Macquarrie and E. Robinson (1973), says, "Phenomenology is . . . ontology" (p. 61). Husserl, in *Ideas*, trans. W. R. Boyce Gibson (1962), sec .153, draws a close correspondence between phenomenology and ontology, while in *The Crisis of European Sciences*, trans. D. Carr (1970), sec. 51, p. 173, phenomenology is described as a special type of "ontology of an *a priori* science." Nor do I use 'ontology' in the sense of expressions like 'the ontology of physics is space, time, and matter.' It is more like 'The ontology of Berkeley's world consists of the subject and its ideas.'

2. As can be found in Husserl's *Crisis*, secs. 8–12., n.2.

3. A and B, as usual, refer to the pages of the first and second editions of *CPR*, respectively, and I have used the Kemp Smith edition, *Immanuel Kant's Critique of Pure Reason* (1953), modifying the translation where necessary.

4. L. E. Loemker, ed., *Gottfried Wilhelm Leibniz: Philosophical Papers and Letters* (2 vols., 1956), 2:1050. For *Nova Dilucidatio*, cf. trans. F. E. England, in *Kant's Conception of God* (1929), appendix, props. 1–7.

5. "The radical origination of things," in Loemker, ed., *Leibniz*, p. 791. For Leibniz, cf. also my *Metaphysics and the Philosophy of Science* (1969), chap. 7, sec. 2.

6. *Kant: Selected Pre-Critical Writings*, trans. G. B. Kerferd and D. E. Walford (1968), pt. 3, sec. 2 (2). Where necessary, I have modified the translation.

7. Ibid., p. 52.

8. *Nova Dilucidatio*, note 4, sec. iii, 2: The Principle of Coexistence, prop. 13, p. 248.

9. B256.

10. Thus, *Critique of Judgment*, trans. J. H. Bernard (1951), introduction, sec. 5, speaks of "body [being] thought through ontological predicates," i.e., the categories (p. 17). Cf. also A846/B874. By contrast, at A246/B303, Kant says that "the name of an ontology . . . must give place to [that of an] Analytic of the Pure Understanding."

11. The first two Kant himself distinguishes as "general" and "special metaphysics of nature"; cf. *Metaphysical Foundations of Natural Science*, trans. J. Ellington (1970), preface, p. 6. Systems metaphysics or ontology is treated in *CPR*: "Appendix to the Transcendental Dialectic" (A642/B670ff.), and in the two introductions to the *Critique of Judgment*. Cf. my *Metaphysics*, note 5, sec. 4(c); also my "The Conception of Lawlikeness in Kant's Philosophy of Science," in *Kant's Theory of Knowledge*, ed. L. W. Beck (1974), pp. 128ff., and my "Neo-Transcendental Approaches Towards Scientific Theory Appraisal," in D. H. Mellor, ed., *Science Belief and Behaviour* (1980), pp. 1–21.

12. For this, cf. note 11, my "The Conception . . . "; also my "History of Science and Criteria of Choice," in R. H. Stuewer, ed., *Historical and Philosophical Perspectives of Science* (*Minnesota Studies* 5 [1970]), sec. 3.

13. I published a first account, of the concept of reduction only, in *Kant-Studien, Acts of the Fourth International Kant Congress* (1974), Part I, as "Transcendental Reduction: A Concept for the Interpretation of Kant's Critical Method," pp. 28–44.

This paper not only stops short of 'realization' but is in many other respects seriously flawed. A very abbreviated prologue to the present paper appeared in *Acts of the Sixth International Kant Congress* (1981), pt. I.1, "The Dynamical Version of Kant's Transcendental Method," pp. 394–406. And cf. also my chapter in Mellor, ed., *Science Belief*, sec. 6, n. 11. The much fuller account of the present essay owes considerably to the helpful and sympathetic audience of my Cambridge Kant Seminar during the last two years.

14. Edmund Husserl, *The Idea of Phenomenology*, trans. W. P. Alston and G. Nakhnikian (1964). Not too much should be made of this reference to Husserl, since for the most part I am confining myself to a simple adaptation of his terminology and some of the basic ideas of his philosophical methodology, as defined by his terminology. I am not concerned with the degree to which the details of Husserl's 'reduction followed by constitution' resemble or differ from the concepts which have here been adopted to explain the basic structure of Kant's method. Husserl himself thought that he was developing some ideas of Kant's, especially those contained in the pages of the first edition of *CPR*, A104–109 (cf. *Crisis*, sec. 27, n. 2., and especially sec. 28, p. 104). *Per contra*, Kant's procedure in *CPR*, when considered in terms of Husserl's general methodology, will actually emerge as something more radical, as will become clear in what follows. More ironically, the hermeneutics of the situation is such that my Kantian interpretation of 'reduction' will be found to be a considerable aid in grasping Husserl's sometimes rather unclear and long-winded presentation of his own technique.

15. Husserl, *The Idea of Phenomenology*, pp. 27–29, n. 14. Husserl eventually settles for a formulation, according to which we must show *in what sense* transcendence constitutes a possibility. It should be noted that wherever the domain and character of the *actual* is taken for granted, the tracing out of the conditions of its possibility becomes a kind of 'descriptive metaphysics,' though involving a 'justificative' status vis-à-vis the claimed *conditions* of this possibility.

16. Ibid., p. 31, n. 13.

17. Cf. *Crisis*, secs. 41–42, n. 1.

18. Cf. *Nova Dilucidatio*, "Additions to Problem IX," p. 238, n. 4.

19. As we shall see, this is really a conflation of two contentions of Kant's: (1) that this form of idealism fails to supply an independent ontology of space and time, to yield the genuine notion of "outside" in an "empirically external" sense; and (2) that it does not make allowance for any notion of a 'thing' *which appears* (merging, as it does, thing and idea), unlike Kant's construal of this 'thing' *qua* transcendental object, "outside us in the transcendental sense" (A272–73). This may serve as a good illustration of the need to read between the lines of such (at first sight) astonishing appraisals by Kant of his opponents.

20. *A Treatise of Human Nature*, ed. L. A. Selby-Bigge (1888), p. 84. Cf. also Berkeley's declaration, in *Principles of Human Knowledge*, sec. 3, that "we perceive [and hence, analytically, there is nothing] besides our own ideas." Of course, there is a difficulty in Hume: if impressions are creations, how come the mind is also said to be 'passive' with respect to them? And I think that Kant wanted to bring this unresolved difficulty out into the open, without letting in by the back door the now-exploded notion of the 'external object' in the sense of position 2, fig. 1. Indeed, it is because of the difficulties concerning this 'external object' that Kant frequently lumps together, as "material idealism," the "problematic idealism" (B274) of Descartes and Locke and the "dogmatic idealism" of a Berkeley or a Hume; e.g., B274.

21. In this essay I have attempted to confine my exposition of the usual stock-in-trade outline of the basic elements of the *Critique* to an absolute minimum—just

sufficient to imply something about the power of *RRP* to illuminate the structure of the Kantian argument.

22. Cf. a similar move in H. Putnam's *Meaning and the Moral Sciences* (1978), p. 133.

23. No. 6286; cf. *Kants Schriften*, Ak. ed., 20: 361. I owe this reference to Oliver Leaman.

24. It will be noted that in this account the reduction moves from $T_a \rightarrow O_t$, whereas before the transition was from $O_w^o \rightarrow O_r$ ($= O_t$). This does not, of course, alter the essentials of the process.

25. It will be helpful to the reader to consult fig. 2, to be discussed in more detail below.

26. And cf. *Opus postumum* (*Kants Schriften*, Ak. ed., vol. 22), where Kant speaks of the "dynamic function" of the cognitive framework (here the modes of sensibility) to generate something as "appearance," with the added reminder that the "thing in itself = x" (here clearly O_t), though "contrasted" with the former, is "not a separate object but only a particular aspect [Beziehung] (*respectus*) for the purpose of constituting [*constituiren*] itself as object" (p. 44). This, written in the year 1800, could hardly be bettered as a *locus classicus* for our 'realization approach.'

27. E. Adickes, *Kants Lehre von der doppelten Affektion unseres Ich* (1929). Cf. also Gerold Prauss, *Kant und das Problem der Dinge an Sich* (1974), chap. 3, sec. 10; and R. P. Wolff, *Kant's Theory of Mental Activity* (1963), bk. 1, chap. 3, pp. 169–73.

28. Prauss, *Kant*, secs. 10–11, n. 27.

29. It should be noted that in all these accounts the word 'object' itself functions merely as an 'incomplete expression,' standing simply for a sort of x (similar to the fx of first-order calculus)—as it is indeed described by Kant at A104, A250, and several other places.

30. In later sections we shall, of course, pick out from this scheme only such details as have presented the most serious obstacles to attempts at analyzing Kant's procedure.

31. For a fuller account of the significance of the Second Analogy, cf. my *Metaphysics*, chap. 8(*e*), n.5; my "The Kantian 'Dynamic of Reason,' with Special Reference to the Place of Causality in Kant's System," in *Kant Studies Today*, L. W. Beck ed., (1969), especially sec. iv; and my "Conception of Lawlikeness," secs. i, ii., n. 11. It will be seen that the account given here provides a very neat 'proof' (and rather clearer) of the position taken in these earlier publications.

32. Here, and in what follows, it will be understood that sensibility, imagination, and understanding are always to be viewed as functions of, and due to, an activating process on the part of an 'ego', the notion of this 'ego' itself in such a context being a myth for the need in the whole account to take for granted the existence of an *actual occasion* of cognition or experience—at least, in principle. The latter is the kingpin on which the whole Kantian scheme rotates; it being remembered, however, that in this scheme 'cognition' and 'experience' are themselves not explicatable without reference to the world of objects; cognition and object are thus always held in a mutual, and internally balancing, tension.

33. See note 32 above.

34. Henry E. Allison, *The Kant-Eberhard Controversy* (English translation of Kant's "On a Discovery . . . ," 1973), p. 130.

35. Graham Bird, *Kant's Theory of Knowledge* (1962). See especially pp. 68–69, 76–81.

36. Letter to Kant, November 5, 1797; in Arnulf Zweig, ed. and trans., *Kant: Philosophical Correspondence, 1759–99* (1967), p. 242. I owe this reference to Timothy Woods.

37. Ibid., p. 243.

38. Ibid.

39. There is no need here to make special mention of another of Kant's prime objectives, viz., to deduce the "objective validity" of the categories, and the corresponding principles of the understanding, with synthetic a priori status. This follows with such obviousness from our account that it is hardly worthwhile to spend any time on it. Kant's own constant emphasis on this aspect has had the unfortunate result of diverting attention from the far more central and seminal aspects of his doctrine.

40. Leibniz's monads (A264/B320, A270/B326, A276/B332); Locke's and Descartes's external object; finally, Berkeley's 'ideas', the last for the reason that space is derivative on and a property of the ideational object (B274; cf. B270–71); and Hume, since by Hume, Kant remarks, "objects of experience [are taken] for things-in-themselves" (*Critique of Practical Reason*, trans. L. W. Beck [1956], p. 54). Moreover, Humean objects, being the result of what I have labeled 'ideational realization,' do not permit, any more than do objects under the Leibniz and the Descartes-Locke interpretations, of a double-realization procedure and hence fail "to hold open . . . a vacant place," subsequently to be "filled . . . by practical reason" (ibid., p. 50). Once you operate with objects *qua* things in themselves, *in the sense* of T_s*—be it well noted the 'critical' T_s sense is, of course, part of a double realization interpretation!—there is no room for the 'appearance' alternative.

41. P. F. Strawson, *The Bounds of Sense* (1966). References in the text are to this edition.

42. Günther Patzig has recently drawn attention to the importance of this model; cf. his remarks in *Transcendental Arguments and Science*, ed. P. Bieri et al. (1979), pp. 72–73.

43. For the *locus classicus* of this distinction in Kant, cf. A327–30.

44. Peter G. Lucas, trans., *Immanuel Kant: Prolegomena* (1953), p. 121.

45. Notice the difference in function between—the different "transcendental locations" of—"transcendental ground" and "transcendental framework"; the former operates (as $O_t\,(m, f)$) at the t_o level; the latter concerns the material detailed in column 2 of fig. 2, i.e., the t_t-level apparatus of sensibility, imagination, and understanding.

46. Passages such as these have too often been treated as though they expressed no more than a 'verbal' contention that the concept of appearance requires constrasting with 'nonappearance', with something 'in itself.' But, as will now be appreciated, a much richer implication is intended: the fact that T_a is not fully articulated apart from the transitional sequence $O_t \rightarrow T_a$.

Kant's Notion of Transcendental Presupposition in the First Critique

A. C. GENOVA
University of Kansas

Recent attention to issues connected with so-called epistemological foundationalism has led to a resuscitation and reconstruction of Kant's notion of transcendental argument (*TA*) as a possible device by which foundational principles might be given an adequate epistemic justification. This recourse to *TA*'s has become controversial in its own right. The reconsideration of *TA*'s has focused on four interrelated issues: (1) what Kant meant by a *TA*; (2) whether there are or could be any valid *TA*'s; (3) if valid *TA*'s are possible, whether their validity requires the assumption of some version of a verification principle; and (4) whether there is some unique, logical form of argument that certifies a legitimate *TA* as a form of argument distinct from other forms of argument.[1]

In this article I shall discuss the relation between transcendental argument and transcendental presupposition. I shall argue that the notion of presupposition is the key to understanding Kant's rather cryptic formulation of a *TA* and that, consequently, an analysis of transcendental presupposition is a prerequisite to any relevant criticism of *TA*'s with respect to their validity or logical form.

I

Issues related to epistemological foundationalism have been among those traditionally construed as definitive of the discipline of epistemology. The central questions of this discipline concern the analysis and justification of knowledge claims; and when this justification involves claims with an imputed universality of scope and modality of necessity—that is to say, claims that have the epistemic status of fundamental principles—then the view that such principles admit of epistemic justification is epistemological foundationalism. This implies that there is a systematic epistemology that can delineate the foundations of the sciences, morality, and art by legitimizing universal standards of rationality and objectivity for these disciplines and adjudicating their conceptual claims. Such principles can be construed as a body of core propositions that characterize or constitute a conceptual scheme with respect to a specified domain of objects. It is generally acknowledged that the relevant domain may be a real domain (like Kant's theoretic manifold of empirical objects or his practical manifold of actions and ends) or an ideal domain (a system of formal objects as in pure mathematics or logic). Of course, what might be called the epistemic force of such principles is itself a question of some controversy. Some philosophers relativize such schemes to variable contexts so that with respect to a successor context a different scheme applies, and sometimes they argue that there are alternative schemes for a given context. Others contend that the conceptual core is unique and invariable in relation to the specified context and even that the specified context is invariable. The former way of talking corresponds to what has been called "modest foundationalism"; the latter, to "immodest foundationalism." What is clear is that Kant, with respect to the domain of possible experience, for example, was an immodest foundationalist.

The central problem with epistemological foundationalism —especially with the so-called immodest kind—has to do with how foundational principles can be epistemically warranted in a way that has a reasonable chance of being convincing to an epistemological skeptic. An appeal to self-evidence has obvious shortcomings. Reliance on empirical derivation will not do because the point of foundationalism is that all empirical determinations presuppose the conceptual scheme. Logical deduction seems inappropriate as well because if the principles were deducible from higher premises then they presumably would not be foundational after all, and the problem of justification would simply reemerge at the level of the supporting premises. Are such principles merely conventional maxims expressive of alternative linguistic frameworks and selected, as needed, just insofar as they serve as successful instruments for our understanding of the world? But it can be shown that to invoke this option of pragmatic justification involves the countenancing of semantic rules in the framework's metalanguage, thus implying more fundamental concepts that are independent of the resulting framework and accordingly require justification in their own right.

Confronted with these and similar difficulties, some contemporary philosophers, reminiscent of some earlier existentialist thinkers, apparently concluding that a rational solution to the problem of epistemic justification is hopeless, have adopted a nonrational one. Thus Richard Rorty argues that systematic epistemology is an impossible discipline, based on a fundamentally mistaken correspondence theory of truth and a pseudomodel of knowledge as the mirror of nature, to be replaced by the "successor subject" of hermeneutics that equates truth with "social coherentism" and seeks edification and self-expression through interparadigmatic conversation.[2] And Stanley Cavell, thinking that the standards of the epistemological skeptic are impossibly high, argues that the typical stance of the philosophical foundationalist occurs in a "nonclaim context"—an artificial context in which no real claim is involved—and aside from the putative knowledge established by the certified procedures of science, there is no persuasive rational procedure to justify the general possibility of knowledge itself, and hence we must recognize that our general relation to the world is not a cognitive one but rather one of "acceptance" and "acknowledgement."[3] These recent theses deserve detailed examination, but with respect to my present concerns it may be enough to note that they seriously compromise our traditional intuitions concerning both philosophical and scientific objectivity. Before a serious reconsideration of the nature of transcendental inference, it would be premature to forgo the possibility of a public, discursive account of the justification of foundational principles.

Another group of contemporary philosophers, rather than abjuring epistemology as a possible discipline, no longer take so-called foundational questions seriously and instead espouse what they call "naturalized epistemology."[4] For these epistemological naturalists problems about the justification of epistemic claims become translated into proposals for the justification of empirical knowledge in terms of the actual conceptual processes that characterize scientific inquiry and the reconstruction of the tacit paradigmatic models that underlie the history of scientific progress. But to limit epistemology to an account of the actual conceptual practices of scientists and then merely legitimize empirical claims with reference to those standards still leaves open questions about the epistemic justification of the conceptual practices of science that serve as the standards. Moreover, since the epistemological naturalists typically interpret the notion of justified belief in terms of beliefs produced by some reliable causal process, their analyses appear to involve a serious conflation of the causal processes that produce belief as a psychological event with the normative practices of justification that gound true or epistemologically warranted beliefs.

It is in this recent and contemporary context that the attempts to revive Kant's transcendental style of argument have emerged. *TA*'s are particularly promising in connection with foundational questions because the general idea of a *TA* is basically that of a self-referential, antiskeptical style of argument whereby one tries to give epistemic justification to certain core propositions or primitive concepts by showing that they are necessary presuppositions for the possibility of meaningful discourse in relation to a specified domain of objects, so that skeptical attempts to deny these principles presuppose the principles as a condition of meaning, and, hence, such denials are self-defeating or disingenuous. This general formulation, although comparatively clear in the abstract, is not very helpful and can even be misleading. It is not very helpful because it is compatible with interpretations of *TA*'s that either are irrelevant to the central problem of epistemological foundationalism or are based on an illegitimate paradigm of a *TA*; and of course to that extent, they are not Kantian.

Interpretations of *TA*'s are irrelevant when they construe a *TA* on the model of conditional proof, i.e., as a hypothetical argument that is relativized to a variable context so that there are alternative conceptual schemes presupposed by a given context dependent upon different possible interpretations of the context.[5] Such formulations are relatively uncontroversial because the purported *TA* has epistemic force only on condition that one accepts a particular interpretation of the context. But the central foundational problem concerns the justification of a unique, invariable conceptual core that is necessarily presupposed for all possible interpretations of the context. On the other hand, interpretations of a *TA* are illegitimate when they represent the argument as requiring a dubious verificationist premise for its validity. It is then made to appear that all *TA*'s face an uncompromising dilemma: If a *TA* is to be valid, it must invoke a dubious verification principle and therefore is probably unsound; otherwise, the *TA* is invalid with respect to what it is supposed to prove.[6] The point is that on this analysis the purpose of a Kantian-modeled *TA* is correctly construed as that of establishing the so-called objectivity thesis, viz., that the categorial features of the conceptual scheme are not merely necessary presuppositions for meaning but also objectively valid. But then, because an illegitimate paradigm of a *TA* is employed, it is thought that the objectivity thesis requires a verificationist premise. Without this premise the paradigm under analysis will fail to refute the epistemological skeptic. At best it will only prove that the skeptic, like the rest of us, must think in conformity with a certain conceptual scheme for meaningful utterance, but not that it is *true* that objects exist independently and actually have properties corresponding to the categorial features of the scheme or that we *know* this to be the case. If so, the skeptic would be free to concede the *subjective* necessity of the scheme while still insisting that its *objective* necessity has not and cannot be demonstrated.

Now I agree that a gratuitous verification principle would be a dubious premise indeed, especially since the very idea of a Kantian *TA* directed to objectivity is to establish its conclusion quite apart from any verificationist premise. On the contrary, an appropriately qualified version of a verification principle is a consequence, not a premise, of the argument. But it is not the case that the absence of such a premise, on that account, would necessarily make a *TA* invalid with respect to the objectivity thesis and be sufficient only to establish subjective necessity. To think so is to confuse what Kant called a metaphysical deduction with his transcendental deduction. To be sure, a metaphysical deduction is one kind of *TA*, but it does not have the burden of proving the objectivity thesis. Its task is the prior task of identifying and justifying the system of categories as an exhaustive and exclusive set of primitive concepts that correspond to the a priori logical functions of judgment and that in turn function as necessary principles of synthesis for the empirical manifold of intuition. It does not prove, nor is it designed to prove, that the categorial concepts have objective validity in the sense required for the objectivity thesis. Its purpose, if you will, is to establish a subjectivity thesis or to yield, as Kant says, "the transcendental clue to the discovery of all pure concepts of the understanding" (A67/B92–A83/B109). If so, these purely formal concepts are components of a unique conceptual scheme that satisfies Kant's logical requirements for the uniquely a priori, viz., "unrestricted universality and unqualified necessity" (B4). We would then have a unique, invariable core, but, after all, it consists only of concepts, not objects. But what right do we have to construe this core as constitutive of real objects in the world? Even if these categories *are* the necessary modes of the way we perceive, think, and make judgments, why should we be obligated to think that the objects themselves are constituted in accordance with the subjective necessity of these categories? These skeptical questions are Kant's (A85/B117–A91/B123, A94/B127, B160, B167–68, A765/B793). They express the central problem of his subsequent transcendental deduction, viz., providing a proof of the objectivity thesis. Thus, it is this second kind of Kantian *TA*—a transcendental deduction

—that is the appropriate paradigm for an objective *TA*; and it should be clear that it must ground the objective relevance of the categories on some basis other than some verification principle whose presence would make the argument a blatant *petitio*. Consequently, if one's paradigm of a *TA* is an argument, in whatever guise, that is acknowledged to be directed to the objectivity thesis but whose epistemic force is insufficient for objectivity just in virtue of the absence of a verificationist premise, then such verificationist attacks on *TA*'s are employing an illegitimate paradigm that is analogous to a metaphysical rather than a transcendental deduction.

Finally, the general formulation of a *TA* with which I began this discussion can be misleading because the refutational context of responding to the epistemological skeptic is very conformable to the logical form of indirect proof, and this has led several critics to think that *TA*'s must have this *reductio* form if they are to be genuine *TA*'s[7]. I have no serious objection to this general way of characterizing the logical form of *some TA*'s, especially since most of the recent examples—Strawson's arguments for a public world of spatiotemporal material objects, Shoemaker's arguments about pain, Malcolm's arguments for the inconceivability of mechanism, Hampshire's isolation of the presuppositions of language, etc.—do occur in this refutational context. But I have argued elsewhere that legitimate *TA*'s having a logically indirect form are actually derivative from and presuppose a more fundamental form of *TA* that does not have the form of indirect proof.[8] The upshot is that once a *TA* proves the objectivity thesis the refutation of the skeptic is easily accommodated by a shorthand indirect proof; but without the more fundamental objective *TA* the derivative indirect proof will not suffice on its own. As Kant says, in such proofs ". . . the game played by [empirical] idealism has been turned against itself" (B276). Perhaps the best example of an indirect *TA* for Kant is found in the second-edition *Refutation of Idealism* (B275). But we are reminded explicitly by Kant that such indirect proofs will not suffice on their own because transcendental proofs (deductions) "must never be *apagogical*, but always *ostensive*" where the latter is "that which combines with the conviction of its truth insight into the sources of its truth" and where the former, "while it can indeed yield certainty, cannot enable us to comprehend truth in connection with the grounds of its possibility" (A789/B817). Kant calls the apagogical "an extremely easy mode of proof" because rather than "reviewing the whole series of grounds that can lead us to the truth of a proposition by means of a complete insight into its possibility" we need only exhibit the overt logical form of contradiction (A790/B818–A794/B822). Confronted with a paradigm that typically manifests this indirect form, critics like Stroud, Gram, and Walker not surprisingly find the argument insufficient to establish the objectivity thesis.

In summary, the fact is that within the broad formulation of a *TA* there are four distinct transcendental styles of argument, each with a different purpose and structure. I label the first kind a *hypothetical deduction*, which is directed to justifying a particular conceptual framework as a necessary presupposition of some contingent interpretation of the domain of possible experience. The second is (to borrow from Kant) a *metaphysical deduction*, which provides an a priori justification of a unique conceptual scheme that is a necessary presupposition of all ·possible contingent interpretations of experience. The third—the kind for which Kant is notorious—is a *transcendental deduction*, which provides an a priori justification for the objective validity of a unique conceptual scheme. This is the argument that attempts to establish the objectivity thesis, viz., that there cannot be anything satisfying our requirements for experience without it also being the case that at least part of this is experience of objects and events which exist independently of the perceiver and conform to the specifications of the categorial scheme. The fourth kind of *TA* is a *transcendental refutation*, which has the form of a *reductio* and the purpose of refuting skeptical challenges to a preestablished scheme or one of its necessary conditions—a scheme that typically admits of independent justification via a hypothetical, metaphysical or transcendental deduction.

I have been arguing that the only legitimate paradigm of a *TA* is a transcendental deduction and that it is only this kind of argument that has relevance to the central problem of epistemological foundationalism. Accordingly, in the next section, I shall essentially use the abbreviation *TA* as synonymous with "transcendental deduction." For similar reasons to those reviewed above, it is also this kind of argument that must be the primary *analysandum* with respect to the recent issues concerning the validity and logical form of *TA*'s. Other paradigms are inappropriate because they either represent irrelevant kinds of *TA*'s or represent as complete what is actually an incomplete stage or derivation from a complex argument that is taken out of context and, consequently, cannot serve as a basis for generalizations about the nature of *TA*'s. In the sequel I shall argue that, with respect to a *TA* construed as a Kantian transcendental deduction, it is Kant's notion of transcendental presupposition that makes a *TA* a unique form of argument.

II

Let us first take account of Kant's general criteria for *TA*'s and then sketch the general form that these criteria, as well as other relevant considerations, suggest for Kant's central *TA* in the *Critique of Pure Reason*. Kant's basic criteria are threefold. First, there is the requirement that *TA*'s always involve rational justification (*Rechtfertigung*) of a right or warrant with respect to a claim (*Anspruch*)—a question of right (*quid juris*) concerning the employment of certain a priori synthetic principles; and this is contrasted to contingent and problematical derivations that establish a claim on the basis of factual evidence—a question of fact (*quid facti*) that concerns how we actually come to possess a certain concept (A85/B117). This rules out what Kant called an "empirical deduction." It also rules out some versions of what I have called a hypothetical deduction and poses serious questions involving naturalistic fallacy issues for the recent epistemological naturalists. Second, there is the apagogical-ostensive distinction already alluded to and which rules out the mode of indirect proof as the primary form for a *TA* (A789/B817). Stated positively, this limitation comes to this: A *TA* must include premises that directly appeal to and overtly manifest the exemplication of transcendental principles in possible experience; and this requirement that there be at least one epistemic premise having reference to possible experience is precisely what Kant means by calling this form of proof "ostensive" and "direct" (A790/B818). Third, Kant says that a transcendental proposition (what is proved to have objective validity and be a necessary presupposition for the possibility of experience) is always a principle (*Grundsatz*), never a theorem (*Lehrsatz*), because "it has the peculiar character that it makes possible the very experience which is its own ground of proof, and that in this experience it must always itself be presupposed [*vorausgesetzt*]"; and further, such principles are established "not however directly from concepts alone, but always only indirectly through relation of these concepts to something altogether contingent, namely, *possible experience*" (A737/B765).

Now the puzzling issues relating to the logical form of a *TA* derive essentially from the third-mentioned criterion—the principle-theorem distinction. What exactly is Kant ruling out here, and what are the implications for the general form of a *TA*? The criterion has at least two crucial and equally controversial, interrelated components: (1) the idea that a TA is somehow significantly different from the standard deductive proof of what Kant calls a theorem because the justified transcendental principles are "presupposed" by the premises and (2) the idea that the transcendental principles which are proved by the TA have a modality of necessity while the epistemic premises are "altogether contingent." Indeed, in my judgment, it is precisely these two aspects that make a TA transcendental, viz., that the conclusion somehow expresses a modality of necessity but only in relation to what is contingent (possible experience) and the transcendental principles expressed in the conclusion are presupposed, in some way, for the possibility of the epistemic premises. Kant's principle-theorem criterion has led some philosophers to argue that a TA must be some unique, noninductive, nondeductive form of argument—or perhaps that the premises must "presuppose" the conclusion in some way or other that makes saying that a conclusion of a TA is deductively entailed either flatly false or not quite right.[9] This puzzle has generated arguments designed to show that Kant's criteria fail to distinguish distinctively transcendental from deductive proofs and, moreover, that no possible argument can satisfy Kant's criteria and succeed in doing what a TA is supposed to do.[10] After all, if the argument is not deductive, then how can it have the epistemic force Kant claims for it? But if it is deductive, how can the a priori synthetic principles be entailed? If the premises were empirical, the conclusion could not be nontrivially a priori; if the premises were analytic, the conclusion could not be synthetic; and the premises could not contain an a priori synthetic component because that there *is* such a connection is presumably what is supposed to be proved.

Besides this difficulty associated with the modality of a TA, there is the related difficulty associated with the postulated presuppositional connection between the premises and the conclusion of a TA. The difficulty has to do with what it can possibly mean to say that in a TA a transcendental principle is a presupposition of its own ground of proof. The problem is that there appears to be no satisfactory interpretation of this notion as a logical relation between propositions that will serve as the form of such an argument. Let P designate the epistemic premise(s) and Q the transcendental principle. Then what does it mean, in this context, to say that P presupposes Q? I shall rely here on the collective insight of recent critics.[11] "P presupposes Q" cannot mean (as Arthur Pap thought in his *The A Priori in Physical Theory*) simply "*Q* is a necessary condition for *P*," i.e., "*P* implies *Q*" no matter how one reads "implies." If "implies" means "materially implies," then "*P*" would presuppose any true proposition, and any false proposition would presuppose *Q*—not at all what transcendentalists have in mind. On the other hand, if "implies" means "logically entails" and this is synonymous with "presupposes," then a *TA* would be a straightforward deduction from premises (proof of a theorem) and would have no distinctive logical form at all. Further, the previously discussed problem of modality would arise. Besides, since the *Q* in a *TA* is supposed to be an a priori principle (one which is necessarily true independent of empirical considerations), it must remain true regardless of the truth value of *P*; but in the locution "*P* logically entails *Q*" we affirm the truth of *Q* only on the condition that *P* is true. Nor can "*P* presupposes *Q*" mean "*Q* is a necessary condition for the truth or falsity of *P*" as Strawson's analysis, in his *Introduction to Logical Theory*, suggests. If this means "*P* or not *P* materially implies *Q*," then, again, it would still be the case that every true proposition would be transcendentally presupposed; and moreover, since "*P* or not *P*" is a tautology, it is vacuous to say that it has necessary conditions because it is invariably true. Alternatively, if Strawson's interpretation means "*P* or not *P* logically entails *Q*," then "*Q*" would also have to be analytic (a tautology) because tautologies entail only tautologies—hardly the character Kant wanted for a transcendental principle. Finally Strawson's criterion cannot be rendered "*P* and not *P* entail *Q*" because then, since "*P* and not *P*" has the form of a contradiction, any proposition whatsoever would be presupposed. In any event, the nonequivalence of presupposition and entailment, as far as I am concerned, was satisfactorily established by John Austin: If "John's children are bald" presupposes "John has children," then, unlike entailment (*pace* Russell), it is the case that "John's children are bald" and "John's children are not bald" alike presuppose "John has children," and it is not the case that the negation of "John has children" presupposes "John's children are not bald."[12] For entailment, if "The cat is on the mat" entails "The mat is under the cat," then it is the case that "The mat is not under the cat" entails "The cat is not on the mat," and it is not the case that both "The cat is on the mat" and "The cat is not on the mat" alike entail "The mat is under the cat."

If we are to make any progress on the problems of modality and presupposition in *TA*'s, it is necessary to fill in what I would call

Kant's transcendental context. Let us assume with Kant that the relevant domain for his transcendental principles is possible experience. Then Kant's *TA* must show that a certain conceptual scheme possessing certain categorial features applies objectively to and is logically presupposed by the domain of possible experience. That is to say, the argument must show that, with respect to this specified domain, certain concepts are objectively primitive, i.e., are nontrivially instantiated whenever any other concept is instantiated, or that certain propositions are objective core propositions, i.e., are true whenever any other proposition is true or false. Because the domain is possible experience and Kant requires the proof to be "ostensive," we have already seen that the proof must contain at least one epistemic premise that expresses one's consciousness or awareness of subjective experience. As Gram correctly points out, this premise must express Kant's "weak" sense of experience—experience as the subjective apprehension of appearances prior to any necessary synthesis in accordance with rules and which corresponds to his weak sense of an object as the intentional content prior to necessary categorial synthesis (A91/B123)—not his "strong" sense of experience as the synthetic connection of appearances insofar as this synthesis is necessary and grounded on the transcendental notion of an object as "that in the concept of which the manifold of intuitions is united" (B127).[13] The premise set must express the weak sense of experience because otherwise the *TA* would be circular; and the conclusion must refer to the principles that ground the strong sense of experience because otherwise it would lack objective validity. But Gram is wrong in thinking that this condition for a valid *TA* can never be satisfied because there is an unbridgeable gap between the subjective validity of the premises and the supposed objective validity of the conclusion. To think that this is the case, as I argued above, is due to the employment of an illegitimate paradigm for the testing of *TA*'s. At any rate, the strategy of a *TA* is to show that in order to account for experience in the weak sense (something that is presumably conceded on all sides) it is necessary to presuppose experience in the strong sense. In addition to the required epistemic premise(s), the premise set will contain other premises—perhaps some propositions already proved by the preceding metaphysical deduction, some analytic propositions, and some uncontested empirical generalizations.

It is generally acknowledged that a conceptual scheme must provide criteria for reference and predication so that the objects of the specified domain can be identified and something can be said about them concerning their properties and relations.[14] In other words, the scheme must provide criteria specifying what is to count as an object in the domain, how to individuate a distinct object from all others in the domain, how to differentiate objects from their properties and relations, and sometimes how to distinguish the subject of experience from the experience of the subject. These criteria are formulated as fundamental principles or rules that constitute the logical structure of the scheme. I take it that, for Kant, the criteria for individuation are provided by the concept of space and time (the a priori forms of intuition), while the criteria for the identification and interrelation of the objects of the domain are provided by his system of categories. Of course, the justification of the objective validity of the forms of intuition and the categorial concepts—respectively the sensible and intellectual conditions of representation—is not completed until the problem of application is resolved (what Kant deals with in his discussion of schematism in the first *Critique* and his analogous treatment of the "typik" of practical reason in the second *Critique*) because, with respect to any conceptual scheme, one will need some procedure by which the purely formal framework can be related to the concrete, material domain. And finally, a transcendental consequence of the argument will be that there is a mutual reflexivity between the schematized categories (the principles) and the relevant domain, because, just as the principles are presupposed for the intelligibility of the domain, there is no justified procedure for the employment of the principles beyond the scope of the domain. Thus a complete *TA* is a very complex argument involving at least five stages: (1) the identification of the relevant manifold, (2) the justification (metaphysical deduction) of the conceptual scheme as an a priori presupposition, (3) the justification of the objective validity of the scheme, (4) the application of the scheme to the manifold, and (5) the limitation of the principles to the specified domain—this last feature being the consequence that I earlier suggested can be construed as a qualified version of a verification principle because cognitive meaning, for Kant, thereby becomes tied to possible empirical verification.

A careful reading of Kant's criteria will show that, just as Kant rules out indirect proof as the primary vehicle of transcendental inference, he equally does not rule out the deductive form of argument for *TA*'s. I contend that the conclusion of a *TA* is logically entailed by the premises and that, therefore, a *TA* has a deductive form. What makes a *TA* unique is not its nondeductive form but the fact that it is a very special kind of deductive argument, viz., one that proves that transcendental principles are objectively valid, necessary presuppositions for the truth of the epistemic premises that ground the deductive proof. The truth of the conclusion makes possible the very argument that justifies it. This is why *TA's* are seen as self-referential.[15] Kant's theorem-principle distinction does not distinguish deductive proof from some unique, nondeductive form of proof; nor does it require that in the proof of a principle the premises are related to the conclusion by the relation of presupposition rather than entailment. I contend that the primary, entailed conclusion of the proof is some proposition to the effect *that* certain principles are objectively valid presuppositions for the possibility of experience. To be sure, there *is* a relation of presupposition between these justified presuppositions and the epistemic premises, and the *TA* is designed to show deductively that this is the case. It is also true, of course, that Kant construes the transcendental principles as having a modality of necessity—they express a priori synthetic propositions. But the entailed conclusion of the *TA* is not itself an explicitly modal proposition in the context of the argument. Given this primary conclusion, the argument can then be extended so as to detach the transcendental principles. Since the conclusion affirms (in part) that the principles are necessary conditions for the possiblity of experience, this can be reformulated as saying, "If experience is possible, then . . . ," where " . . . " is a placeholder for a statement consisting of the conjunction of the principles. Then, with the assertion "Experience is possible" (because it is actual), the principles follow.

I am arguing that the *TA's* conclusion—the proposition that expresses the objectivity thesis—states what is the case, not what necessarily is the case. There is a definite sense in which it is correct to say: that *these* principles (or any principles, for that matter) are objectively constitutive for human experience, is, after all, something that *could* have been otherwise. The argument cannot establish the logical impossibility of all other alternatives; it can only show what is the case for human cognition. Given the sensible nature of human intuition, the discursive nature of human cognition, and the general descriptions of experience expressed in the epistemic premises, the conclusion is entailed. In the context of the argument the *relevant* issue of modality concerns the transcendental principles, not the claim to the effect that they are transcendental principles. This becomes clearer if we consider how

111

this modality comes about in a transcendental context like Kant's. Since the categorial propositions at issue are universal principles having existential import with respect to the objects of the contingent domain, they cannot be true in virtue of their analyticity but must be synthetic. But if true, neither can they be a posteriori statements because they express conditions to which all a posteriori statements about objects in the relevant domain must conform. Consequently, with respect to what is true within the domain that presupposes the conceptual scheme, these statements are a priori. Thus the principles are a priori synthetic statements, and that is the only way that sense can be made of this modality in the transcendental context. This is the point of Kant's specification that in a *TA* the proved principle is necessary, but only in relation to what is contingent. On the one hand, the argument shows that the objective possibility of a certain kind of logical connection—an a priori synthetic connection—*follows* from the epistemic premise set precisely because the sensible and intellectual conditions for representation (and, therefore, possible experience) are the source of the *x* that grounds and mediates the subject-predicate tie in an a priori synthetic proposition (A766/B794, A782/B10). On the other hand, the argument shows that the objective, synthetic unity that results from categorial synthesis in accordance with rules is a *presupposition* for the epistemic premise set that describes possible experience. That I am aware of a succession of experiences *as* experiences and as experiences of a certain *kind* and as all belonging to *me* presupposes the general condition under which experiences can be united in one self-consciousness (B133)—" . . . the analytic unity of apperception is possible only under the presupposition of a certain synthetic unity" (B133–34).

Am I suggesting that the conclusion of a *TA* is contingent? This would be paradoxical indeed, because, if contingent, must it not then be empirical? And if empirical, then an empirical justification of transcendental principles (precluded by Kant's first criterion) would seem legitimate after all. But this way of formulating the problem is already confused. It can be disambiguated only by keeping in mind how the real modalities applicable to factual knowledge are generated in Kant's transcendental context. It is only in this special context that the distinctions between analytic and synthetic, concept and intuition, appearances and things in themselves, the "ought" and the "is," mechanism and teleology, real possibility, actuality and necessity, etc., are meaningful, all of which are due to the "peculiarities of our cognitive faculties"—the *fact* that human intuition is sensible and human understanding is discursive.[16] Thus the modality of an a priori synthetic proposition is both a function of its relation to the specified domain of objects and the given character of the cognition in virtue of which these objects are apprehended. Questions about real or objective modality (not merely logical modality), taken in abstraction from Kant's transcendental context, lack significance. This is why critics and commentators have often been puzzled about the status of the propositional content of the *Critique* itself, especially that found in Kant's Transcendental Logic. The conclusion of a *TA* is a component of what Kant calls "transcendental knowledge"—knowledge about the preconditions of knowledge. In Kant's words, "Not all cognition a priori must be called transcendental, but instead only that by means of which we recognize that and how certain ideas (perceptions and concepts) are a priori applied and possible."[17] We probably would call this "metaphilosophical" knowledge today, but this second-order knowledge about the precondition (presuppositions) for the possibility of human experience cannot be a priori synthetic in the relevant sense in which the justified principles themselves are shown to have this modality in a *TA*. The point of the *TA* is to demonstrate, for the domain of possible experience, "that and how" the objective validity of principles with this modality is a transcendental presupposition for the domain. And part of the point of the transcendental context of the *Critique* itself is that the notion of modality, in abstraction from this context, is a purely logical notion. To construe it as more than that is to confuse logic with fact—an error Kant attributes to Leibniz and other rationalists. So from the perspective of Kant's transcendental context it is correct to say both that (1) transcendental knowledge (including the conclusion of a *TA*) is "contingent" in the sense that, from the standpoint of all possible worlds, it is logically possible that the conceptual scheme could have been otherwise than it is but not that it is a posteriori and that (2) such knowledge is "a priori" or even "a priori synthetic" in the sense that, from the standpoint of the actual world, it expresses what is preconditional with respect to possible factual knowledge but not that it is thereby exempt from the need to justify its objectivity. In any event, it is not the case that a conclusion of a *TA* (if it is construed as a priori synthetic) is a modal statement in the logical context of the *TA*. It is not a statement with "It is necessary that . . . " as a prefix. Its a priori modality derives from Kant's transcendental context, not from the premise set of the *TA*. The relevant reason why transcendental principles (Kant's

Axioms, Anticipations, Analogies, and Postulates) are not the *primary* conclusions of *TA*'s is not because they would then have an unwarranted modality in the logical context of *TA*'s but because the first order of business for a *TA* is to establish a second-order truth about the principles.

Kant's principle-theorem criterion means no more than this: (1) the conclusion of a *TA*, unlike the proof of a theorem, is not merely a deductive consequence but a deductive consequence that expresses something that *makes possible* the truth of its premises; (2) such conclusions, unlike theorems, must be based on at least one epistemic premise— "not directly through concepts alone but indirectly through relation of these concepts to something altogether contingent, namely, possible experience"—because the *TA* must appeal to the actual exemplification and employment of the principles in possible experience; and (3) the principles are not derived analytically from higher principles of the same kind with prior epistemic authority because there are none, but theorems are so derived from higher-order theorems or axioms.

If what I have argued is correct, the problems concerning the modality of the conclusion and the purportedly unique presuppositional relation between premises and conclusion in a *TA* are not to the point. To say that a conclusion asserts that certain other propositions (in relation to a specified domain) have a modality of necessity is not to say that the conclusion itself is a modal proposition. Similarly, to say that certain foundational principles are presupposed by the premises of an argument that justifies the principles is not to say that the conclusion of the argument is itself related to the premises by the relation of presupposition rather than entailment.

Although we have seen that a *TA* is a complex affair and therefore, the analysis of abstract expressions like "*P* presupposes *Q*" can hardly suffice for the clarification of the notion of transcendental presupposition, nevertheless, I suppose that the upshot of my position can be stated as follows: If, once more, *P* designates the premise set and *Q* a transcendental principle, I reject the idea that the general, logical form of a *TA* is best conveyed by "*P* presupposes *Q*." I say that this more appropriately designates the form of the primary conclusion and that the paradigmatic form is better represented as "*P* entails '*P* presupposes *Q*.' " If so, then if *Q* is a presupposition for *P*, this does not entail that the primary conclusion of the *TA*, viz., "*P* presupposes *Q*," is itself a presupposition for *P*. It could only entail this if the truth of the presupposition Q entailed that P presupposes Q. But, clearly, to say that the truth of a presupposition entails the statement expressing its presuppositional relation is counterintuitive for our use of "presupposition." "John has children" does not entail " 'John's children are bald' presupposes 'John has children.' "

The argument of the preceding section supports the thesis that the key to understanding Kant's transcendental style of argument is the relation of transcendental presupposition. It is this that gives a TA its self-referentiality when the argument is treated as a valid sequence of statements in the formal mode, and it is this that grounds the reflexivity between possible experience and transcendental principles when the argument is treated in terms of what the argument is about in the material mode. Of course, the epistemic force of the argument rests on the fact that the justification is meant to hold for all possible interpretations of human experience (within the transcendental parameters of sensible intuition and discursive understanding) and pertains to an invariable conceptual core. It is not then a hypothetical deduction that achieves its epistemic force in reference to particular interpretations of experience correlated with variable or alternative conceptual schemes. In order to complete my analysis of Kantian presupposition, it is necessary for me to say something more about presupposition as a relation between statements and then relate Kant's notion of presupposition to what I have called his transcendental context.

In the context of the analysis of arguments, it is fashionable to treat presupposition as a relation applicable to sentences, statements or propositions in the formal mode, not as a relation that applies to what these linguistic and conceptual items are about. Presuppositions typically function as preconditions for the truth value, meaning, existence or successful assertion of sentences where this depends on the kind of presupposition purported to be involved. I suppose that the central question concerning presuppositions concerns whether there are any. For example, Russell maintained that a proper analysis of so-called presuppositional sentences would show that this notion is expendable because the presumed presuppositional relation is no more than logical entailment. If one argued, with Strawson, that "The King of France is wise" presupposes (not entails) that the King of France exists (because otherwise "The King of France is wise" would have no truth value and therefore would not achieve statementhood), Russell would counter that part of the meaning of "The King of France is wise" includes the assertion that the King of France exists. Any meaningful sentence already has its truth value, and, consequently, cases of so-called presuppositional failure are simply cases of false statements requiring no special accommodation. Frege, of course, also adopted the presuppositional account for sentences containing names or singular referring expressions but felt that presuppositional failure was a defect endemic to natural languages—something that simply would not occur in an ideal canonical notation where the conditions for well-formed formulae would rule out the occurrence of singular expressions that might fail in reference. Many contemporary linguists and semanticists, although agreeing that a provision must be made for the role of presupposition in natural language, reject the notion that presuppositional failure is a defect of natural language rather than being due simply to the limitations on our knowledge of the world.[18]

In my judgment attempts to dispense with any distinct notion of presupposition become plausible to the degree that the analysis of language is abstracted from the contextual background in which language as an activity occurs. I mean, if sentences are treated exclusively in terms of their propositional content and construed as symbolic representations that already convey meaning, then the conditions for meaningfulness and the conditions for statementhood become identified. If a sentence is meaningful through its conformance to a set of minimal rules that determine what is to count as a sentence in the language, then the sentence is a statement that expresses a proposition, i.e., has a truth value. But if, instead, like Frege, Strawson, Austin, Grice, or Searle, the analysis of language treats sentences as signs of linguistic acts that occur in the contextual setting of natural language now construed as an institutional fact, then the condition for statementhood will be stronger than the abstracted conditions for meaningfulness; or alternatively, meaning conditions will not include considerations of illocutionary and perlocutionary force, the conditions for the performance of speech acts, etc. It is in this context, I contend, that the notion of presupposition becomes particularly prominent because the relation of presupposition obtains only with reference to some contextual background, conventional or otherwise.

Accordingly, in the linguistic context, presuppositionalists typically divide into two groups: semantic presuppositionalists and pragmatic presuppositionalists. Presuppositions are generally seen as implied propositions which certain sentences are not primarily about but the truth of which is, in some sense, a precondition for the utterance of those sentences; and one central theme that runs through the literature is that the presuppositional component is a dimension of meaning that is distinct from the kind of semantic content that constitutes the typical domain of truth-conditional semantics.[19] Semantic presuppositionalists analyze presupposition in the linguistic context of the syntactic and semantic rules of a natural language and treat the problem of presupposition as part of the broader problem of explaining the compositionality of sentence meaning.[20] From this perspective, as Katz says, presupposition is a semantic property of a sentence that applies to the Fregean senses of certain declarative sentences—a necessary condition for the statementhood of certain sentences, viz., the condition of successful reference—and a semantic presuppositionalist like Katz attempts to relegate all legitimate cases of presupposition under the heading of Fregean existential presuppositions.

Pragmatic presuppositionalists typically construe presuppositions either as preparatory conditions for speech acts (following Austin and Searle) or as conventional as conversational implicatures (following Grice).[21] Here the presuppositional context is or is part of the external institutional or social overlay in which natural language exists, and presupposition is interpreted as a necessary condition for successful communication. Searle delineates necessary conditions for utterance acts, the propositional acts of reference and predication, and illocutionary acts— input-output conditions, propositional content conditions, sincerity conditions, preparatory conditions, meaning conditions, and so on. Grice's notion of an implicature can be grasped by saying that if a speaker's utterance of P licenses the inference that Q even though Q expresses content beyond what the speaker actually said, then the speaker has implicated that Q and Q is an implicature of P. Such implicatures occur in virtue of certain lexical items and grammatical constructions in P that contribute to its conventional meaning in the context of a language game or in virtue of certain particularized and generalized conversational contexts in which the participants cooperatively observe maxims of discourse. Examples of conventional presupposition would involve certain particles like "even" or "also" and certain factive verbs like "realizes," "remembers," or "knows." Thus, "Even Carter likes Reagan" presupposes that others like Reagan; and "Carter remembers that he lost the election" presupposes that Carter lost the election. Presumably, existential presuppositions that accompany quantifiers would also fall in this class. On the other hand, a conversational implicature is exemplified by saying that "Carter criticized Reagan for his radical cut in social programs" presupposes that Reagan made a radical cut in social programs, or by subjunctive conditionals which are said to presuppose the falsity of their antecedent clauses.

The range of linguistic phenomena associated with the semantic and pragmatic accounts of presupposition resist rigid classification and criterial precision. Controversy concerning the existence and character of presupposition as a component of sentence meaning persists among linguists, philosophers, and mathematicians. The reason for this, I think, is that very diverse phenomena have been labeled "presuppositions" depending upon the context of analysis and the philosophical orientation of particular advocates. What is relatively clear is that those who subscribe to the legitimacy of this notion do seem to adopt, in some sense or other, a "use" theory of meaning that addresses the question of meaning in terms of some broader context that provides the basis and criteria for the role of presupposition in natural language. If so, then the notion of presupposition is primarily tied to a contextual background. This is why neither the relation of material implication nor logical entailment is sufficient in itself to capture the logical character of presupposition. The well-known logical behavior of these relations is quite perspicuous when expressed as "P implies Q" or "P logically entails Q," because they do not depend, at least in the same variable and indefinite way that presupposition does, on contextual background. When one is asked what "P presupposes Q" means, the question begs for a context. The presuppositional context might be specified in terms of the formal semantic and syntactic rules for a natural language, the regularities that informally govern a particular language game, the pragmatic maxims that guide successful communication, or the conceptual framework that embodies the preconditions for knowledge. Presuppositions are inherently *contextual*.

A second common feature of presuppositional occurrence is that the logical behavior of a presupposition will depend on *what* it is that the presupposition is a presupposition for. Meaning? Truth? Truth value? Successful assertion? The existence of something? If we do not specify that in virtue of which one statement presupposes another, any attempt to explicate the logical behavior of a presupposition will be futile. Once again this points to the uselessness of the paradigm "*P* presupposes *Q*" taken in abstraction from its context and without any specification about what is at stake. For example, with respect to the existential presupposition expressed in the claim that "John's children are bald" presupposes that John has children, it is true that "John's children are not bald" has the same presupposition; but with respect to the sincerity condition for speech acts expressed by the claim that my saying "The cat is on the mat" presupposes that I believe it is; it is not true that my saying "The cat is not on the mat" still presupposes that I believe it is. Presuppositional failure in the first case results in a lack of truth value; in the second case we simply have infelicity with respect to assertion. In other words, all presuppositions carry a *relevance condition*. That is to say, unless we know what it is that is relevant to the presuppositional relation, the function of the presupposition remains opaque.

A third feature of presupposition is its nonequivalence with implication. For reasons already discussed, we have seen that "presupposes" cannot be synonymous with "implies" in either the material or the logical sense. But this is not to say that if *P* presupposes *Q* then *P* cannot imply *Q*. It seems clear that a presupposition is a necessary condition for that which presupposes it—either a material or a logical necessary condition. I think that all presuppositions are material necessary conditions and some presuppositions are logical necessary conditions. It is tempting to say that the presupposition is logically entailed when it derives from the meaning of certain lexical or syntactic elements in the presupposing sentence, while it is only materially implied when it derives from criteria related to a broader contextual background. Thus it would seem to be logically inconsistent to say "Even Carter likes Reagan, and nobody else does." But to say "The King of France is wise, and he doesn't exist" is, as Strawson says, a different kind of absurdity. If the presupposition relevant to the latter example were entailed, then its falsity would entail the falsity of "The King of France is wise," contrary to the presuppositionist claim that this sentence would merely lack truth value.

Finally, the most-pronounced characteristic of presupposition is that it grounds the real possibility of what it is a presupposition for. It *makes possible* whatever corresponds to the content expressed in its relevance condition, and it does this on the basis of criteria generated in its presuppositional context. Of course, it is also the case that any deductive conclusion, as a necessary condition for the truth of its premises, "makes possible" the truth of the premises in the sense of that which must be true if something else is to be true. Similarly, the premises "make possible" the truth of the conclusion in the sense of that which is sufficient for the deduction of the conclusion. "Makes possible," like "logically prior" is equivocal. Presuppositions are logically prior to what presupposes them and make possible what is presuppositionally relevant in a much stronger sense than what is conveyed merely by their status as necessary conditions. They make something possible in virtue of their status as real preconditions—as something which must *already* be the case if what presupposes them is to be the case. They are logically prior not merely with respect to their truth-conditional relation to what presupposes them but in the sense that they constitute the foundation for the possibility and compositionality of that which presupposes them. In short, presuppositions are principles.

Now Kant's *TA* is not an inductive generalization grounded on the pervasiveness of spatial-temporal and categorial features. It is not an argument based on our psychological inability to imagine a different scheme with different conditions. It is not an Aristotelian intuition of an essential connection between objects and categorial features. It is not a relativized or conditional argument applicable to some postulated or conventional interpretation of experience. It is not a deductive argument based on higher cognitive principles that possess higher epistemic authority. It is not a case of pragmatic abduction concerned with how well a given conceptual scheme "fits" an already cognized system of facts. It is deductive argument that attempts to establish the irreducible and nonderivative conditions for its own possibility that has applicability to any possible human experience, and, consequently, it must justify the original legitimacy of objectively valid first principles from *within* a framework that presupposes the principles, and that is why it is called "transcendental." So the transcendental principles are the presuppositions, and the presuppositional context, for Kant, is the epistemological (not linguistic) context in which knowledge claims are normatively justified. But it is not merely an epistemological context in which particular empirical claims are warranted, but a transcendental context in which the preconditions for the very possibility of such claims are justified. If so, then the relevance condition associated with *these* presuppositions will pertain to the existence, meaning, truth value, and assertability of any affirmative or negative epistemic premise that describes any aspect of experience. The objectively valid principles will be constitutive of and foundational for the possibility and compositionality of any epistemic description.

Still, this description of the argument only tells us *that* but not *how* it proves the objectivity thesis. It is still vulnerable to the skeptical charge that at best it can only prove that the foundational scheme is subjectively necessary, not objectively valid. In that case, it would be merely an elaborate, conceptual smoke screen for a metaphysical deduction. How does it demonstrate that independent objects exist and actually conform to the requirements of the categorial scheme? Note that this skeptical challenge construes the problem in terms of proving that a subjectively necessary conceptual apparatus corresponds to the characteristics of utterly distinct, preexistent objects. If the *TA* is to succeed, Kant needs a way to replace this paradigm of metaphysical realism with a paradigm in which this formulation of the skeptical challenge makes no sense. What the argument needs is a way of making a logical connection between the cognitive conditions of knowledge and the concept of an object in general. It needs to show that there can be no consideration of objects independent of the conditions of our knowing them. And what is crucial to see is that this requirement cannot be merely a postulate or assumption that is then imposed on the skeptical paradigm but rather must be a constituent of an entirely different epistemological paradigm. If this can be provided, then the kind of epistemological gap between subjective necessity and objective validity that worries the metaphysical realist will be closed.

For Kant the required paradigm is provided by the fundamental orientation of the Critical Philosophy, viz., what Kant called the Copernican Revolution in Philosophy (Bxvi–Bxviii, A126). This metaphor corresponds to what I have called Kant's transcendental context, and it is precisely what serves as the presuppositional context for a *TA*. It is this epistemological context that yields the criteria for transcendental presupposition. The point is that the Copernican paradigm provides a new criterion of objectivity. What is to be construed as an object of knowledge is no longer something that is given independently of our cognitive activity. It is not such objects that are given but only "representations" (*Vorstellungen*), which then must be submitted to the epistemological test of whether or not they can be "referred to an object," i.e., can be connected with each other in certain ways in accordance with necessary rules applied by the activity of judgment. This move is analogous to Wittgenstein's replacement of word-world connections with word-word connections. Thus Kant's picture is not one of an epistemological isomorphism between categorial concepts and distinct things in themselves. When representations represent an object (in contrast to being merely subjective), there is not thereby some correspondence between representations and some nonepistemic, transcendent entities, but instead a determinable nexus between the representations and other representations in accordance with universally shared rules. So the object referred to in Kant's "reference to an object" is an epistemological resultant—an epistemic *product* of the activity of intelligence—and that is why Kant can say that an object is "that in the concept of which the manifold of intuition is united."

Kant's transcendental context entails the principle that, from a philosophical point of view, questions concerning the possibility, conditions, and limitations of knowledge are logically prior to any determination of the existence and nature of the objects known. As Kant interprets it, this principle, when applied to human cognition, involves two interrelated facets: the first is a philosophical prescription concerning method that stipulates that what is to be construed as an object of knowledge will be a function of what results from a prior analysis of the epistemological conditions of human cognition; the second is apparently an empirical generalization, but nevertheless is so well established that Kant treats it as uncontestable (B146), viz., that, unlike what he calls an "intuitive understanding," human cognition is conditioned by sensibility, and, consequently, the content of experience will consist of objects insofar as they appear, not objects independent of the conditions of cognition. On the other hand, given the fact that human cognition has this character, it is an analytic truth (the "first principle" of understanding) that such cognition must proceed by combining representations into a synthetic unity under concepts (B139, B145); i.e., it involves the application of discursive concepts to an empirically given content. Now these statements, as well as the general Copernican framework in terms of which they make sense, may or may not appear as explicit premises in a Kantain *TA*. The important point is that they constitute the general fabric of the transcendental context without which the argument could not demonstrate the status of transcendental principles as objectively valid presuppositions. Kant's transcendental context provides the following criterion for transcendental presupposition: Given the nature of human cognition and our Copernican paradigm of objectivity, what is it that must be acknowledged as a necessary condition that functions as a preestablished foundation that makes possible and accounts for any empirical descriptions of the content of experience? The answer: the schematized principles of the categorial scheme that function as the universally normative rules for the synthesis of representations in general. Subjective descriptions of experience are possible only if objective judgments of experience are possible. And each transcendental principle—because of its universal scope, its logically unique function with respect to the kind of synthesis it grounds, and its status as a cognitive principle (*Grundsatz*) of the highest epistemic authority—will be *sui generis*. This is what Kant meant by the rarely noticed additional criterion for transcendental proofs, viz., "that only one proof can be found for each transcendental principle" (A787/B815).

I have argued that the primary vehicle of transcendental inference is neither an indirect proof nor a nondeductive proof. It is a deductive argument having a self-referential character that is designed to establish (1) the relation between a priori synthetic connection and possible experience, (2) the objective validity of the transcendental principles, and (3) their status as transcendental presuppositions for the possibility of experience. Kant's strategy is to show that it is not possible to account for the experience we do have without it also being the case that our experiences at least sometimes refer to real objects that conform to the categorial scheme (previously identified in the metaphysical deduction) and exist in a single objective spatiotemporal world. I have also maintained that this thesis—the objectivity thesis—is vulnerable to the challenge of the epistemological skeptic only if we ignore the transcendental context of the argument that derives from Kant's Copernican paradigm. But within this transcendental context the *TA* can succeed in making an identification between the formal unity of the concept of an object in general and the formal unity of any object that can possibly fall under this concept. As Kant says, "The conditions of the possibility of experience in general are likewise conditions of the possibility of objects of experience, and that for this reason they have objective validity in a synthetic a priori judgment" (A158/B197).

In light of this, if a skeptic still persists, *in this context*, with his claim that the argument shows only subjective necessity, then he is either disingenuous or has missed the point. For Kant has shown that it literally no longer makes sense to ask whether or not there are external objects that *really* correspond to the scheme. It is not as if there are or might be utterly distinct "objects" that might be recalcitrant to the imposition of the categorial scheme. The invariable conceptual core is not justified in relation to some postulated system of things in themselves having an ontologically independent status, but it is the conceptual core that grounds our notion of an independent object. As we have seen, to argue on the basis of the mere *logical* possibility that things could have been different from what they are is beside the point. That there might be unknowable objects in some other possible world is irrelevant. What *would* count against Kant's argument is the possibility that objects might not conform and yet still be objects in our world or in any world possible for us. But if the formal principles *are* the norms for objectivity, then what counts as an object for us is identical with what counts as a possible object for us. The skeptic needs to show that there might be real objects in our world that are unknowable, and he needs to do this while assuming an invariable conceptual scheme that entails the opposite. Thus the skeptic's claim that the *TA* has demonstrated only what we must believe (not what we can know) employs a nonepistemic notion of an object and sets systematically unsatisfiable conditions on the use of "know." If so, then the validity of Kant's *TA* does not depend on any verificationist premise to the effect that we can know that utterly distinct objects exist and conform to the categorial scheme.

To interpret Kant's argument as one that establishes a unique categorial scheme as a necessary subjective apparatus which is then somehow imposed on things in themselves is to transform Kant's argument into a transcendental subjectivism which must then bridge the gap between necessary concepts and independent entities. It is to construe Kant's scheme as a system of innate ideas that characterizes individual minds and makes contact with reality only in virtue of some kind of ontological guarantee or preestablished harmony—an interpretation that Kant explicitly warns us against in his "Outcome of the Deduction of the Categories of the Understanding" (B166–68). To offset this, Kant employs a biological analogue to characterize his transcendental idealism (empirical realism) as a system of "the epigenesis of pure reason." The point is simply that an object is an epigenetic product of the use of intelligence just insofar as this use conforms to the universal criteria that ground the objectivity of judgments in general.

Many recent critics who fault Kant for his failure to prove the objectivity thesis either confuse Kant's transcendental deduction with his metaphysical deduction or misinterpret Kant's doctrine as a form of what I have called transcendental subjectivism. They want some ontological guarantee, over and above the conclusion of his central TA, that objects exist and conform to the framework as a matter of fact. But given the transcendental context of the argument, the notion of "fact" makes sense only as an epistemological function of the framework. Such objections therefore play on a nonepistemic notion of an object that transcends the possibility of any determination in the argument and as such invoke the very doctrine—transcendental realism—to which Kant's whole Copernican paradigm is an alternative. The realist metaphysics in these objections would need a defense in its own right at an entirely different level. That is fair philosophical game, and I do not deny that the paradigm of metaphysical realism can be defended, but this would take entirely different kinds of argument from most of those that have been mounted against the immodest epistemological foundationalists.

NOTES

1. This study was supported by University of Kansas General Research Allocation #3059-20-0038. All quotations from Kant's *Critique of Pure Reason* are taken from the Norman Kemp Smith translation (London, 1956).

2. Richard Rorty, *Philosophy and the Mirror of Nature* (Princeton, N.J.: Princeton University Press, 1979).

3. Stanley Cavell, *The Claim of Reason* (New York: Oxford University Press, 1979).

4. Examples include: Jay Rosenberg, "Transcendental Arguments Revisited," *Journal of Philosophy* 72 (1975): 621–22; W. V. Quine, "Epistemology Naturalized" and "Natural Kinds," in *Ontological Relativity and Other Essays* (New York: Columbia University Press, 1969); Alvin Goldman, "Discrimination and Perceptual Knowledge," *Journal of Philosophy* 73 (1976): 771–91; Alvin Goldman, "What Is Justified Belief?" in G. Pappas, ed., *Justification and Knowledge* (Boston: Reidel, 1979), pp. 1–23; and Hilary Kornblith, "Beyond Foundationalism and the Coherence Theory," *Journal of Philosophy* 72 (1980): 597–612.

5. See, e.g., Stephen Körner, "The Impossibility of Transcendental Deductions," in L. W. Beck, ed., *Kant Studies Today* (La Salle, Ill: Open Court, 1969), pp. 230–49; Richard Rorty," Verificationism and Transcendental Arguments," *Nous* (1971): 3–14; and Rosenberg, "Transcendental Arguments Revisited."

6. See Barry Stroud, "Transcendental Arguments," *Journal of Philosophy* 65 (1968): 241–56; Judith Thomson, "Private Languages," *American Philosophical Quarterly* 1 (1964): 20–31; M. S. Gram, "Must Transcendental Arguments Be Spurious?" *Kant-Studien* 65 (1974): 304–17; and Ralph C. S. Walker, *Kant*, (The Arguments of the Philosophers) ed. Ted Honderich (London: Routledge & Kegan Paul, 1978), p. 130.

7. For example, Stroud, in "Transcendental Arguments," argues that if Strawson's argument for the continued existence of material objects is straightforward deductive (not indirect) then it is not a transcendental proof (p. 247); see also M. S. Gram, "Transcendental Arguments," *Nous* 5 (1971): 15–26; and Henry Ruf, "Transcendental Logic: An Essay on Critical Metaphysics," *Man & World* 2 (1969): 38–64.

8. "Transcendental Form," *Southwestern Journal of Philosophy* 11 (1980): 25–34.

9. Besides Stroud, Gram, and Ruf, see Patricia Crawford, "Kant's Theory of Philosophical Proof," *Kant-Studien* 62 (1961–62): 257–68; Martin Kalin, "What Makes an Argument Transcendental?" *Idealistic Studies* 7(1977): 172–84; and T. E. Wilkerson, "Transcendental Arguments," *Philosophical Quarterly* 20 (1970): 200–12.

10. Gram, especially his "Must Transcendental Arguments Be Spurious?" pp. 315–16.

11. This "collective insight" is essentially a composite of the various objections set forth by Gram, Crawford, and Ruf, but I do not attribute to them my formulation of the composite.

12. John Austin, *How to Do Things with Words* (New York: Oxford University Press, 1962), pp. 49–50.

13. Gram, "Must Transcendental Arguments Be Spurious?" p. 316.

14. See Körner, "The Impossibility of Transcendental Deductions." I have followed Körner's general description of the requirements for a conceptual scheme.

15. For an excellent discussion that emphasizes this aspect of self-referentiality, see Rüdiger Bübner, "Kant's Transcendental Argument and the Problem of Deduction," *Review of Metaphysics* 25 (1975): 453–67.

16. *Critique of Judgment*, "Dialectic of the Teleological Judgment," sect. 76 and 77, trans. J. H. Bernard (New York: Hafner, 1951), pp. 249–58.

17. *Prolegomena to Any Future Metaphysics*, sec. 13, remark 3; and the first *Critique* (A71).

18. Jerrold J. Katz, "A Solution to the Projection Problem for Presupposition," in Choon-Kyu Oh and David A. Dinneen, eds., *Syntax and Semantics*, vol. 2, *Presupposition* (New York: Academic Press), pp. 91–126. My characterization of the way the semantic presuppositionalist sees his contrast to Russell is basically taken from Katz.

19. See Lauri Karttunen and Stanley Peters, "Conventional Implicature," in Oh and Dineen, eds., *Syntax and Semantics*, vol. 2, *Presupposition*, pp. 1–3.

20. Katz, "A Solution to the Projection Problem for Presupposition," p. 91.

21. See Karttunen and Peters, "Conventional Implicature"; and H. P. Grice, "Logic and Conversation," text of William James Lecture at Harvard University (unpublished manuscript, 1968), excerpted in D. Davidson and G. Harmon, eds., *The Logic of Grammar* (Encino, Calif.: Dickenson, 1975), pp. 64–75.

What Kant Really Did to Idealism

MOLTKE S. GRAM
University of Iowa

Kant's arguments against Idealism have had a hard life. We are allegedly unclear about what the conclusion of those arguments is. We are supposedly even more in the dark about what kind of logical structure the proofs have. As if that were not enough, we have been occasionally told that, even if we were to agree about the conclusion or the structure of the proofs, the arguments in the A and B editions of the first *Critique* are mutually inconsistent: either the premises or the conclusions, or both, are mutually incompatible.

These are the three major issues facing anyone wanting to defend one or the other of Kant's arguments against Idealism. The first has several parts. Does Kant argue to the existence of objects outside us?[1] Or does he argue for the existence of material objects, which may not be outside us?[2] Or, finally, does his Refutation of Idealism supply an argument for the existence of things in themselves?[3] You can find somebody in the tradition who supports one or another of each of these interpretations. And what about the logical structure of the arguments in the first *Critique*? Is it a straightforward deductive argument, or is it a candidate for what Kant elsewhere calls a transcendental proof? Here again the tradition is divided.[4] Finally, suppose the arguments in A and B to be mutually incompatible. Does this arise from the character of the premise sets of the two proofs or from their respective conclusions?[5]

My case, put bluntly, is this. Kant's arguments in both the A and the B editions succeed in refuting Idealism as he understands it. Yes, he tries to accomplish this by proving the existence of objects outside us. No, he does not attempt in either edition to use his Refutation of Idealism as proof of things in themselves. In both editions he attempts to prove that there are material things outside us that exist independently of their being perceived. No, the arguments he offers are not mutually inconsistent either in the premises or in the conclusion to which Kant argues from those premises. But the kinds of premises he uses in the arguments differ. No, Kant's arguments against Idealism are not transcendental in his sense of the term. They are deductive because each exhibits a distinctive form of deductive reasoning. This is what Kant really did to Idealism. He offers us three logically distinguishable arguments against that view. Take them in turn.

I. *The* Nova dilucidatio *Argument*

This is Kant's first serious attempt to refute Idealism.[6] It assumes a battery of distinctions which Kant deploys at the beginning of *Nova dilucidatio*. To determine (*determinare*) anything is "to affirm a predicate with the exclusion of its opposite."[7] A reason (*ratio*) is what "determines a subject with respect to a certain predicate."[8] Reasons are either antecedent (*rationes cur*) or consequent determinations (*rationes quod*).[9] The former tell us why something is; the latter, how we know it.

Kant's Jupiter Example illustrates this distinction.[10] The eclipses of the satellites of the planet Jupiter provide us with a way in which we know (*ratio cognoscendi*) the successive propagation of light taking place at an assignable velocity. But this is only a consequent determination, for light would have still been propagated in time from Jupiter even if its satellites did not exist at all. The behavior of the satellites assumes and does not provide a reason (*ratio fiendi*) why the transmission of light is connected with an assignable lapse of time.

The Jupiter Example can be generalized. You can give an explanation of something whenever you specify whatever causes you to come to know that phenomenon occurs. This can be done by specifying a criterion for detecting instances of it. But the specification of a criterion for identifying instances of something does not tell you the nature of what you may be able successfully to identify any more than a thermometric measurement of temperature can tell you what the nature of temperature is. So much for the background distinctions.

The Kant of *Nova dilucidatio* gives us what he identifies as three distinct refutations of Idealism. The differences are, however, philosophically inconsequential. Proposition 12 of section 3 is said to follow from the Principle of Sufficient Reason and is essential to all three versions of the argument in *Nova dilucidatio*. Kant calls it the Principle of Succession and states it this way: "Nulla substantiis accidens potest mutatio, nisi quatenus connexae sunt, quaram dependentia reciproca mutuam status mutationem determinat" [No change can happen to substances except insofar as they are connected with others, their reciprocal dependence determining the mutual change of state].[11] There are three stages of the argument which are supposed to rest on this proposition.

1. Assume a simple substance which contains internal determinations that are mutually compatible and are posited on internal grounds.

2. Suppose that another determination succeeds the determinations already posited on internal grounds.

3. The succession of determinations requires another ground which by virtue of premise (1) must be inherent in the substance.

4. But since succession is the transition from one determination to its contrary, both cannot be simultaneously contained in the internal ground of the substance.

5. Therefore, no simple substance can both change and exist in isolation from any other substance.

The argument continues:

6. Things posited by a determining reason (*determinatum*) must be posited simultaneously with the reason (*rationatum*).

7. Therefore, both *determinatum* and *rationatum* must coexist.

8. Change (*mutatio*) is a succession of determinations in which some determination arises which did not previously exist.

9. This change cannot arise through what is to be found intrinsically in the substances because of premises 3 and 4.

10. Therefore, change assumes the existence of an external connection of one substance with another.[12]

The argument concludes:

11. The mind undergoes internal changes in internal sense.

12. These changes cannot arise from the *nature* of the mind because of premises (5) and (10) of the foregoing stages.

13. Therefore, the mind must be connected with other things that are outside of it (*extra animam*).

14. Change of perceptions takes place in conformity with external motion.

15. Therefore, ". . . [I]it follows immediately . . . that a human mind apart from a real nexus of external things would obviously be incapable of any change of internal state."[13]

This, then, is Kant's initial attempt to refute Idealism.

First, some explanations. Kant tells us that he is giving three different refutations. He does not. What he *does* construct is one proof which he delivers in three stages. The pivotal premises of each of the three stages are so many variations on one and the same premise, the premise, namely, that if you assume change to be a succession of one property by its contrary then the reason (*ratio*) cannot lie in the nature of the substance. Assume otherwise and you would be unable to account for the transition from, say, a's having f at time t and a's having g at t'. Internal determinations are sempiternal. Whatever follows from the internal determinations of a substance is timeless. But no deductive implication can account for the transition from something's having different properties at different times. What is crucial to Kant's argument in *Nova dilucidatio*, then, is the distinction between what he calls determinations in the nature or reason of a substance and determinations that occur in the temporal succession from one state of that substance to another. The former can explain why something has the properties it has if you can deduce those properties from the internal determination of a thing. But the latter can explain the temporal transition of the possession of one property to another only by reference to the action of one substance upon another. And this assumes that there must be substances external to one another. Thus the logical relation between what Kant calls the Principle of Succession and the Principle of Sufficient Reason.

But all of this could equally hold in a world in which there are no minds. Does Kant's argument show not merely that any case of change requires the externality of one substance from another but also that there must be material substances external to the temporal transition that occurs from one mental state to another? The third stage of the argument is compatible with there being only mental substances and their states. This vitiates the *Nova dilucidatio* argument—but only on the assumption that the argument is supposed to prove the existence of *material* objects outside us rather than the existential independence of objects apart from anybody's acts of awareness. The phrase *extra animam* obscures this distinction. Something could exist independently of a mind without being a material substance. This distinction does not, however, undermine the *Nova dilucidatio* argument. It shows only that the argument is incomplete. Let me explain.

You can try to show, as Kant does, that the fact of a temporal transition from one state to another requires the existence of entities that are existentially independent of one another. What you will have shown is that there are objects in the world which exist independently of being perceived. Whether such objects are material or mental is irrelevant to the *Nova dilucidatio* argument. To show that there must be substances existing *extra animam* is to show the *possibility* of the existence of material bodies. This is all that the argument purports to show. That our perception of material bodies is a necessary condition of our perception of a temporal transition in our own mental states is an extension of the argument which Kant had yet to make.

II. *The Fourth Paralogism Argument*

We have seen how what Kant calls the Principle of Succession is the basis of his earliest serious argument against Idealism. We have also seen that the principle applies equally to the transition of events in what Kant calls our internal sense and to events in which only material objects are involved. But we have also had to conclude that the *Nova dilucidatio* argument proves at most the possibility of material objects existing outside of us and not that, as Kant later was to show, we directly perceive material objects or the existence of material objects, as a condition of our ability to perceive a temporal transition from one of our mental states to another.

Both the premises and the conclusion of the argument in the Fourth Paralogism are compatible with their logical counterparts in the *Nova dilucidatio* version of the argument. But the arguments differ radically in strategy. The former moves from a fact about change of properties in time; the latter, from a fact about the status of all perceptions, irrespective of temporal transition, to the possibility of direct perception of external objects. The argument in the Fourth Paralogism, accordingly, is this:

1. No outer appearance (*äusserliche Erscheinung*) is immediately perceived [*ex hypothesi*].
2. Therefore, we must infer the existence of outer appearances as the causes of what we do immediately perceive.
3. Therefore, the existence of outer objects (read: "spatial objects," A373) is doubtful because it always remains doubtful whether the cause of what we immediately perceive is external or internal. [*Lemma*: The inference from a given effect to a determinate cause is always uncertain.]
4. But outer appearances, thought empirically real, are transcendentally ideal. [*Lemma*: Conclusion of the Transcendental Aesthetic, A41–B59ff].
5. If we assume the transcendental ideality of all appearances, then outer appearances are as epistemically immediate as inner appearances.
6. Hence, spatial objects can be the objects of immediate awareness.[14]

The argument is cogent, but it demands supplementation. Three major objections threaten it. For one thing, step 4 assumes that what Kant calls the transcendental ideality of all appearances entails an immediate awareness of things outside us and that it does so because it entails the empirical reality of all appearances. There is, however, no evidence in the argument as it presently stands that any such claim is true.[15] For another, even if we assume that there is such an entailment and hold that no external objects exist independently of possible human experience, steps 2 and 3 might still obtain even within a world in which all appearances are transcendentally ideal just because the causal relation can hold between an outer and an inner appearance.[16] For yet another, to say that all appearances are transcendentally ideal seems to imply, not that we can be directly aware of outer appearances, but rather that we can be aware of things in themselves. For if what appears to us is something independent of our mental acts, then it might be alleged to be something that exists altogether independently of the forms of our intuition. So far from proving that we are aware of phenomenal objects outside us, what the argument in the Fourth Paralogism proves is that we are aware of objects which cannot be objects of possible perceptual experience. This, then, is the indictment. But none of it is true. Take the items seriatim.

Return to steps 4 and 5 of the Fourth Paralogism Argument. Here we are told that what makes external or spatial objects capable of immediate perception is that they share one feature in common: they are one and all transcendentally ideal. This is said, further, to imply the empirical reality of such objects. And so we can supposedly say that we immediately perceive any object which is transcendentally ideal and still say that there is a distinction between our perception of objects in internal and in external sense.

But does transcendental idealism imply what Kant calls empirical realism? A transcendental idealist holds "the doctrine that appearances are to be regarded as being, one and all, representations only, not in themselves, and that time and space are therefore only sensible forms of our intuition, not determinations given as existing by themselves."[17] A transcendental realist holds that space and time are "given in themselves, independently of our sensibility."[18] An empirical realist holds that we are directly aware of objects outside us. "Matter is with him [the empirical realist], therefore, only a species of representations (intuition), which are called external, not as standing in relation to objects *in themselves external*, but because they relate perceptions to the space in which all things are external to one another, while yet space itself is in us."[19] An empirical idealist, on the other hand, regards appearances as "representations produced in us by their objects."[20] And this implies that it is impossible for us "to see how we can come to know the existence of objects otherwise than by inference from the effect to the cause."[21]

Transcendental idealism does imply empirical realism. And it does not *imply* the existence of material objects. If you say that all objects of experience are transcendentally ideal, you are saying that we can directly perceive both material and mental objects in our experience. You cannot be giving a proof that, say, material objects exist *schlechthin*. Kant's proof of the Fourth Paralogism shows that we directly *perceive* material objects. The two conclusions are importantly different. Transcendental idealism proves, on Kant's own showing, that both material and mental objects are just objects of possible experience. This supposedly follows from the claim that space and time are forms of our intuition and not properties of things independently of possible experience and, further, that any appearance must exhibit one or the other of these forms in order to be itself an object of possible experience. This may show that appearances of both mental and material objects are transcendentally ideal. But does it show that there are material objects? Emphatically not. Nor does Kant's argument in the Fourth Paralogism require such a demonstration.

The argument does not show that there are material objects. The demonstration of that proposition by the invocation of transcendental idealism assumes and does not show that there are such objects. It tells us only that objects of outer intuition, like those of inner intuition, are transcendentally ideal and not things in themselves. This tells us something about an essential characteristic of outer intuition. It does not show us that there is anything in the world that has that characteristic.[22]

This establishes not the logical fatality of Kant's argument but only the infelicity of the way in which he states it. The inference from the transcendental ideality of all appearances shows that the objects of inner and outer sense share an epistemically important property: they are both objects of direct awareness. The issue involved in the Fourth Paralogism is whether we can directly perceive objects outside us rather than having to infer their existence from mental deputies which such objects cause to occur in our mental histories. Kant's own words appear to contradict this. Thus A371: "[E]xternal things exist as well as I myself . . . ." But this is dangerously misleading. Compare what he also says at A371: "In order to arrive at the reality of outer objects I have just as little need to resort to inference as I have in regard to the object of my inner sense."[23] There is a clash here, but it is only apparent. Kant needs only to show that we do not require a causal inference from an effect to its probable and congenitally problematic cause in order to refute what he calls problematic idealism. This move shows that our awareness of material objects is no more or less direct than our awareness of our inner states. The two passages, typical of Kant's statement of what he is doing in the Fourth Paralogism argument, do not, then, really clash. The former contains the crucial qualification " . . . exist as well as I myself [Also existieren ebensowohl äussere Dinge, als ich selbst existiere . . .]." We are as directly aware of things outside as we are directly aware of our own mental states. But this assumes that there are material things outside us. Transcendental idealism can assure us that the problematic idealist can undermine our claim that there are such things by an appeal to our alleged inability to be directly aware of them. But this cannot be construed as a proof that there *are* material things outside. Proof of the former, not the latter, is the thrust of Kant's argument at this stage of its development.

The argument in the Fourth Paralogism may escape the charge that Kant illegitimately moves from the possibility of our immediate perception of material objects to the conclusion that there are such objects. But this alone does not assure its success. It can and has been argued that the conclusion of Kant's argument commits him to saying—which sharply conflicts with what he says elsewhere—that we can be perceptually aware of things in themselves.[24]

The objection runs as follows: If we claim that all appearances are transcendentally ideal, what appears to us must be not phenomenal entities in space and time but rather things in themselves. Since space and time are forms of our intuition, the objects of our intuition which appear to us as spatial and temporal cannot be phenomenal objects. Kant's argument allegedly forces us to reduce what we ordinarily call a phenomenal object into something which has either spatial or temporal parameters but which is not itself either spatial or temporal, and this is a certifiable thing in itself.

If you try to escape from this conclusion by saying that phenomenal objects, not things in themselves, appear under our forms of intuition, Kant's argument would seem to be no better off than it was before. Suppose that the forms of intuition we have are imposed on phenomenal objects. This merely reproduces the problem. We began by asking what there is in the world to account for the presence of an object which is spatially and temporally located. We then said that what is there is just the phenomenal or spatial-cum-temporal object. But the very phenomenality of the object engendered the question in the first place. The only way out for Kant would seem to be an illegitimate recognition of things in themselves in order to make his argument in the Fourth Paralogism work. And this will not do.

Indeed not. But the objection shows only that Kant's argument is ambiguous. It does not show that it is irretrievably fallacious. The source of the confusion lies in the interpretation that is to be given to Kant's argument in the Transcendental Aesthetic for the transcendental ideality of our forms of intuition. The arguments which Kant gives us at A33/B49 and A26/B42 are the source of that ambiguity. At A33 we are told that space and time cannot be things in themselves because such a conclusion would force us to say that they are actual without being actual objects. Kant draws the decisive conclusion at A43: Space and time are "conditions which are originally inherent in the subject." This reading of Kant's description of a thing in itself is that it is a kind of object. Call it the Ontological Interpretation.[25]

But there is also what I shall call the Criteriological Interpretation of the relation between things in themselves and phenomenal objects. At A31, Kant says that time is merely "a necessary representation that underlies all intuitions." And at A24 he says the same about space. The shift is crucial. *The Ontological Interpretation requires us to acknowledge the existence of things which are neither spatial nor temporal. The Criteriological Interpretation requires only that we describe a thing in itself as an object the characteristics of which are not available to possible experience.* The latter, unlike the former, does not commit us to saying that such objects are neither spatial nor temporal. The latter interpretation is completely neutral about the ontological issue of whether space and time do in fact exist apart from possible human experience.

The distinction between what I have called the Criteriological Interpretation and the Ontological Interpretation of the relation between phenomenal objects and things in themselves removes what would otherwise be a fatal ambiguity in Kant's attempt to refute Idealism. The argument in the Fourth Paralogism proves, after all, that there are things *extra animam*. It does not, however, prove that they are things which are nonspatial and nontemporal. That argument moves from what we are given in perception to what exists outside the mind. And what exists outside the mind can be a thing in itself on what I have called the Criteriological Interpretation without having to qualify as a candidate for the Ontological Interpretation.

There is, however, yet another problem facing Kant's argument in the Fourth Paralogism. It may be true, as we have seen, that Kant needs only establish the capacity to perceive objects outside us as directly as we can perceive our mental states. It may also be true that Kant's argument against Idealism in the first *Critique* does not assume an illegitimate perceptual awareness of things in themselves. But both parts of Kant's argument rest on the validity of the Kantian proof that our forms of intuition are transcendentally ideal and the further contention that the assumption of their transcendental reality leads to the unwanted conclusion that empirical idealism is true.

You might argue that the idealistic threat arises whether we say that space and time are transcendentally ideal or real. For, so the objection might run, whether spatiality is transcendentally real or ideal, you still have the problem of relating a mental act to what is external to that act. Kant in fact seems to perpetuate the very problem which his argument in the Fourth Paralogism purports to solve, for at A372 we are told that outer appearances are produced in us by things in themselves.[26]

But even though the forms of our intuition are, as Kant argues, transcendentally ideal, the relation between what directly appears to us under those forms and the objects to which it is referred can still be questioned all over again. Even if you say that both external and internal objects of consciousness can qualify as objects of immediate awareness, you can still ask how the objects of which we are immediately aware, though they are one and all transcendentally ideal, relate one to another within the overreaching panoply of transcendental ideality. And this is just the problem which a transcendental doubting Thomas raises.

The objection is instructively wrong. It merely succeeds in underscoring the importance of Kant's theory of the transcendental ideality of our forms of intuition for dialectically defusing step 3 and its attendant lemma in the Refutation of Idealism contained in the Fourth Paralogism. The empirical idealist's pivotal assumption is that every act of perceptual awareness must be an inference from an effect to a cause which can never be the object of direct awareness. And what gets empirical idealism off the ground is what is allegedly the irredeemable dubiety about any inference from an effect to a cause.

Transcendental ideality is supposed to change all of this. Here there is admittedly a gap in Kant's argument. He tells us that the endemic faultiness of inferences from effects to causes can be removed once we come to realize that the forms of both inner and outer sense are mental; hence, the problem about relating something in our mental history to something that is outside that history evaporates.[27] But nothing in this claim as it stands in Kant's text explains just why making things outside us into transcendentally mental items of our world makes the inference from a perceptual effect to a perceptual cause any more or less faulty than the assumption that our forms of intuition are transcendentally real—that, namely, they are characteristics of things independently of possible human experience.

But an argumentational gap is not necessarily an irreparable flaw in an argument. The assumption of the transcendental ideality of our forms of intuition implies that the relation between an act and an object of perception is not exclusively causal. If you say with Kant that all perceptual objects are transcendentally ideal, you are saying that perceptual objects which are spatial are as immediately available as mental objects. External (read "spatial") objects do not initiate a causal chain the effects of which are all that can constitute objects of immediate perceptual awareness. This is not to deny, however, the causal chains are involved in the relation of objects external to us terminating in events of immediate perceptual awareness. The transcendental-ideality clause of the argument in the Fourth Paralogism shows that the causes of what we perceive on any occasion can be as immediately available to us as their effects on our sensory apparatus. And this is what step 3 of the argument, buttressed by its lemma, falsely denies.[28]

Kant's statement of his Refutation of Idealism in the A edition of the first *Critique* yields, then, a sound if anamolous conclusion: *It does not prove the existence of material objects or the existence of objects outside us. But it nonetheless does refute Idealism.* It shows that we can be as directly aware of material objects as we are of mental objects. The argument, as we have seen, does not move from the transcendental ideality of space and time to the conclusion that there are material objects. It goes, rather, from the possibility of our ability to perceive such objects directly to the conclusion that the empirical idealist's claim that all perception must be an inference from an effect that we directly perceive to a cause that we can never directly perceive is false.

Nor does Kant's refutation founder on the objection that we must covertly vouchsafe to ourselves the ability to intuit things in themselves as a necessary condition of the success of that argument. The distinction, which Kant assumes but does not overtly make, between what I have called the Ontological Interpretation and the Criteriological Interpretation of the relation between things in themselves and phenomena shows that the refutation moves only to our ability to intuit phenomenal things. And, finally, we have also seen that the transcendental ideality of our forms of intuition does not reproduce the problem it is intended to solve by forcing the issue raised in step 3 of Kant's argument all over again. It admits a causal model of perception but shows that such an admission does not prevent the cause of any perceptual effect from being directly perceived.

III. *The Argument in the Postulates: B275 and All That*

At B275 Kant claims that the *"mere, but empirically determined, consciousness of my own existence proves the existence of objects in space outside me"* (italics in text). The proof runs as follows:

1. I am conscious of my own existence as empirically determined in time.[29] [Assumption]

2. All determination in time presupposes [*setzt voraus*] something permanent [*etwas Beharrliches*] in time.[30]

3. This permanent cannot be something in me because it is the necessary condition of my ability to determine my existence in time.[31]

4. The existence of things of actual things which I perceive outside me is a necessary condition of my consciousness of my existence in time.

5. Therefore, I must perceive something outside myself in order to be able to determine my existence in time.

6. Therefore, my consciousness of my existence is at the same time an immediate consciousness of other things outside me.[32]

This, then, is the gross anatomy of the argument against Idealism in the Postulates.

This version of Kant's argument differs dramatically in both strategy and content from its predecessor in the A edition of the *Critique*. The important differences are these. First, in A, Kant tried to show that immediate awareness of objects outside us is possible because of the transcendental ideality of space and time. In B, however, nothing in Kant's argument turns on whether our forms of intuition are transcendentally ideal or transcendentally real. We can have the epistemic ability to determine our existence empirically in time whether we are transcendental realists or idealists.

Second, in A the immediacy of our perceptual awareness of things outside us is made to follow from the results of the Transcendental Aesthetic. All of this is changed in the B version. Kant appeals to facts about our ability to ascribe events we experience to our respective mental histories. The crucial inference in A is from transcendental ideality to immediacy. In the B version, however, the crucial inference is from our ability to distinguish between events in our own mental histories to events that occur independently of those histories. Finally, the strategy of the refutation in A is to show that Idealism is false because objects of outer sense are as directly perceivable as those of inner sense. In B, however, Kant seeks to refute Idealism by showing that our awareness of the objects of inner sense is inferred from our direct acquaintance with the objects of outer sense.

The argument in the Postulates comes, then, to this. We begin by assuming that there is some subject—in particular, myself—having a set of representations which are ordered in time. This subject is at least potentially aware of the fact that these representations are his and that he has these representations at different times. These representations are states of the subject's consciousness and cannot, therefore, supply the ground (logically necessary condition) for the fact of the subject's self-awareness. But inner experience cannot be a ground for self-awareness without circularity: Facts of inner experience are what, according to the argument, are to be grounded and hence cannot themselves supply that ground.

Assume that, say, r is a representation logically entailing that r has a possessor. This entails, at most, the existence of a subject, not the existence of a subject that is self-aware. The entailment between "r is a representation" and "r has a possessor" does not, then, further entail that anybody ascribes psychological properties to himself. As an empirically self-conscious subject, I am restricted in my knowledge to my representations and their relations. But these relations cannot enable me to distinguish ascriptions of certain states to myself and ascriptions of states to something else. My ability to make such a distinction requires me to determine a permanent in perception. And this permanent requires spatial as well as temporal relations.

I must, so the argument continues, be potentially aware of the fact that the *r*'s that I ascribe to myself are being ascribed to myself as a permanent. In being aware of this permanent, I am aware of the relations in which any *r*'s do or do not stand. The ability to ascribe *r*'s to my own self and to distinguish them from other *r*'s requires both that I be aware of something as a necessary condition of my being aware of the *r*'s which I ascribe solely to my own mental history. The object of this awareness cannot be just another element in my own mental history. It must be an event in the history of objects that exist independently of me. Thus I must be aware of material substances as a necessary condition of being aware of myself.

But the version of the refutation in the Postulates looks less like a demonstration than a batch of demonstrational promissory notes. It is, in its present condition, vulnerable to some initially plausible and powerful objections. Take them in turn.

A. Consider step 2, which tells us that all determinations in time assume that we are conscious of something permanent in time. Distinguish between what I shall call continuous and momentary items. Something is continuous just in case it is numerically identical through time; momentary, just in case it exists at one and only one point in the time series. The objection runs like this. The Realism-Idealism issue can be raised and settled in a world in which there are only momentary items and even in a world like ours in which there are momentary items called stages of continuants as well as continuants. Kant's argument relies, however, on a successful logical transition from step 1 to step 2, and this involves the recognition of a permanent in time. That recognition implies the existence of the only permanent objects available to us in our experience, namely, material objects.

But the issue here would seem to be quite independent of the distinction between continuants and momentary items in our experience. We can ask about our ability to distinguish between knowing if something belongs exclusively to one's own mental history or exists independently of that history with respect to either momentary items or continuants.

Nor is this all. Not only can we raise the Realism-Idealism issue restricting ourselves solely to a consideration of momentary items; but we *must* also in any case resolve that issue with respect to each momentary epistemic situation as a necessary condition of our ability even to raise the issue for epistemic situations involving continuants. If you begin by asking for the conditions for empirically determining your existence *through* time, you must know how to determine your existence empirically at any given point *in* time. You would otherwise not be able to state the conditions under which you have the ability you are assumed to have in step 1 of the argument. This question arises on each occasion of an awareness of what we are given in inner sense. For even in cases in which what is before us is a continuant, our lack of a God's-eye view of the entire history of that continuant prevents us from having anything more than an acquaintance with a temporal stage of that continuant. And this, too, is a momentary, not a continuous, item.[33]

B. The burden of the argument against Idealism in the Paralogisms is, as we have seen, to establish the inference from one's ability empirically to determine his existence in time to the necessity of there being something independent of him, from this to the existence of something permanent outside him, and finally to the conclusion that the permanent in question is a material thing. Grant for the sake of argument that our awareness of something external to us is a necessary condition of our ability to ascribe events that occur in inner sense to our respective mental histories. But does this *imply* either that what is external to me is a spatial object or that it is a material object? The objector thinks it does not.

The conditions of the argument require only that I be aware of something permanent existing independently of myself. And this does not show whether objects having these characteristics are material. Kant's conditions can be satisfied in a world populated solely by temporal items. The consequence of this possibility for Kant's argument is fatal even in a world like ours that contains both mental and material objects. For it does not show how the objects of inner sense, which are exclusively temporal, require anything more than an awareness of another object like them in order to enable me to determine my existence in time. For permanence involves only the notion of time and pertains only accidentally to spatiality. We can, therefore, provide the ground for ascription of mental states and still consistently deny that there are any material objects.[34]

C. Kant's argument relies heavily on the entailment of our ability to ascribe mental states to ourselves with a parallel ability to ascribe states to objects external to us. We are allegedly being told that our possession of the latter is a necessary condition of our possession of the former. The idealist denies this; therefore, he cannot consistently assume that we can empirically determine our existence in time.[35]

The critic assumes this to be true, but he points out that it feeds on

141

an ambiguity about what it is to have an ability which we could but do not exercise because the relevant actual conditions are not given and having an ability the conditions for the actual exercise of it are given. Kant's argument requires only that we can know what it is like to ascribe states to objects external to us. This does not imply that we ever actually exercise that ability or that we ever need to exercise it. Step 1 of the argument in the Postulates concedes to the idealist that there are actual situations in which we exercise the ability to ascribe states to our own mental histories. We have the ability to ascribe states to things that are not episodes in our own mental histories. But do we ever encounter actual situations in which we are called upon to do this? The idealist denies that we ever find ourselves in such situations. He tolerates only selves and whatever temporally ordered properties they may have. And yet we might still be able in such a world to ascribe characteristics to things that exist outside us without ever actually having to exercise such an ability. This is an egregious modal shift. And it allegedly vitiates Kant's argument.

There is a pattern in these arguments, and it has an ironic twist. We are told that Kant's argument fails because the conditions for the ability each of us has empirically to determine his existence in time can be met by (1) the existence of momentary objects alone, (2) the assumption that there are any objects, material or mental, outside each of us, or (3) the existence of permanent objects which are temporal but not spatial. The pattern is significant. None of these objections shows that Kant has failed to establish the existence of objects external to us. They purport to establish only that Kant's argument fails to show that such objects are material.

All these arguments rest, however, on a false assumption about what Kant must do in order to refute Idealism that is as common as it is false. They all assume that the strategy of the argument moves deductively from a demonstration of the existence of permanent and independent objects to the conclusion that material objects exist outside us. Kant's strategy moves from the independence and permanence of an objective time order to the conclusion that there must be a world of objects having those characteristics in order for me to perceive the succession of my mental states and only then goes on to show that material objects are the only available candidates for such objects. The details of this strategy require exposition.

Begin by distinguishing two senses of "substance." Something counts as a substance$_1$ or continuant just in case it is numerically one through time. There is a sense that notion in which what is to count as a substance is sempiternal (substance$_2$): it has no past nor future. Substances$_1$ endure through time. Substances$_2$ do not endure through time any more than time itself endures through time. For a substance$_2$ is the time order itself. Suppose that the time order itself were a substance$_1$. It would then be part of another time order, and that higher-order time order would then be a part of yet another time order. The generation of time orders would, accordingly, proceed to infinity. The infinite regress, however, would be vicious. The succession of one element upon another in the time order assumes the permanence of the time order itself. There could otherwise be no succession at all. If every time order were placed within another time order, then there would be no ultimate time order in which to measure the change from one such order to another. And this would prevent temporal succession from occurring at all. There must be, therefore, one overarching time order which is independent of whatever temporal suborders there might be. And this time order must be sempiternal.[36]

This conclusion is decisive for the proper interpretation of Kant's argument in the Postulates. Recall step 2, in which Kant claims that the very notion of a determination in time assumes something permanent. But let us suppose, as Kant's idealist does, that all succession in time is subjective. The idealist allows me only an acquaintance with the sequence of my representations in my mental history and nothing more. But he also allows that when I perceive the succession of r's in inner sense, I know that one of them *succeeds* the other. But if there are as many time orders as there are subjects which have inner sense, even so much as an awareness of a mere succession of r's in my inner sense would be impossible. There must be, therefore, something external to me if I am to witness what the idealist vouchsafes me in step 1 of the argument. And this must be a substance$_2$ which is permanent in the relevant sense and which, further, is independent of the succession of the states constituting my mental history.

It is no answer to this conclusion to argue either that it might be possible for each of us to identify his time order with what is supposed to be the single time order or to claim that, for all Kant's argument shows, the putatively objective time order is merely imaginary and not real. The former breaks down on the stubborn fact that the mental histories of all of us are anchored in the objective time order just because the subjects themselves are members of a larger time order, even though the sequence in which they perceive their respective mental states differs from subject to subject. And the latter collapses in the same fact. Even imaginary objects have a place in the objective time order because they have a place in the temporal order to which all the subjects belong, no matter what they imagine.[37] There can be as many time orders as there are subjects, but none of them can contain the basis of a perception of succession without being placed within one permanent time order independent of all the others. And we conjure up the representation of a time sequence in our imagination. But the conjuring is still done within the objective time order.[38]

When we perceive our own mental states, then, we are aware that they are determined in a time which is external to them, where by "external" is meant that time exists before a mental state begins and after it has ceased. But time itself cannot be perceived.[39] Assume the contrary and you will have succeeded only in launching yourself on another vicious infinite regress. Suppose that time itself were, *per impossible*, to be an object of perceptual awareness. Both time itself and the act by which I am supposedly aware of it would be in time: time itself would be grasped by a cognitive act which precedes other such acts and is succeeded by still others. But then there would be a time before which time itself became an object of awareness and another time at which it would have ceased to be such an object. The absurdity is patent and blatant: the situation I have just described requires that time itself be a part of the series constituting the objective time series. Time would then be a part of itself. This is internally contradictory; hence, time itself cannot be perceived.

But if the independent and objective time series is perceptually unavailable to us, then how can Kant argue without futility that we must be perceptually aware of something external to ourselves if we are to be aware of the sequence of *r*'s in inner sense? Kant's argument requires not merely the existence but also the perceptual availability of permanent substances existing independently of my mental history. Here the argument in the Postulates is exasperatingly skeletal. It nevertheless admits of this supplementation. Kant must find something which is permanent and which is also perceptually available to us if his argument against Idealism is to go through. He has four candidates for a permanent which we can perceive. Let me begin by eliminating the first three.

Suppose that the permanent in time which we must perceive in order to ground our awareness of a succession of *r*'s in our mental histories is a permanent self. This can be rejected immediately

144

because no permanent self is given to us in intuition.[40] What I perceive when I look inward is, *pace* step 1 of Kant's own argument, only a succession of momentary items, none of which gives any indication that I am being presented with anything that is numerically identical through time. An appeal to states of consciousness is no more helpful. No state of consciousness is continuous in the required sense, for none is temporally continuous, and it is precisely this lack of continuity in the succession of our states of consciousness that requires us to seek a ground for our ability to perceive a succession of such states in a source external to our mental mentories. And Kant's argument is no better off than it was before if we transform a series of conscious states into a series of selves each of which is permanent for a short duration. This alternative merely duplicates the problems which plague its predecessors. The duration, however short, in which any self which is a member of the bundles of selves constituting experience in inner sense must still be grounded. Even the self of short duration has the same problem of perceptual availability as its cousin self of greater longevity. And even this short-termed self breaks up into a sequence of individual acts of consciousness —which raises the problem facing Kant's argument all over again at another level.

Kant's argument takes a sensitive turn. Continuous selves, momentary states of consciousness, and even bundles of selves cannot supply Kant with the permanence the awareness of which is a necessary condition of our ability to perceive the succession of our mental states. The objective time order can do this. But, as we have seen, that order cannot itself be an object of perceptual awareness without generating a contradiction. What remains to Kant is the community of substances$_2$ in the objective time order. This appears at first blush to be questionable, but it is not. Kant's argument requires that there be a permanent in time in order to ground the truth of step 1 in his argument. He needs the existence of a sempiternal permanent in order to move from our perception of a succession of states in our mental histories to something which exists both permanently and independently outside us. This conclusion must be derived solely from what is asserted in step 1. He could not reach such a conclusion by moving from that step alone directly to the further conclusion that there are substances$_2$, for material substances are subject to the same epistemic restrictions as mental substances, and both are substances$_2$. Thus the need for the bridge which only substance$_1$ can provide.

But Kant does not move directly from the existence of substances$_2$ in time to the conclusion that they are spatial.[41] There is an intermediate premise which does not emerge clearly in the argument of the Postulates but which presides over the entire argument. Time, Kant constantly tells us, is the form of inner sense; space, the form of outer sense.[42] It may be true to say that every act of awareness of objects in inner sense is temporal, but it is not the case that every temporal object in our experience is an awareness of one of our own mental states. Objects of outer sense are temporal as well as spatial. The distinction is obviously important. It shows that we cannot *define* awareness of objects given in inner sense by saying that they are merely temporal and not spatial, even though it may be true that all objects of inner sense have temporal and even exclusively temporal parameters. Objects of outer sense are also temporal, but since this is so, then the proof that our awareness of our mental states, combined with the proof that the only externally permanent objects of which we can be directly aware are substances$_2$, does refute Idealism. All Kant needs to show is that there is an independent and permanent time order if he is to refute Idealism. The independence and objectivity of the time order transfer to objects of outer sense. Time, though *the* form of inner sense, is also *a* form of outer sense. This guarantees the possibility of our direct awareness of material objects.

This reconstruction of Kant's argument in the Paralogisms enables us to defuse the three arguments which threaten Kant's own demonstration. Return to argument *A*, according to which Kant's refutation fails because an idealist can state his position without having to recognize the existence of substances$_2$. He can retreat to the claim that there are only momentary entities in the world, concede that we are never aware of a transition in our awareness from the perception of one momentary item to that of another, and then raise the whole issue of the existence of an external world all over again with respect to every momentary entity of which we are aware in inner sense.

The three objections initially threatening Kant's argument in the Postulates can now be answered. We were told in argument *A* that Kant's refutation of Idealism collapses because the issue about the possibility of our awareness of a succession of one of our mental states can be raised with respect to our apprehension of each of the momentary states which are members of that succession and, further, that any solution of the problem concerning the former assumes a solution of the problem with respect to the latter. Right, but for the wrong reasons. My awareness of a state of affairs belonging to my mental history at any given time assumes my awareness of that state as occurring at a certain time. And this, in turn, assumes my awareness of the fact that what I now perceive has followed upon something else prior to it and precedes something that may follow upon it. The solution of the Realism-Idealism issue does, then, assume our ability to resolve that problem with respect to momentary items in our mental histories as a necessary condition of resolving that problem with respect to our perception of a succession of such items. But the resolution of one is the resolution of the other just because my awareness of any one of my mental states at a given time contains within it an awareness of the fact that the state in question follows upon something else and will be succeeded by something else. Our awareness of succession is built into the very notion of our awareness of a momentary mental state as such.

Argument B goes the way of its predecessor. The argument is that Kant bases his refutation of Idealism on an illicit logical move. He may, we are told, be able to show that what is required by step 1 in his refutation is an awareness of the something that is both permanent and external to my mental states as a necessary condition of my ability to be aware of the fact that they are my mental states. But there is no foundation in this for the further conclusion that these objects are either spatial or temporal. This alleged flaw in Kant's refutation of Idealism is fatal. The absence of any logical connection between my awareness of something external to my mental history and something that is either spatial or material would vitiate any attempt to move from step 1 to the conclusion of that argument.

But the initial plausibility of such an allegation is ultimately illusory. Kant moves, as we have seen, from our awareness of the succession of our mental states in time to an objective time order. He then moves from the necessity of recognizing the existence of such a time order to the conclusion that there must be an immediate awareness of permanent things outside us because time itself, however objective it may be, cannot itself be an object of perceptual awareness. But since time is not only the form of inner sense but also one of the forms of outer sense, he is entitled to conclude that whatever is given to us in outer sense is objective and material. This conclusion assumes that whatever can be given to us in outer sense is material. But the assumption is not, as the proponent of argument B contends, an illicit inference from externality as such to spatiality or materiality. The operative inference here is, rather, from the fact that temporality is also an essential part of what it is for anything to be material to the conclusion that the objectivity of the time order guarantees our ability to be directly aware of material objects external to us. This is not a move from externality to materiality. It is the logically defensible transition from the fact that we can be directly aware of an objective time order to the conclusion that material objects must be in that order because part of what it is to be a material object is to be a part of that order.

Argument C remains. We can have an ability to ascribe characteristics to things in an objective time order. But here our critic claims that we can have abilities that we never have occasion to use, and he exploits a concession which Kant makes to the idealist at the very outset of his refutation of Idealism in the Postulates. Step 1 of that argument allows us only an acquaintance with our respective mental states and their succession one upon the other—and nothing else. This step allows us an awareness of a *representation* of material things outside ourselves, but it does not grant us a direct awareness of the *object* of that representation.

The argument founders on the subtle but brutal fact that even the act of awareness of a representation of a material object outside ourselves rather than of the object itself is caught up in the objective time series, the representation of which, I am aware, may admittedly belong only to my mental history with no connection to anything external to that history. But the *act* of awareness belongs to the objective time order. And this is enough to establish what Kant's refutation purports to do, namely, to show that there is an objective time order and that the existence of such an order makes it possible for us to perceive material objects directly. Not only do we have the ability to perceive material objects directly, but we must perceive them even though we can conjure up imaginary material objects in our dreams and imagination.

IV. *Dubia*

We have been able to distinguish three stages in the development of Kant's refutation of Idealism. The first stage of the argument relies on the fact that the transition from one state to another cannot be accounted for deductively and must, accordingly, assume the existence of antecedent states which are causally responsible for the change in any substance from one state to another. This proves, as we have seen, only that changes of this kind require the existence of causal agents external to the bodies which undergo the change. But, as we have also seen, Kant's argument applies equally to material and to mental substances. It is incomplete, but it is not invalid.

The second stage fills the lacuna in the structure of Kant's initial attempt to do away with Idealism. Here the move is from the transcendental ideality of all appearances to the conclusion that objects of both inner and outer sense are epistemically equal. The idealist grants that we are directly aware of our own mental states in time but argues that we cannot transfer this capacity to our awareness of spatial objects. But if space is as transcendentally ideal as time, then the epistemic discrimination between the kinds of awareness we have of the two kinds of object ceases. Material objects are as directly available to us as our mental states.

Kant's final solution of the problem proves that we are directly aware of objects external to our inner sense as a condition of our being able to have direct awareness of the succession of our mental states in inner sense. The critical turn here is the move from our awareness of a succession of our mental states to the existence of an objective time order and only then to the final conclusion that our awareness of objects of outer sense is a necessary condition of our awareness of objects of inner sense. We saw that, for the first time in the development of Kant's argument, his attack on Idealism did not stop short of completeness, as it had in the first stage of that development, and that the argument of the third stage undertook to prove, not just the possibility, but the actuality of our direct awareness of material objects outside us.

This account of Kant's development has, however, been sharply disputed. Some have argued that the conclusion of the argument in the Paralogisms is logically incompatible with the conclusion of the argument in the Postulates.[43] Others have claimed that both arguments assume, illegitimately, that there are things in themselves.[44] Still others have claimed that the fate of both of these arguments depends upon the existence of an argument structure called distinctively transcendental.[45] These claims are one and all false. Let me eliminate them one by one.

First, the claim that the arguments in the Paralogisms and the Postulates are mutually contradictory. The former rests on the assumption, we are told, that the external world does not exist but is completely specified by the sequence of our representations. The latter works to the conclusion that there is an external world and that we are directly aware of these objects. Kant speaks with a forked tongue, for he supposedly uses the notion of an external world in two mutually incompatible ways. He tells us in the

Paralogisms that the external world is nothing but our representations, but he says in the Postulates that the external world consists of things that are independent of our representation. And this is an ambiguity that is only a verbal fig leaf for a contradiction.

Ambiguity, yes. Contradiction, no. The proof in the Paralogisms shows that the objects of outer sense are like the objects in inner sense because both are transcendentally ideal. The external world in this sense is a collection of transcendentally ideal representations, but this does not imply our inability to distinguish within the class of transcendentally ideal representations one subclass from another, and so, when the Kant of the Postulates says that he is proving the existence of an external world independent of our representations, he is only claiming that external objects, though they exist independently of the states of our inner sense, still exist independently of those states. And this is compatible with the fact that the objects of both senses are representations.

Does Kant illicitly assume in the arguments of both editions of the *Critique* that there are things in themselves and smuggle that assumption into the proof for the existence of things outside us in order to achieve by surreptitious postulation what he can only rightfully attain by argumentation? If any of the premises assumes the existence of things in themselves, Kant could conclude immediately that there are permanent things which exist independently of our mental states. But that would assume an independent demonstration of the existence of things in themselves. This would give us the refutation of Idealism Kant propounds without having to invoke either of the arguments he gives us in the first *Critique*. But if Kant does invoke either of those arguments, his argument succeeds only in moving in a circle.

The truth is that neither version of Kant's argument assumes or proves the existence of things in themselves. His argument in the Paralogisms does, to be sure, assume the results of the Transcendental Aesthetic, according to which time and space are transcendentally ideal. But this has already been established in the Transcendental Aesthetic. It has as a consequence that things in themselves are distinct from appearances. But the argument in the Paralogisms can be formulated all over again for the relation between things outside in space and things in inner sense without assuming that there are things in themselves. And the same applies to the argument in the Postulates. There the purpose of the argument is to show that we must be aware of an objective time order if we are to be aware of a succession of our mental states. That time order may involve the existence of things in themselves because it is transcendentally ideal, but this is not an assumption of the argument, for it is stated totally within the context of elements in our experience both of which are transcendentally ideal. The issue here is, therefore, raised and settled totally within the context of empirically real entities without any reference to the distinction between things and themselves and appearances.

There is, finally, the claim that the attempts of Kant in his Critical Period to refute Idealism stand or fall with the viability of a distinctively transcendental mode of argumentation and that this kind of argument must be strictly separated from what we usually understand by deductive reasoning. There may be genuine cases of transcendental arguments, and they may be distinguishable from cases of deductive reasoning. It may also be the case that Kant's arguments can be cast in a transcendental mould. But those arguments can also be stated in a straightforwardly deductive way. The cogency of the arguments does not, therefore, depend upon the existence of a distinctively transcendental mode of reasoning.

NOTES

1. Norman Kemp Smith, *A Commentary to Kant's* Critique of Pure Reason (New York: Humanities Press, 1962), pp. 314ff., reviews most of the relevant older literature. There are, however, significant omissions. Cf. Henry Sidgwick, "The So-Called Idealism of Kant," *Mind* 4 (1879): 408ff., where he argues—wrongly, as we will see—that Kant confuses material objects in space with things in themselves. Cf. also Henry Sidgwick, "Kant's Refutation of Idealism," *Mind* 5 (1880): 111ff.; and Arthur Balfour, M.P., "Transcendentalism," *Mind* 3 (1878): 480ff., for a similar view. See also Emil Arnoldt, *Kant nach Kuno Fischer's neuer Darstellung* (Königsberg: Ferd. Beyer's Buchhandlgung, 1882), pp. 40, that Kant argues for the external of material objects in both the A and B editions of the *Critique*. Cf. also C. D. Broad, *Kant* (Cambridge: Cambridge University Press, 1978), pp. 190; Henry Allison, "Kant's Critique of Berkeley," *Journal of the History of Philosophy* 11 (1973): 43ff.; and Friedrich Kaulbach, "Kants Beweis des "Daseins der Gegenstände im Raum ausser Mir," *Kant-Studien* 50 (1958–59): 323. H. A. Prichard, *Kant's Theory of Knowledge* (Oxford: Clarendon Press, 1909), pp. 322ff., also claims that Kant trades on an ambiguity inherent in "things external to me" in the attempts to refute Idealism, not clearly telling us whether he is attempting to prove the existence of things in themselves or merely material things outside us.

2. Hans Vaihinger, "Zu Kants Widerlegung des Idealismus," *Strassburger Abhandlungen zur Philosophie* (Tübingen: J. C. B. Mohr, 1884), pp. 87ff.; H. W. B. Joseph, "A Comparison of Kant's Idealism with that of Berkeley" *Proceedings of the British Academy* 15 (1929): 213ff.; and G. E. Moore, "Proof of an External World," *Proceedings of the British Academy* 25 (1939), reprinted in *Philosophical Studies* (London: George Allen & Unwin, 1959), chap. 7, passim, for a defense of this claim.

3. Cf. Benno Erdmann, ed., *Immanuel Kant's Prolegomena* (Leipzig: Leopold Voss, 1878), pp. lxxiff.; Benno Erdmann, *Kant's Kriticismus* (Leipzig: Leopold Voss, 1878), pp. 199ff.; and, finally, Henry Sidgwick, *Mind* 5 (1880): 111ff., who argue for this interpretation.

4. Cf. T. E. Wilkerson, "Transcendental Arguments," *Philosophical Quarterly* 20 (1970): 200ff., T. E. Wilkerson, *Kant's* Critique of Pure Reason (Oxford: Clarendon Press, 1976), chap. 10, passim; and my "Transcendental Arguments," *Nous* 5 (1971): 15ff., for an argument that Kant's refutation in the Postulates is a paradigm of a transcendental argument. Cf. Jaakko Hintikka, "Transcendental Arguments: Genuine and Spurious," *Nous* 6 (1972): 274, for the other side of the story.

5. See Norman Kemp Smith, *A Commentary*, pp. 308ff.; Vaihinger, "Zu Kants Widerlegung des Idealismus," pp. 133ff.; and A. C. Ewing, *A Short Commentary on Kant's* Critique of Pure Reason (London: Methuen & Co., 1938), pp. 178ff., for representative views of the character of the alleged contradiction between the argument in the Postulates and the argument in the Paralogisms. See Wolfgang Müller-Lauter, "Kants Widerlegung des materialien Idealismus," *Archiv für Geschichte der Philosophie* 46 (1964): 60ff.; Douglas Langston, "The Supposed Incompatibility Between Kant's Two Refutations of Idealism," *Southern Journal of Philosophy* 17 (1979): 359ff.; and James D. Stuart, "Kant's Two Refutations of Idealism," *Southwestern Journal of Philosophy* 6 (1975): 29ff., for equally representative specimens of the argument for the compatibility of the two refutations. See Alfons Kalter, *Kants vierter Paralogismus* (Meisenheim am Glan: Anton Hain, 1975), passim, who presents the unitarian interpretation of the problem. We are repeatedly told that there is no problem because where a contradiction seems to exist in Kant's views we have only to infer that he wrote them at different times. The disadvantage of the hermeneutical principle guiding Kalter is that Kant cannot contradict himself as long as we assign different dates to what he said.

6. This is the full title: *Principiorum primorum cognitionis metaphysicae nova dilucidatio*. I cite the Academy Edition, 1:385ff. The only English translation known to me is in F. E. England, *Kant's Conception of God* (New York: Humanities Press, 1968), appendix.

7. *Nova dilucidatio*, Academy Edition, 1:391 (sec. 2, prop. 4); England, *Kant's Conception of God*, p. 220. I consciously exclude consideration here of Kant's attempts to refute Idealism in the form in which he represents it in the *Inaugural Dissertation* and the *Metaphysik Herder*. In the former he infers from the fact that something appears to us to the conclusion that there must be something that appears. And this is an object which exists outside of us. True, but tautalogous. To say that there are things that appear when we are appeared to leaves it a completely open question whether what appears to us is physical rather than mental. The Kant of the *Inaugural Dissertation* shores up his argument by drawing the further conclusion that what appears to us must exist independently of our mental acts. But this is still not enough to undo Idealism. We can all agree that what appears to us exists independently of its appearing, but we can nonetheless be divided about what does appear to us is mental or material. The argument in the *Metaphysik Herder* (Academy Edition, 28:42ff. [cap. 2 sec. 1]) merely states the argument for Idealism. There is no attempt to refute it. The exposition of the argument runs like this. All sensations (*Empfindungen*) of bodies outside us are merely appearances in our soul. The reasons: (1) secondary qualities are definable in terms of primary qualities (e.g., colors are definable in terms of the behavior of light waves emitted from a light source), and (2) dreams are at times livelier than veridical perception. Maybe so, but this merely gives two highly

questionable prima facie grounds for accepting Idealism. The grounds themselves are as *sub judice* in this dispute as the conclusion they are supposed to support.

8. Ibid.

9. Ibid.

10. Ibid.

11. *Nova dilucidatio*, Academy Edition, 1:410 (sec. 3, prop. 12); England, *Kant's Conception of God*, p. 244.

12. *Nova dilucidatio*, Academy Edition, 1:411 (sec. 3, usus); England, *Kant's Conception of God*, p. 247.

13. Ibid.

14. *Kritik der reinen Vernunft*, Academy Edition, 5:A367ff. The translations of the first *Critique*, unless otherwise indicated, are to the Norman Kemp Smith translation of that work. References to the work are given hereinafter by citation only of the A and B editions. CF. A42/B59 for the claim that both inner and outer appearances are transcendentally ideal but empirically real. See also my "Kant's First Antinomy," in Lewis White Beck, ed., *Kant Studies Today*, (La Salle, Ill.: Open Court, 1969), pp. 210ff., for a discussion of this problem in another but related context in the *Critique*. I bypass the argument against Idealism which Kant presents in the *Prolegomena*, par. 13, notes 2 and 3 (Academy Edition, 4:287ff.). This does, however, warrant an explanation. Kant tells us there that an idealist is anyone who maintains that there is nothing more in the world than thinking beings. But everything given to us as a perceptual object must be given in intuition. We can really know only appearances. But every appearance is the result (*Wirkung*) of the affecting of our sensory apparatus by a thing in itself. The Kant of 1783, therefore, finds Idealism false just because the relation of affection assumes the distinction between things in themselves and appearance. Despite the temporal difference, Kant's argument in the *Prolegomena* (1783) does not differ at all from his argument in the *Inaugural Dissertation* (1770). Cf. note 7 above.

15. Cf. H. A. Prichard, *Kant's Theory of Knowledge*, p. 322.

16. Cf. Hans Vaihinger, "Zu Kants Widerlegung des Idealismus," pp. 140ff., and my "The Myth of Double Affection," in W. H. Werkmeister, ed., *Reflections on Kant's Philosophy* (Gainesville, Fla: University Presses of Florida, 1975), pp. 29ff., for an exposition and a refutation, respectively, of this view.

17. A369.

18. A369.

19. A370.

20. A372.

21. A372. I pass over the issue about the relation between the relation of transcendental reality and transcendental ideality in Kant's argument at A371. There Kant says that transcendental reality "gives way [*sieht sich genötigt*] to empirical idealism. The allusion, obscure as it is, does not require exegetical attention for my purpose. For the relationship between transcendental ideality and empirical idealism is irrelevant to the cogency of the Fourth Paralogism. Suppose that space and time are, after all, properties of things existing independently of our experience. This does not entail either the truth or the falsehood of the claim that all objects of direct perceptual awareness are mental. Nor does it entail that the relation between material objects and our awareness of them must be reduced to the relation between a cause and the effect it has on our sensory receptors. Kant says that, if you hold the transcendental reality of space and time, you must then hold that what we immediately perceive is the last link in a chain beginning with the object which we

take ourselves to perceive but which we cannot directly perceive. The relation between transcendental idealism and empirical idealism is, however, totally independent of the issue concerning the causal relation of an object which exists in itself to the object of our immediate perceptual awareness. You can hold that, in order to perceive anything, there must be a causal chain of events beginning with the object and ending with its last link somewhere in the cerebral cortex. But this is totally neutral with respect to whether or not what we perceive is an idea or the object which initiated the causal chain resulting in our perception of the idea. And, no matter what the outcome of either of these considerations may be, the success of the argument in the Fourth Paralogism turns on whether the assumption of transcendental ideality implies empirical realism. This makes the problems surrounding the relation between transcendental reality and empirical idealism inconsequential for Kant's argument.

22. What I say here echoes the ill-fated Garve-Feder review of the 1781 edition of the first *Critique*. Cf. Immanuel Kant, *Prolegomena zu einer jeden künftigen Metaphysik*, ed. Karl Vorländer (Hamburg: Felix Meiner, 1957), app. 2, passim. The authors of that review held that we cannot distinguish real from imaginary elements in our experience without finding a mark in sensation itself. And they advise us to pick out the most enduring sensation and take it to be the apodictic evidence for what is externally real. Kant allegedly fails here because he conflates inner and outer sense by claiming that endurance through time can belong only to outer sense. The review deserves its fate. Kant does not claim that permanence belongs only to objects of outer sense and then turn around and assimilate those objects to inner sense, which for him does not enjoy an epistemic permanence. He says only that both appearances of inner and outer sense have the same epistemic status.

23. Cf. A375 and B291.

24. Cf. S. F. Barker, "Appearing and Appearances in Kant," in Beck, ed., *Kant Studies Today*, pp. 274ff. See also my "How to Dispense with Things in Themselves," *Ratio* 18 (1976): 1ff., for an attempt to remove this difficulty from Kant's theory.

25. This is given more detailed attention in my "Kant's First Antinomy," pp. 210ff.

26. Cf. Ewing, *A Short Commentary on Kant's* Critique of Pure Reason, pp. 178ff., for an exposition of this view.

27. Cf. A378ff.

28. Cf. my "The Myth of Double Affection," pp. 33ff.

29. B275. Cf. Luise Cramer, *Kants rationale Psychologie und ihre Vorgänger* (O. R. Reisland, 1914), for the historical roots of this problem.

30. Ibid.

31. Ibid. Kant alters the formulation of this step in the preface to the second edition of the first *Critique* (Bxln.). In a sense, but not as such.

32. Cf. an earlier attempt of mine to state this argument in my "Transcendental Arguments," *Nous* 5 (1971): 20–21. Cf. also Hintikka's summary dismissal of the refutation of Idealism in the Postulates in his "Transcendental Arguments: Genuine and Spurious," *Nous* 6 (1972). He writes (p. 276) that the refutation of Idealism is "not very illuminating of the nature of his [Kant's] main arguments" and then goes on to say that "[t]he charitable way of looking upon this particular piece of Kantian argumentation is perhaps to think of it as an *ad hominem* argument against an idealist which[sic!] in the very process of formulating his doctrine is using concepts which according to Kant presuppose the contrary." Wrong on both counts. So far from failing to illuminate the nature of Kant's main arguments, the argument in the Postulates *is* one of those arguments. The historical evidence for this is unmistakable,

154

for the Grave-Feder review of the first edition of the *Critique* not only irritated Kant but moved him to alter entire sections of the *Critique*. The substitution of the argument in the Postulates for the argument in the Paralogisms attests to Kant's opinion of the importance of that argument.

It is, furthermore, hardly a piece of charity to Kant or to his argument to say, as Hintikka does, that the argument is *ad hominem*. The argument is not that some concepts assume other concepts but rather that the idealist's application of those concepts assumes the truth of propositions, the truth of which he denies.

33. Cf. A. E. Balfour, M.P., "Transcendentalism," *Mind* 3 (1878): 480ff.; Patricia Crawford, "Kant and the Refutation of Scepticism," in Pierre La Berge, ed., *Collection Philosophica* (Ottowa: University of Ottowa Press, 1976), pp. 344ff.; and H. A. Prichard, *Kant's Theory of Knowledge*, p. 323, for the view that Kant's argument in the Postulates can be settled without assuming the distinction which Kant makes in the First Analogy between change (*Veränderung*) and succession (*Wechsel*). This is both true and irrelevant. Kant's step 1 in his argument in the Postulates does not depend upon his ability to distinguish between change and succession. That step requires only that we be able to know that one mental event follows another in our own mental history. And this is compatible with there being no permanent element in what we perceive in that history at all.

34. Cf. my "Categories and Transcendental Arguments," *Man and World* 6 (1973): 268ff., for what I now believe to be a simplistic statement of the issue.

35. Cf. Jonathan Bennett, *Kant's Analytic* (Cambridge: Cambridge University Press, 1966), pp. 204ff., and Broad, *Kant*, pp. 191ff., both of whom claim that Kant's argument succeeds on the assumption that you guarantee someone's ability to ascribe properties to public objects as a necessary condition for that person to be able to ascribe a mental property to himself. The solution they give us is unexceptionable as far as it goes, but it does not go far enough. We may be able to ascribe properties to things outside ourselves in order to know on any occasion when we correctly ascribe properties to our own mental histories. This does not exclude the possibility that the external objects to which we ascribe properties that we refuse to ascribe to our own mental histories may themselves be mental and not material. The issue of the dependence of private ascription of properties on our ability to ascribe those same properties to objects which exist independently of us can be raised without any reference to the distinction between how we know what belongs to our mental histories and what belongs to the histories whatever exists independently of us.

36. Cf. Jonathan Bennett, *Kant's Analytic* (Cambridge: Cambridge University Press, 1966), chap. 13, passim, for the elaboration of this distinction. Cf. also Peter Strawson, *The Bounds of Sense* (London: Methuen & Co., 1966), pp. 129ff., for a similar argument.

37. Cf. B275 and the extraordinary footnote at xl.

38. Arthur O. Lovejoy is a good example of this kind of criticism. See his "On Kant's Reply to Hume," in Moltke S. Gram, ed., *Kant: Disputed Questions* (Chicago: Quandrangle Press, 1967), pp. 296ff., where he argues that the distinction between perceptual permanence and our perception of change can occur in illusory as well as veridical perception. True, but irrelevant. We can, indeed, distinguish between succession and change in our dreams. But step 1 of Kant's argument in the Postulates does not assume this distinction. It assumes only that we are able to ascribe successive mental states to ourselves, and this has nothing to do with whether we are in a dream or waking state.

39. The argument is to be found in the Transcendental Aesthetic, A183–B226. It is repeated in B225, where Kant argues that time in itself cannot be perceived.

40. Cf. A349.

41. See A. H. Smith, *Kantian Studies* (Oxford: Clarendon Press, 1947), chap. 2 passim, for the opposing view.

42. Cf. A33/B49ff.

43. Cf. note 1 above.

44. Cf. note 2 above.

45. Cf. my "Do Transcendental Arguments Have a Future?" *Neue Hefte fur Philosophie* 14 (1979): 23ff., for a review of this issue.

Kant's Tactics in the Transcendental Deduction

PAUL GUYER
University of Illinois at Chicago Circle

We all know Kant's strategy for the transcendental deduction of the categories, or the proof of their *a priori* yet objective validity: "The transcendental deduction of all *a priori* concepts has . . . a principle according to which the whole enquiry must be directed, namely, that they must be recognized as *a priori* conditions of the possibility of experience" (A94/B126),[1] precisely because "the *a priori* conditions of a possible experience in general are at the same time conditions of the possibility of objects of experience" (A111).[2] But what are Kant's tactics for executing this strategy, the particular maneuvers which will prove that certain concepts really are *a priori* conditions of the possibility of experience itself? On this point there has never been much agreement, nor will I attempt to remedy this situation by advocating some single argument as *the* argument of the deduction. On the contrary, I will argue that the two main ideas of Kant's strategy, the idea of experience and the idea of constructing a transcendental deduction by discovering the *a priori* conditions of its possibility, are ambiguous and that the unresolved existence of this dual ambiguity allowed—or condemned—Kant to attempt four different types of argument in behalf of his strategic goal.[3] I will not deny, of course, that Kant revealed some preference among these four tactics by giving special prominence to one or another on various occasions, but I will argue that, though the tactic which Kant made most prominent in the *Prolegomena to Any Future Metaphysics* is rather obviously flawed, there are also less obvious but equally fatal flaws in the two tactics on which Kant based much of his argumentation in the 1781 (A) and 1787 (B) editions of the Transcendental Deduction in the *Critique of Pure Reason* itself, and that the only tactic which can actually execute the strategy of the deduction is one which Kant indeed suggested in the Transcendental Deduction but to which he devoted very little of his direct effort there.

To classify the four varieties of argument I want to discuss, I must explain the two ambiguities which generate these four possibilities.

First, Kant is actually unclear about the exact nature of a transcendental "proof" (cf. A782–83/B810–11) as one which discovers the *a priori* conditions of the possibility of experience, and this unclarity suggests two different conceptions of the premises which must be assumed by a transcendental deduction. On the one hand, in explaining the distinction between a "metaphysical exposition" and a "transcendental exposition" which he introduced into the Transcendental Aesthetic in 1787, Kant says, "I understand by a transcendental exposition the explanation of a concept, as a principle from which the possibility of other *a priori* synthetic knowledge can be understood" (B40), and this explicit reference to *other* synthetic *a priori* knowledge suggests (*A*) not merely that a transcendental deduction *produces* some synthetic *a priori* knowledge but also that it *presupposes* some—that the condition of the possibility of which the transcendental deduction discovers is itself some claim to synthetic *a priori* knowledge (thus the existence of an *a priori* intuition of space is the condition of the possibility of the already established fact that geometry is "a body of *a priori* synthetic knowledge" [B41]). On the other hand, Kant's statement in "The Principles of Any Transcendental Deduction" (Section 13) that such a deduction is "the explanation of the manner in which concepts can . . . relate *a priori* to their objects" (A85/B117), though it distinguishes such an argument from a merely empirical deduction by the fact that it *produces* synthetic *a priori* knowledge, does not in fact imply that such a proof *presupposes* any knowledge which is itself synthetic *a priori*. Similarly, Kant's statement in the Doctrine of Method that the "proofs of transcendental synthetic propositions" proceed "by showing that experience itself, and therefore the object of experience, would be impossible" without "the possibility of arriving synthetically and *a priori* at some knowledge of things which was not contained in the concepts of them" (A782–83/B810–11) does not imply that such a proof *begins* by assuming some premise which is itself a claim to synthetic *a priori* knowledge. Thus these definitions leave open the possibility (*B*) that a transcendental deduction is an argument which shows that *a priori* knowledge of the validity of certain categories is a condition of the possibility of some other knowledge which is itself thoroughly empirical.

That Kant's different definitions of transcendental exposition, deduction, or proof allow this pair of alternatives seems obvious, but I think this fact has not always been recognized, nor have the problems it may occasion been adequately understood. Thus, such writers as Bird and Strawson[4] see the deduction as concerning the conditions for the self-ascription of experiences but do not consider that it may depend upon some claim about such self-ascription which is itself *a priori*, while others, such as Kemp-Smith and Henrich,[5] clearly recognize that (at least one key version of) the deduction turns on a claim about the identity of the self which is assumed to be known *a priori* and with "Cartesian certainty" but do not realize what difficulties there are in supposing that this claim is indeed genuinely synthetic and yet known *a priori*.

Before we can consider such problems, however, we must also consider the ambiguity of Kant's key concept of "experience" itself. For not only is it unclear whether Kant intends the very concept of experience itself to (A) already imply some *a priori* premise or (B) not imply such a premise, but it is also unclear just what this concept is. This unclarity is far more often acknowledged than is the one just mentioned but is less quickly documented. Basically, however, the question is whether the concept of experience (I) already includes a reference to *objects* as in some sense distinct from subjective representations or (II) does not—whether, we might say, Kant's claim that "all experience does indeed contain, in addition to the intuition of the senses through which something is given, a *concept* of an object as being thereby given" (A93/B126) is meant as (I) a *definition* or a *premise*, evident from the very concept of experience itself, from which the deduction can begin or as (II) a synthetic claim representing only some part of the *conclusion* of an argument beginning with some weaker, subjective conception of experience. Thus it is also unclear whether Kant intends his transcendental deduction (I) to answer an empiricist who concedes the possibility of valid judgments about objects distinct from himself and questions only whether any *a priori* knowledge of such objects is required by those judgments or (II) to answer a skeptic who concedes only the possibility of judgments about his own states but does not recognize that knowledge of objects, let alone *a priori* knowledge of objects, is a condition of the possibility of experience in this weaker sense.

It seems that Kant actually defines the concept of experience to include a reference to objects, as, for instance, when he begins the "Analogies of Experience" in 1787 by stating that "experience is an empirical knowledge, that is, a knowledge which determines an object through perceptions" (B218), and thus that he can only intend the deduction as an argument of type I which shows that some *a priori* knowledge of objects is a condition of the possibility of any judgment about them at all, having already assumed that experience is knowledge of objects. In the next sentence but one after this, however, the term "experience" is used in what is clearly a more subjective sense, for it says that in "experience indeed perceptions come together only in accidental order, so that no necessity determining their connection is or can be revealed in the perceptions themselves" (B219); here experience seems to be equated with the mere occurrence of perceptual states rather than with the judgment that perceptions represent an object. Indeed, as Lewis White Beck has pointed out,[6] this ambiguity is present in the very first lines of the *Critique*, for only by such an equivocation could Kant have written that

> there can be no doubt that all our knowledge begins with experience. For [otherwise] how should our faculty of knowledge . . . work up the raw materials of our sensible impressions into that knowledge of objects which is called experience? [B1]

Unless Kant is first using "experience" to mean merely the subjective states which may or may not represent objects and only then using the same word to connote knowledge of objects, this passage is incoherent. But if he does use "experience" in this systematically ambiguous way, then the definition of a transcendental deduction as a proof that certain concepts are the conditions of the possibility of experience allows for the two radically different types of argument (I and II) described above.

Further, none of the terms which Kant sometimes uses in place of the disputed word "experience" permit a simple resolution of this ambiguity. He sometimes argues that *a priori* knowledge of the categories is a condition of the possibility of the "unity of consciousness," yet this phrase too seems capable of connoting both a connection among representations in virtue of which they can represent an object and also the mere fact that several representations are recognized to constitute a manifold of representations, whether or not this manifold represents an object. Thus at A107, after first introducing the concept of "transcendental apperception" as a "consciousness of self," Kant says that "there can be in us no cognitions, no connection of one cognition with another, without that unity of consciousness which precedes all data of intuition," thus suggesting that the "unity of consciousness" is a consciousness of a connection that representational states have even regarded merely as such, whether or not they are taken to constitute experience of an object (see also

A108). At A109, however, Kant says that "that unity which must be met with in any manifold of knowledge which stands in relation to an object . . . is nothing but the necessary unity of knowledge," suggesting that there is at least a material equivalence between unity of consciousness and consciousness of an object.

The term "apperception" itself is also used in a systematically ambiguous way. Thus, as we just saw, the concept of transcendental apperception is officially introduced as a "consciousness of self" (A107), and at A113, for example, "original apperception" is explicitly described as a "transcendental representation" of "self-consciousness," from which indeed "numerical identity is inseparable" and which "is *a priori* certain." This suggests that some claim, indeed an *a priori* claim, about the identity *of the self* in its different subjective states is the premise of the deduction. Yet just before first formally introducing the term "apperception" at A107, Kant actually first *uses* it, in discussing the rule by which we construct a triangle, in saying that "this *unity* of rule determines all the manifold, and limits it to the conditions which make unity of apperception possible," and this suggests that the unity of apperception is that form of connection among representations by which *an object* is represented. Even more remarkably, Section 18 of the deduction in B equates the "transcendental unity of apperception" with an objective *as opposed to* subjective unity (B139), and Kant then continues in Section 19 to suggest that this difference is precisely that between that kind of relation among representations by which an object distinct from those representations is presented and a relation of representations which represents merely "the state of the subject" (B142).[7] These examples suggest that, in spite of the apparent reference to an explicit consciousness of subjective states connoted by the original Leibnizian use of "apperception," Kant in fact equates this concept with a strong sense of "experience" equivalent to knowledge of objects and intends his deduction to argue only that if one presupposes the possibility of making judgments about objects then one must also concede the *a priori* validity of the categories.

Kant's statement that "the possibility, indeed the necessity, of these categories rests on the relation in which our entire sensibility, and with it all possible appearances, stand to original apperception" can thus be substituted for his claim that "the categories . . . are nothing but the conditions of thought in a possible experience" (A111) without precluding this interpretation, for Kant uses the word "apperception" just as ambiguously as he uses the word "experience" itself. Nevertheless, it is clear that Kant sometimes argues for the categories as conditions for the possibility of at least a certain form of self-consciousness as well as of the consciousness of objects, without first equating these two conceptions, and that in at least some versions of his argument the reference to self-consciousness is indispensable. Thus the sentence following that linking the categories with "original apperception" just quoted continues:

> In original apperception everything must necessarily conform to the conditions of the thoroughgoing unity of self-consciousness, that is to the universal functions of synthesis, namely of that synthesis according to concepts in which alone apperception can demonstrate *a priori* its complete and necessary identity. [A111–12]

Sometimes Kant is content to argue only that the possibility of judgments about objects requires *a priori* knowledge of the categories, even to label as a "complete deduction of the categories" an argument which maintains only that,[8] without mentioning apperception at all, and sometimes he is satisfied to treat the possibility of apperception as equivalent to the possibility of judgments about objects. There are, however, many other places, and indeed places where Kant explicitly claims to present the deduction in "systematic interconnection" (A115), where the concept of apperception as consciousness of the identity of the self in contrast to knowledge of objects is employed in the fundamental premise of the deduction.

If we combine the two possibilities for argument allowed by the ambiguity of such terms as "experience" and even "apperception" itself with the other pair of alternatives, that a transcendental deduction either does or does not assume a premise which itself embodies synthetic *a priori* knowledge, we see at once that four tactics are available, at least in principle, to prove that *a priori* knowledge of the categories is a condition of the possibility of experience. The proof may begin by equating experience with knowledge of objects given by perception and assuming the possibility of judgments about such empirical objects and then, depending on whether or not it also assumes that this already involves a synthetic *a priori* premise, or a near relative, take the form:

I*A*: Judgments about empirical objects are possible, and these assume some synthetic *a priori* knowledge (or a near relative), which implies the further *a priori* knowledge of the categories;

or

IB: Judgments about empirical objects are possible, and although these do not themselves assert any *a priori* knowledge, they do imply *a priori* knowledge of the categories.

Alternatively, the possibility of experience may be equated with only the possibility (cf. B131–32) of apperception as a form of self-consciousness rather than consciousness of objects other than the self, and then we have the two further forms of argument:

IIA: The possibility of apperception as a form of synthetic *a priori* knowledge itself implies *a priori* knowledge of the categories and indeed of their application to objects regarded as distinct from the self;

and

IIB: The possibility of apperception even as a form of merely empirical knowledge of the self implies (at least relatively) *a priori* knowledge of the categories and indeed of their application to objects regarded as distinct from the self.

In what follows I shall show that Kant explicitly formulated versions of tactics IA, IB, and IIA and at least suggested the possibility of IIB but that, although he was willing on occasion to advance IA or IB or IIA as *the* argument of the deduction, the only one of such arguments which is neither question-begging nor fallacious and does not rest on an unfounded premise has a conclusion which is too weak for Kant's purposes. Thus only an argument of type IIB can ultimately be regarded as a plausible tactic for the execution of the strategy of the deduction—even though, as my parenthetical qualification is meant to suggest, its conclusion is also not quite as strong as what Kant himself thought he could reach.[9]

With this fourfold classification before us, we are almost ready to enter the field of battle and see how Kant's tactics actually fare. Before we begin, however, we should notice that Kant does intend all aspects of his campaign to be governed by a single underlying premise. This is the premise that any form of knowledge whatsoever involves a connection of diverse representations and that such a connection requires a mental act of combination. The first clause of this premise is well stated in the Deduction in A, where indeed Kant puts it in two forms: first he says that "knowledge is a whole in which representations stand compared and connected," so that "if each representation were completely foreign to every other, standing apart in isolation, no such thing as knowledge would ever arise" (A97); then he adds the interesting claim that, since it is *by time* that the diverse representations are separated, "for each representation, *in so far as it is contained in a single moment*, can never be anything but absolute unity," it is therefore *in time* that all representations "must be ordered, connected, and brought into relation" (A99). The second clause of Kant's underlying assumption is made most clear in B, when he says that "the combination (*conjunctio*) of a manifold in general can never come to us through the senses, and cannot, therefore, be already contained in the pure form of a sensible intuition," for "it is an act of spontaneity," and therefore "all combination—be we conscious of it or not, be it a combination of the manifold of intuition, empirical or non-empirical, or of various concepts—is an act of the understanding" (B 129–30).[10] In a way Kant's various kinds of arguments differ by how much is assumed to follow how directly from the fact that combination is the work of the understanding and, in the end, by how much emphasis is laid on the temporal separation of representations and the temporal form of their combination.

IA

I begin by considering arguments which infer the *a priori* validity of the categories from not only an assumption of the possibility of empirical knowledge but also a characterization of the latter which already claims some other *a priori* knowledge or a near relative thereof. I speak somewhat generally here because several different Kantian arguments fall under this heading, not all of which assume *a priori* knowledge in an equally direct form. In fact, in only one of the three types of argument that I am about to describe is an assumption of the existence of some form of *a priori* knowledge distinct from that of the categories completely explicit; but in the others something so closely related to an outright assumption of apriority—namely, an assumption that empirical knowledge is universal and/or necessary—is built so directly into the premise of the argument that it will be most illuminating to regard these lines of thought under the present heading.

1. The first argument I will consider avoids the question-begging which in fact generally threatens tactic IA by assuming an *a priori* knowledge of objects which is indeed distinct from *a priori* knowledge of the categories themselves but is really not meant to stand on its own. This argument is suggested in Kant's discussion of

"The Synthesis of Reproduction in Imagination" in A, where Kant suggests something like this: As part of the combination of the manifold which by his underlying assumption is necessary to produce knowledge, reproduction of relevant past representations is required, and "this law of reproduction presupposes that appearances are themselves subject to . . . certain rules" (A100) (here is where this argument presupposes another and, as IB(1) below will show, problematic one); but if *a priori* intuitions are included among those which must be so reproduced, then the rules according to which this synthesis of reproduction takes place must also be *a priori*—and, although this is not stated, such rules can only be the categories. Thus Kant implies that we may first derive knowledge of *a priori* concepts from their role in our knowledge of objects of *a priori* intuitions and then extend this *a priori* knowledge to objects of ordinary empirical intuition as well:

For if we can show that even our purest *a priori* intuitions yield no knowledge, save in so far as they contain a combination of the manifold such as renders a thoroughgoing synthesis of representations possible, then this synthesis of imagination is likewise grounded, antecedently to all experience, upon *a priori* principles; and we must assume a pure transcendental synthesis of imagination as conditioning the very possibility of all experience. [A101]

The problems with such an argument, however, are obvious. Leaving for later the underlying question why the reproduction of a manifold of representations should require any rules at all, the question immediately arises, Why should our *a priori* knowledge of, say, the geometry of empirical objects require any *a priori* rules *other* than those which geometry itself contains? To take the examples with which Kant himself follows the passage just quoted, what could the *a priori* rules needed "to draw a line in thought . . . or even to represent to myself some particular number" (A102) possibly have to do with the kinds of *a priori* concepts Kant is supposed to be deducing, categories like reality and negation, inherence and subsistence, or causality and dependence (A80/B106)? The answer appears to be, Nothing; and the present argument, though it may anticipate a later argument about the *scope* of the application of the categories turning on our *a priori* knowledge of the unity of space and time,[11] appears to be of questionable relevance to the goal of the deduction.

Kant must have been aware of the implausibility of this argument, for we do not find it repeated. On many other occasions, however, Kant was satisfied to offer as complete deductions of the categories two other kinds of argument, which use as their premises not our *a priori* knowledge of the pure manifolds of space and time but a conception of empirical knowledge which includes an element of universality and necessity that comes as close to an outright assumption of *a priori* knowledge as it could—and which does, of course, open Kant to charges not of irrelevance but of circularity or at least question-begging. Here I have in mind Kant's frequent arguments that, given the premise that we are indeed entitled to make judgments about empirical objects, we can derive the *a priori* validity of the categories directly from the *concept of a judgment* or even from the *concept of an object* itself.

2. The tactic for the execution of the deduction in which Kant obviously felt the most confidence in the years following the publication of the first edition of the *Critique*, and which held a large part of his confidence even through the publication of the second edition, is the argument that the very idea of judgment itself implies knowledge of a necessary and universal connection which can be accounted for only by *a priori* knowledge of the categories in which judgments are cast. Essentially this argument takes the form that a judgment is a connection among representations which is necessary and therefore universal as well, or universally valid and therefore necessary as well, or simply both necessarily and universally valid, and that this is so even in the case of a judgment on an empirical object. With the premise stated at the start of the *Critique* that no amount of purely empirical evidence ever justifies a claim of genuine universality and necessity (e.g., A1–2), however, it quickly follows that it cannot be the particular content of an empirical judgment which accounts for these characteristics, and so it follows not only that there must be something which is known *a priori* even about empirical objects in order to account for the universality and necessity of empirical judgments but also that this must be some sort of rule or rules valid for both such objects and such judgments independently of their content. From here it is only a short step to *a priori* knowledge of the categories.

We find a confident assertion of the soundness of such an argument in *The Metaphysical Foundations of Natural Science* (1786), in which Kant says that "the problem as to *how* experience is possible by means of those categories . . . can be solved almost by a single conclusion from the precisely determined definition of a judgment in general (an act by which given representations first become cognitions of an object),"[12] and expositions of it in both the *Prolegomena* and the Deduction in B. But we may begin our examination of it by considering versions which appear in two of Kant's reflections from 1783–84, obviously notes associated with the composition of the *Prolegomena*. The first of these is a long sketch which Kant explicitly entitled "Deduction of Pure Cognitions *a priori*." Here Kant begins by contrasting a strong notion of experience as knowledge of objects with the lack of connection characteristic of representations regarded merely as subjective states:

> But the consciousness of perceptions relates all representations only to our self as modifications of our condition; they are therefore separated among themselves, and in particular they are not cognitions of any particular thing, and are not related to any object. They are therefore not yet experience.[13]

Kant then continues to assert that the kind of connection which such subjective but not yet cognitive states lack is precisely the kind of connection which is asserted by a judgment:

> If we question logic as to what can count as knowledge in general, then a concept is a representation which is related to an object and designates it; and when we connect . . . one concept with another in a judgment, we think something of the object that is designated through a given concept, that is, we cognize it when we judge about it. All knowledge, thus that of experience also, consists of judgments. . . . Therefore experience is possible only through judgments.

But then Kant quickly adds that, even though "perceptions to be sure constitute the empirical materials" of such judgments, "the relation of these [judgments] to an object and knowledge of the latter through perception cannot depend upon empirical consciousness alone," precisely because a judgment is now defined as the assertion of a necessary connection:

> But the form of every judgment consists in the objective unity of consciousness of the given concepts, that is, in the consciousness that these *must* belong to one another, and thereby designate an object, in the representation of which they are always to be met with.

And then, since this necessity and consequently universality cannot be derived from the empirical content of the judgments, it can be

167

explained only by *a priori* knowledge of rules in accordance with which they are made:

> But this necessity of connection is not a representation of empirical origin, but presupposes a rule which must be given *a priori*, that is, unity of consciousness which takes place *a priori*. This unity of consciousness is contained in the moments of the understanding in judgment, and only that is an object in relation to which unity of the consciousness of the manifold of representations is thought *a priori*. [This and preceding quotations from *R*5923, Ak. 18, pp. 385–87]

Given both that empirical judgments are possible and that even empirical judgments assert necessary connections, it follows that such judgments must presuppose rules known *a priori*, and these can be furnished only by the categories of the understanding.

Kant offers a similar argument, indeed one which explicitly uses the term "category," as following from the alternative definition of a judgment as the assertion of a *universal* connection:

> [A] category is the representation of the relation of the manifold of intuition to a universal consciousness (to the universality of consciousness, which is really objective). The relation of representations to the universality of consciousness, consequently the transformation of empirical and particular unity of consciousness, which is merely subjective, into a consciousness which is universal and objective, belongs to logic. This unity of consciousness, insofar as it is universal and can be represented *a priori*, is the pure concept of the understanding. This can therefore be nothing other than the universal of the unity of consciousness, which constitutes the objective validity of a judgment. [*R*5927, Ak. 18, pp. 388–89]

Reading this from the end, we have the claim that the objective validity of a judgment consists in its claim to universal validity (though whether by this Kant means that it *applies* to a universal class of *objects* or must be *accepted* by a universal class of *subjects* is unclear[14]) and that such a claim cannot be grounded in the empirical content of consciousness itself. So it must lie instead in a category, and then our knowledge of the objective validity of such a judgment must lie in our *a priori* knowledge of the validity of a category for the object regardless of its empirical content.

In either of these forms Kant's argument to the categories from the mere concept of a judgment already cries out for criticism; but before providing that, we might as well consider the version of this argument which Kant offers in the *Prolegomena*. The *Prolegomena* proceeds by asserting that "experience consists in the synthetical connection of phenomena (perceptions) in consciousness, so far as this connection is necessary" (section 22, Ak. 4, p. 306), and by defining a correlative distinction between the judgments by which such connections can be expressed and those which can only report a form of connection of representations falling beneath this dignity, viz., the distinction between judgments of experience and judgments of perception. The judgment of perception, if it is a judgment at all, reflects "only the logical connection of perception in a thinking subject"; "the objective validity of the judgment of experience," however, "signifies nothing else than its necessary universal validity" (section 18, Ak. 4, p. 298), which Kant here expressly defines to include both necessary intersubjective agreement and the necessary applicability of a judgment of experience to a universal class of objects: my intention in making a judgment of experience is "that I and everyone else should always connect necessarily the same perception[s] under the same circumstances" (section 19, Ak. 4, p. 299). Once again, however, Kant argues that the intuition of an empirical object, a "perception which pertains merely to the senses," is inadequate to ground a claim to such universal and necessary validity, and so, since it nevertheless supplies the content of the judgment of experience, the only solution is that

> the given intuition must be subsumed under a concept which determines the form of judging in general relatively to the intuition, connects empirical consciousness of intuition in consciousness in general, and thereby procures universal validity for empirical judgments. A concept of this nature is a pure *a priori* concept of the understanding. [Section 20, Ak. 4, p. 300]

Only if it is formed by means of one of the categories, in other words, can a judgment the particular content of which is thoroughly empirical claim the status of necessity and universality required by the definition of a judgment of experience; and apparently if it is so formed it must claim this status.[15]

A similar conception of judgment is exploited in sections 19 and 20 of the Deduction in B, and this version of the present tactic solves one problem of the *Prolegomena* by not speaking of judgments with merely subjective validity at all; but since this version of the argument is not meant to be completely self-sufficient, perhaps it should not detain us now.[16] The problem with this tactic is obvious enough already. Even if we ignore the problem about making genuine judgments about subjective states, the question immediately arises, Why should objective validity be taken to consist in universality and necessity of a sort so strong that they can be secured only by the application of *a priori* concepts to empirical objects? Why should not a high but still empirically confirmed degree of agreement be adequate to license an objective judgment as opposed to a subjective report? In other words, what recommends acceptance of such a strong definition of the requirements of empirical judgment to begin with? With such a definition we may have a valid argument for the categories and one that avoids the charge of strict circularity; but without an independent argument for this conception of judgment, which Kant does not provide, his procedure certainly seems question-begging.

3. An alternative tactic that also appealed to Kant was to derive the universal and necessary validity claimed by even empirical judgment not directly from the conception of judgment itself but from the concept of an object for such a judgment. A direct argument to the necessity of *a priori* categories for the knowledge of objects arises when Kant defines an object not just as "that in the concept of which the manifold of a given intuition is *united*" (B137) but as that in virtue of which the several representations constituting such a manifold are *necessarily* connected.[17] We find such an argument both in Kant's *Nachlass* and in the *Critique* itself. In one long note dating from some indeterminate point in the 1780s, for instance, Kant directly links the concept of an object of knowledge with that of necessary connection:

> In the representation of an object which is to contain the manifold of its intuition, the synthetic unity of the manifold is necessary. The representation of this synthetic unity, under which all the manifold in intuition must stand if it is to be knowledge of an object of intuition, is the principle of synthetic knowledge in general, and must itself take place *a priori*;

and then it is the *necessity* of the unity of the manifold presented by an object which requires the use of some *a priori* concepts in application to the empirical content of this manifold:

> A synthesis can never be known as necessary and therefore *a priori* from the representations which are to be synthetically connected, rather from their relation to a third concept, in which and in relation to which this connection is necessary. This third

concept is that of an object in general, that indeed through which this synthetically necessary unity is thought. [R5643, Ak. 18, pp. 283–84]

The mere fact that the relation of a manifold to an object requires a unity in that manifold would not itself appear to entail that this unity must be derived from a concept which can be known to hold of that manifold *a priori*; only the fact that this unity must be necessary is sufficient to require this strong conclusion.

The same sort of argument appears equally clearly in the A Deduction's discussion of "The Synthesis of Recognition in a Concept," for here Kant makes the transition from the unity of a manifold furnishing knowledge, which is required by his basic premise that knowledge is a whole in which representations are connected, to the further claim that this unity must be necessary expressly by the introduction of a strong definition of "an object of representations" (A104). Kant begins this passage by asserting the uncontroversial but thoroughly conditional necessity that *if* the successive apprehension and reproduction of some particular representations are to furnish any knowledge at all there must be some sense in which these representations can be regarded as representations of some single object (A103), so that *if* they are to represent *that* object it is indeed necessary that they be connected in a certain way. But this would be true even if the concept of this object were thoroughly empirical and *a posteriori*. Kant may initiate a slide toward the *a priori* by choosing the concept of a number as an example of the kind of object of which several representations are seen as successive representations, but on the face of the matter there seems to be no reason why, for instance, the concept of my writing pad should not be thoroughly empirical and yet be the concept of the *same object* by which I connect my several representations of yellowness, rectangularity, and stubborn resistance to the motion of my pen as representations of one object.[18] Kant appears to exclude this possibility only by defining the necessity imposed by the concept of an object as an unconditional necessity which cannot be derived from an empirical concept; thus to determine that several representations are necessarily connected is to determine that they are connected *a priori*:

Now we find that our thought of the relation of all knowledge to its object carries with it an element of necessity; the object is viewed as that which prevents our cognitions from being haphazard or arbitrary, and which determines them *a priori* in some definite fashion. For in so far as they are to relate to an object, they must necessarily agree with one another, that is, must possess that unity which constitutes the concept of an object. [A 104–105]

But Kant does not in fact explain why the nonarbitrary connection among representations required for them to represent an object should not be adequately embodied in a conditional necessity such as "If there is a legal pad before me then I must perceive paper which is both yellow and rectangular," for such a statement does claim that a certain succession of representations is not haphazard, without employing a concept which can be known only *a priori*. Kant's assumption that the kind of necessity imposed by an object can be known only *a priori* seems just as question-begging as his assumption that the kind of connection asserted by every empirical judgment can only be so known, and to justify the traditional charge that Kant just took for granted what the empiricist put in doubt.

IB

So now we must see whether Kant did not also suggest arguments which show that *a priori* concepts are necessary for empirical judgments without explicitly assuming that such judgments claim universality and necessity. I will argue that Kant did suggest two types of argument in behalf of this tactic but that the first of these—which it may indeed be somewhat artificial to distinguish from argument IA(3)—though it may have a conclusion as strong as Kant desired, rests on a fatal fallacy; and that the alternative form of argument from a nonaprioristic conception of empirical knowledge, though not subject to any equally obvious fallacy, cannot prove a conclusion of sufficient strength for Kant's purposes. Thus a turn toward arguments based on the concept of apperception will be virtually required by the inadequacy of all the arguments Kant developed without it.

(1) I will consider first Kant's attempt actually to argue that knowledge of an object requires *a priori* knowledge of a necessary connection rather than just to define this requirement into force.[19] This argument is offered in "The Synthesis of Reproduction in Imagination" in A. Here Kant argues that, given the basic fact that knowledge requires a combination, it is also a necessary condition for knowledge of an object that a present representation of the object be able to bring about "a transition of the mind" to one or

more of the other—and past—representations constituting the manifold of the intuition of the object, and that "this law of reproduction" in turn "presupposes that appearances are themselves actually subject to such a rule, and that in the manifold of these representations a coexistence or sequence takes place in conformity with certain rules" (A100). For, as Kant argues, if it were entirely contingent whether or not our senses presented us with repeated patterns of representations, it would be equally contingent whether or not we could ever reproduce them as required for the knowledge of an object; the only alternative is that "there must be then something which, as the *a priori* ground of a necessary synthetic unity of appearances, makes their reproduction possible," and this of course turns out to be the *a priori* principles which ground the "transcendental synthesis of imagination" (A101).

As an argument from a condition of the possibility of knowledge of an object to the necessity of the connection that object imposes, this is clearly fallacious. For, even if we concede that to be able to reproduce representations requires being aware of a regularity among these representations, Kant's argument still requires not just the conditional that

(1) it is necessary that if I am to experience an object, then I must be aware of a regularity among the representations of it,

but the stronger claim that

(2) if I am to experience an object, then I must be aware of a necessary regularity among the representations of it.

Yet (2) is by no means equivalent to (1) and does not seem to be established in any way by Kant's indisputable claim that if, for instance, "cinnabar were sometimes red, sometimes black, sometimes light, sometimes heavy, . . . my empirical imagination would never find opportunity when representing red color to bring to mind heavy cinnabar" (A100–101). Such an example seems to establish only (1), and that implies only the conditional necessity that *if* I am to know an object, then there had better *in fact* be some regularity among the representations of it which I can experience.

To put the matter in somewhat more detail, what Kant's inference to the existence of *a priori* knowledge requires is not just the conditional necessity (1), but an unconditional necessity which we can express by detaching the consequent of (2) and asserting simply that

(3) I am aware of a necessary regularity among the representations of objects;

but this of course cannot be detached from (1) without fallacy.[20] Now there is, of course, a way in which we could reach something like (3) by a valid inference, namely if we were to add to (1) the additional premise that

(4) it is necessary that I experience objects,

for from (4) and (1), using the unexceptionable principle that if p implies q and p is necessary then q is also necessary, we could infer

(5) it is necessary that I am aware of regularity among the representations I have,

and we could then perhaps introduce (3), namely my awareness of necessary connections, as the only possible explanation of (5). The only problem with this argument, however, is that no empiricist of the sort against whom Kant's argument is supposed to be directed could possibly be expected to concede (4), that it is *necessary* that we experience objects; at most, only the *possibility* of knowledge of objects would be conceded. But to explain this, all we need is, once again, (1).

Thus Kant's argument at A100–102 is, as it stands, fallacious: it allows us to infer that reproducibility is a condition of the possibility of knowledge of objects but not that *necessary* reproducibility, and therefore *a priori* principles from which such a necessity could flow, is such a condition. The only way the latter thesis could be established is if Kant could show, by deriving it from *some other* necessity, that there is some way in which (4) is justified, that is, that it *is* necessary that I have experience of objects. And this, of course, means that the argument of the deduction cannot succeed while it confines itself to the examination of what is necessary *if* we are to experience objects—it must find something with respect to which such experience can itself be seen to be not just possible but necessary. This obviously points toward a conception of apperception as a form of self-consciousness which might imply knowledge of objects without itself being equivalent to it.

(2) Before we take this turn, however, we must consider Kant's alternative method for deriving the necessity of *a priori* concepts from the possibility of empirically objective judgments. On this line of reasoning, Kant does not construct an argument that can be saved from fallacy only by the unwarranted assumption that it is somehow necessary that we experience objects; rather, he tries to show that

since all knowledge requires an act of combination *and* since there are certain laws which govern any such act, or only certain forms which its expression can take, it can be known independently of the content of any particular empirical judgment that certain concepts must be employed in it, concepts which are then, obviously, known *a priori*.

In its bluntest—and earliest—form this kind of argument just assumes that there must be rules by which the mind performs its act of combining representations into connected wholes of knowledge, without arguing that combination requires laws, and similarly just assumes that because there are such rules we can know them *a priori*, without proving that the mind's operations must be transparent.[21] More subtly, however, Kant tried to exploit the very notion of combination itself in such a way as to derive both the necessity of *a priori* rules for such connections from the form of their expression and to identify them with rules to which we have indisputable access, namely, the logical functions of judgment. Such an argument, then, begins like that in *R*5923 (see IA(2) above), but makes its inference to *a priori* concepts from only the form and not the assumed necessity of empirical judgments. We may discern it in this note from the period of the *Prolegomena*:

Experience is knowledge of that which is object of sensation (*a posteriori*). Sensations yield, however, no knowledge; therefore something must be added to them if experience is to be possible. [But] to *a posteriori* representations only *a priori* representations from concepts can be added, and this [*sic*] can only be connection (synthesis), in so far as it is determined *a priori*.

If sensations both exhaust the sphere of the *a posteriori* and yet are insufficient to constitute experience or knowledge of objects, in other words, what must be added to them can only come from the realm of the *a priori*. Kant then continues his discussion to specify the identity of this *a priori* element:

The general principle of possible experience is therefore: *all perceptions are determined *a priori* in respect of their connection in one consciousness (for consciousness is unity, in which alone the connection of all perception is possible, and if it is to be knowledge of an object, it must be determined *a priori*). The objective unity of the consciousness of different representations is the form of judgment. Therefore all perceptions, so far as they are to constitute experience, stand under the formal conditions of judgment in general, and the determination of them through this function is the concept of the understanding.

Kant adds two riders to this argument. First, attaching this claim to the asterisk in the passage still being quoted, he identifies the "formal conditions of judgments" with the categories: "*All appearances are, in respect to their connection, determinable *a priori* in accord with the unity of consciousness in all judgments in general, that is, they stand under categories" (R5934, Ak. 18, p. 393). Then, in another note from the same period, he also asserts that *all* the categories identified as forms of judgment must apply to the objects of the understanding: "For the logical form of understanding in judgments must yet precede [experience], and the appearances (as mere representations) must be regarded as determined in respect of every one of these forms, for otherwise no experience can arise?" (R5926, Ak. 18, p. 388). Thus Kant attempts first to argue that there really must be an *a priori* element in the knowledge of objects just insofar as that knowledge requires a combination at all and then to specify this element by equating combination with judgment and the *a priori* element of the former with—all—the forms of the latter.

Of course, the first stage of this argument is not much more persuasive than an outright assumption of the existence of some laws by which the mind performs its operations, even though it reappears even in the B Deduction when Kant writes that

> combination does not, however, lie in the objects, and cannot be borrowed from them, and so, through perception, first taken up in the understanding. On the contrary, it is an affair of the understanding alone, which itself is nothing but the faculty of combining *a priori*. [B134–35]

It makes the ungrounded assumptions, first, that what the mind must add to *a posteriori* representations to constitute knowledge is indeed *another* representation of some sort, and not *just* its own action of combination, and, second, that the division into *a posteriori* and *a priori* is exhaustive, so that if this additional representation is not the former it can only be the latter—and not, for instance, just arbitrary or invented. All of this is a fair amount to assume.

The second paragraph I have quoted does suggest something new, however, namely, an argument that since the connection of representations takes place in judgment the former must be governed by the forms or structures available for the latter. This, it is important to notice, is quite different from the earlier argument

176

(IA[2]) that *since* judgments have necessary and universal validity they must imply the *a priori* validity of certain concepts; this argument does not assume that judgments have such necessity but only that they have certain internal structures and thus that whatever they link must likewise have such forms. And, it should also be noted, the present argument does not seem to assert any unconditional necessity that judgments must be made; it seems to hold only the conditional necessity that *if* experience is to take place it must take the form of judgment and thus that if it is to take place it must take on the specific forms of judgment.

This kind of argument is more plausible than anything we have seen so far. Strangely enough, however, it is *not* one to which Kant gives any prominence in the text of the Deduction itself. It appears, to be sure, in the section of the *Critique* which is supposed to furnish "The Clue to the Discovery of All Pure Concepts of the Understanding," the so-called "Metaphysical Deduction," as when Kant argues that "the same function which gives unity to the various representations *in a judgment* also gives unity to the mere synthesis of various representations *in an intuition*," from which it is inferred that "the same understanding, through the same operations by which in concepts, by means of analytical unity, it produced the logical form of a judgment, also introduces a transcendental content into its representations," so that we are entitled to call these forms "pure concepts of the understanding, and to regard them as applying *a priori* to objects" (B104–105). But there is no hint of an argument from the nature of judgment at all in the exposition of the Deduction in A, and in B we find only the kind of argument (IA[2]) in which the conclusion that judgments must have some forms which can be known *a priori* is derived from the prior assumption that a proper judgment expresses a strong claim to "necessary unity" (B142) and in which it is only afterward pointed out that there are certain specific logical functions of judgment and that "the *categories* are just these functions of judgment, in so far as they are employed in determination of the manifold of a given intuition" (B143). Why does Kant not let the argument that any connection of representations is judgment and that judgments, and thus these connections, have certain forms stand on its own?

The answer to this question can only be that the argument is inadequate to Kant's purposes: it is valid as far as it goes, but it does not go far enough. Even if, ignoring the standard objections,[22] we grant the correctness of Kant's account of the logically possible forms which judgments may take, and even if we concede that it must be possible for us to make empirical judgments, it is clear that certain conclusions which Kant wanted to establish in the Deduction cannot be secured by this kind of argument alone. Perhaps most obviously, Kant's thesis that it is not just possible for us to use some of the functions of judgment but that it is necessary to use them all—what is so clearly asserted to be the case by *R*5926 (above)—cannot be established by this argument. For while it may follow from the fact that knowledge of an object does indeed require a combination of representations and thus *some* form of judgment, it follows neither that any individual cognition must involve *all* the forms of judgment or even that for each form of judgment there must be *some* cognition which employs it. And when we think for a moment about the details of Kant's tables of judgments and categories, the nature of the problem becomes even more evident. For it is Kant's view that only the categorical form of judgment characterizes what we might call atomic judgments, that is, judgments which link particular representations which are not themselves judgments, and that the hypothetical and disjunctive forms of judgment link only other judgments, not particular representations themselves (A73/B98). But then to link representations as demanded merely by the concept of combination itself, it must be sufficient to use the categorical judgment and its associated category of inherence and subsistence, and unnecessary (even if possible) to use the hypothetical and disjunctive forms of judgment—and their associated categories of causality and dependence and community—for this minimal purpose of cognition.[23] If this is so, however, then the deduction can furnish neither an answer to Hume nor metaphysical foundations for natural science.

Second, it is also far from obvious why a deduction of the categories from the mere forms of judgment should imply that our judgments must concern a relation of representations "which is *objectively valid*" and why they should not in fact just express a "relation of these same representations that would have only subjective validity" (B142). On the present account it would seem that the categories could be used to express connections among inner and subjective states regarded merely as such, without applying to any objects intended to be distinct from such subjective states or accessible to other persons. Yet Kant's introduction to the Deduction makes it clear that he wants to demonstrate that the pure concepts of the understanding not only can but even must apply to objects in space as well as to those which are merely in inner sense or time (A87–91/B119–23), and the necessity of making some claims of objective validity, even if it cannot reasonably be made the premise of his argument, is still something Kant wants as a conclusion of it. So a stronger argument than the present one from the logical functions of judgment is clearly required.

But we have exhausted all the tactics which Kant attempts to deploy without bringing in the concept of apperception as some form of self-consciousness. Thus if we are to have any hope of finding an argument for executing the strategy of the deduction which is not question-begging (IA), fallacious (IB[1]), or inadequate (IB[2]), we must now finally consider Kant's arguments from the concept of the transcendental unity of apperception.

IIA

Kant was obviously content to conduct his argument at an essentially superficial level, employing a conception of object or judgment that already has most of his conclusion built into it, when as in the *Prolegomena*, he wanted to hurry on to the critical consequences of his new philosophy. Nevertheless, Kant also attempted to prove our *a priori* knowledge of the categories from a conception of apperception as a form of self-consciousness not immediately equated with empirical judgment about objects. Most readers have found Kant's analysis of apperception too compact and obscure to be as persuasive as it is intriguing, and some have taken this as evidence that Kant was never as interested in the foundations of the "critical philosophy" as in its applications.[24] It seems to me, however, more accurate to conclude that Kant was deeply interested in the deduction of the categories from the nature of self-consciousness itself—a pervasive concern with apperception is evident, after all, in Kant's earliest surviving efforts toward the Transcendental Analytic, the so-called *Duisburg Nachlass* from around 1775[25]—but settled on a brief treatment of the concept in the *Critique* itself because he thought that it permitted a simple deduction from a virtually self-evident *a priori* premise. As we shall see, however, his premise, although it does indeed seem self-evident on first glance, is undermined by the very consideration that Kant needs to generate his argument from it. And this means that Kant's simple argument from a conception of apperception as itself *a priori* knowledge fails, and the only tactic left for the execution of the strategy of the deduction is a more arduous analysis of the conditions of the possibility of apperception as merely empirical knowledge about the self (IIB) which Kant intimates but hardly accomplishes in any version of the Deduction itself.

The apparently unimpeachable premise from which Kant's preferred argument from apperception begins is the assertion that, whatever the contents of any of my diverse representations may be and whatever other knowledge they may provide, I have *a priori* knowledge of the numerical identity of the self to which they belong; whatever else I may know about one of my representations, I know *a priori* that it belongs to the same self to which any and all of my other representations belong. As Kant puts it: "We are conscious *a priori* of the complete identity of the self in respect of all representations which can ever belong to our knowledge, as being a necessary condition of the possibility of all representations" (A116), or "As self-consciousness is a transcendental representation, numerical identity is inseparable from it, and is *a priori* certain" (A113). In the words which introduce the phrase "transcendental apperception," it is a "consciousness of [a] self" which is "*necessarily* represented as numerically identical" (A107). And to make a short story even shorter, Kant's argument is then basically that what has to be represented in such a way "cannot be thought as such through empirical data" (A107), and so must instead be so thought through rules which are known *a priori*.

Before we examine this argument in more detail, one problem must be considered. I am claiming that Kant's argument assumes *a priori* knowledge of the numerical *identity* of the self, yet Kant often speaks of apperception as the transcendental or necessary *unity* of self-consciousness (e.g., B132, 144), and the concepts of unity and numerical identity are not obviously the same. Thus it is not obvious that an argument constructed on the premise of *a priori* knowledge of the numerical identity of the self must be identical with one which merely assumes *a priori* knowledge of its unity[26] or that the flaws of the former must infect the latter. This objection, however, would miss precisely what is both the weakness and yet the potential strength of Kant's argument. In Kant's usage the *concept* of numerical identity is indeed just a species of the general concept of unity, namely, the concept of the unity of an object the states of which are temporally diverse and not just diverse in general.[27] It is also Kant's view, however, that the states of which the unified self consists, namely representations, can be regarded as diverse at all only if they are regarded as temporally diverse. Thus the self can be *regarded* as a unity only insofar as it is *regarded* as numerically identical in diverse representations, and the conditions for recognizing it as the former must be identical with those for recognizing it as the latter.[28] This is a consequence of Kant's premise—of paramount importance both for the failure of tactic IIA and for the possible success of IIB—that "every intuition contains in itself a manifold which can be represented as a manifold only in so far as the mind distinguishes the time in the sequence of one impression upon another; for each representation, *in so far as it is contained in a single moment*, can never be anything but absolute unity" (A99). To think of the representations of the self as diverse at all—which is surely presupposed by any thesis that to think of the self as a unity is to think of a synthetic (B133) and therefore informative or "ampliative" (A7/B11) connection—requires thinking of its representations as being given at different times, and thus its unity can be known only as numerical identity.

Thus Kant's argument from an *a priori* form of apperception must indeed be an argument from an *a priori* knowledge of the numerical identity of a self with temporally diverse (or successive) representational states. Before we can comprehend the consequences of this fact, however, we must see what the argument is which Kant constructs on this premise. In slightly more detail than before, Kant's argument is this:

(1) I have *a priori* knowledge that my different representations are states of a numerically identical self;

but, given what is involved in knowledge of any sort of whole (A97), this means

(2) I know that there is a connection among my representations,

and indeed, because of what we might call the transitivity of *a priori* knowledge,

(3) I know (2) *a priori*.

However, by Kant's premise that all knowledge of a combination requires an act of combination or synthesis (B129–30), (3) means that

(4) I must know that I perform a synthesis upon all my representations,

and indeed

(5) I must know this *a priori*.

But since, of course, I cannot actually perform a synthesis upon any representations before their actual occurrence, I can know (5) only by knowing something to the effect that

(6) There are certain concepts in accordance with which I can connect any of my representations.

Since, further, I cannot know anything about the specific content of my particular representations independent of their actual occurrence, these concepts must concern the structure or relation of those representations.[29] These, however, can be known only through the categories; therefore

(7) I know *a priori* that the categories apply to all my representations and therefore to what is represented by them.

My transition from (5) to (7) may be neater than anything that Kant himself provides, but there can be little doubt that something like this is Kant's favored argument from the premise of transcendental apperception. In the Deduction in A both Kant's summary of the "Preliminary Explanation of the Possibility of the Categories" and his statement of the deduction in its "systematic interconnection" emphasize the inference from our certainty of the necessary numerical identity of the self in its different states to an *a priori* synthesis or synthesis performed according to *a priori* rules on all those states. The first passage reads thus:

> But as self-consciousness is a transcendental representation, numerical identity is inseparable from it, and *a priori* certain. For nothing can come to our knowledge except in terms of this original apperception. Now, since this identity must necessarily enter into the synthesis of all the manifold of appearances, so far as the synthesis is to yield empirical knowledge, the appearances are subject to *a priori* conditions, with which the synthesis of their apprehension must be in complete accordance. [A113]

And in the "systematic" presentation of the deduction we read:

> We are conscious *a priori* of the complete identity of the self in respect of all representations which can ever belong to our knowledge. . . . This principle holds *a priori*, and may be called the transcendental principle of the *unity* of all that is manifold in our representations, and consequently also in intuition. Since this unity of the manifold in one subject is synthetic, pure apperception supplies a principle of the synthetic unity of the manifold in all possible intuition.

This synthetic unity presupposes or includes a synthesis, and if the former is to be *a priori*, the synthesis must also be *a priori* (A116–18),

which can in turn be explained (our transition from (5) to (7)) only if the *"transcendental synthesis* of the imagination" is actually executed by the *"pure understanding"* with its "pure *a priori* cognitions," the *"categories"* (A119).

Exactly the same argument lies at the heart of the Deduction in the second edition:

> The thought that the representations given in intuition one and all [*insgesamt*] belong to *me* accordingly means that I unite them in one self-consciousness, or can at least so unite them; and although this thought is not itself the consciousness of the *synthesis* of the representations, it presupposes the possibility of that synthesis. . . . Synthetic unity of the manifold of all intuitions, as generated *a priori*, is thus the ground of the identity of apperception itself, which precedes *a priori* all *my* determinate thought. [B134]

In each of these passages Kant maintains that I have an *a priori* knowledge of the numerical identity of my self in its different representational states, that this knowledge presupposes a synthesis of these states, but that since this synthesis must be independent of the specific or determinate content of these states, it can only be an *a priori* synthesis or synthesis according to *a priori* concepts.

This argument could be presented with more precision than I have offered, but that is not necessary for my purposes. I want to proceed on the assumption that this argument or a more refined version of it is formally valid, free of the kind of fallacy which has infected some of Kant's other arguments, and focus on the acceptability of its key premises, specifically the assertions (1) that we have *a priori* certainty of our continuing identity in different states and (4) that such knowledge requires a unique synthesis. What I want to argue is that there is no reason to think that (1) is true and indeed that the very reason for accepting anything like (4), namely, that consciousness of one's own continuing identity in different representational states requires judgment according to any specific rules, is precisely what undermines (1); (1) and (4) are not formally contradictory, but the very reason for accepting (4) is a reason for rejecting (1).

The first thing that we must notice is that Kant's claim in B that although "it reveals the necessity of a synthesis," the "principle of the necessary unity of apperception is itself, indeed, an identical, and therefore analytic, proposition" (B135) cannot be accepted, and his earlier admission that what is known *a priori* is the "synthetic proposition, that all the variety of *empirical consciousness* must be combined in one unified self-consciousness" (A117n.)[30] is needed to make Kant's argument even plausible. For if we were to interpret the principle of apperception as strictly analytic, the most that would follow from it is that *if* I am conscious of my continuing identity with respect to several different representations there must be *some* synthesis by which I can connect them, but not that I must know independently of the occurrence and content of any particular representations that I will be conscious of my identity with respect to them, and therefore that I can synthesize them or that there is some specific synthesis—according to the categories—that I can perform on them. In other words, if Kant's claim that "all *my* representations in any given intuition must be subject to that condition under which alone I can ascribe them to the identical self as *my* representations" (B138) *is* taken analytically, it can imply only that *if* I call several representations "one and all *my* representations," *then* I must "apprehend them as constituting *one* intuition" (B135). That does not imply, however, that I can know independently of the occurrence of any given representations that I *will* be able to recognize them *as* one and all my representations and thus does not imply that I can know *a priori* that I synthesize them, *a fortiori* that I synthesize them according to certain rules. What Kant requires is not an analytic claim that if I call several representations mine I must see them as representations of a single self (an explication, as it were, of what it means to call them "mine") but a synthetic claim that, *whatever* representations I have, I *can* call them mine and thus ascribe them to myself as representations of a single self. Only this would require *a priori* knowledge of any synthesis of them.

So the question next arises, Why should Kant have felt entitled to suppose that any such synthetic proposition can be known *a priori* and with certainty? As if admitting that an analytic account of this *a priori* knowledge is inadequate, Kant does offer several reasons for this certainty. The most obvious of these must be regarded as question-begging, but there is a deeper consideration at work that has great initial plausibility. (*a*) The weakest of Kant's arguments for the certainty of his premise (1) is offered just after his "systematic" presentation of the deduction at A116–19; considering the possibility that would defeat (1), namely, that "much empirical consciousness [could] arise in my mind, but in a state of separation, and without belonging to a consciousness of myself," Kant declares that this is "impossible. . . . For it is only because I ascribe all perceptions to one consciousness (original apperception) that I can say of all perceptions that I am conscious of them" (A121). This, however, while it may well be true, is analytic and question-begging, for by referring to representations of which I *can say* that I am conscious, Kant in fact restricts his argument to just those representations for which self-consciousness and its concomitant consciousness of a connection are already conceded and fails to prove what is at issue, namely, that *all* of my representations must be capable of being ascribed to my identical self. (*b*) Another kind of claim which Kant advances in support of the certainty of (1) is that "intuitions are nothing to us, and do not in the least concern us if they cannot be taken up into consciousness" (A116) or that "without its relation to an at least possible consciousness, appearance could never be an object of knowledge for us, and since it has in itself no objective reality, but exists only in cognition, it would be nothing at all" (A120). This is analogous to Locke's claim that "to imprint anything on the Mind without the Mind's perceiving it, seems to me hardly intelligible."[31] But though the ontological claim that a representation can *exist* only as a modification of consciousness may be true, it does not imply that I must be able to *recognize* every modification of my consciousness as such or ascribe it to myself as mine. Many circumstances could arise in which, say, only the report of another about my behavior could convince me that I must have had a representation which I did not in fact recognize as such or ascribe to myself, though, of course, the representation in question would not have existed unless it existed in me.[32]

There is, however, another consideration which persuades Kant of (1) which, though not as clearly stated as (*a*) and (*b*), appears to cut much deeper.[33] This is what is intimated by Kant within his chief presentations of the *a priori* argument from apperception, as when he claims that we must be "conscious *a priori* of the complete identity of the self in respect of all representations which can ever belong to our knowledge" *because* "in me they can represent something only in so far as they belong with all the others to one consciousness" (this is what I omitted from my earlier quotation of A116–18 above), or when he claims, as at B134, that consciousness of the identity of my apperception of my manifold must precede my *determinate* thought of the manifold or that representation of the unity of the manifold "first makes possible" any *particular* combination of it (B130–31).[34] For what Kant is suggesting in these remarks is that whatever the outcome of my empirical investigation of any particular manifold, and thus whether I discover that it does or does not lend itself to any particular claim of empirical knowledge *I must at least know that I possess the different representations the empirically objective content of which I propose to investigate*; and this means that my knowledge of my common possession of these representations must be independent of the outcome of any empirical investigation of them, or synthesis according to merely empirical concepts. It must be certain *a priori* yet, as synthetic, require a synthesis *a priori* or at least according to *a priori* concepts.

This is the only plausible argument which Kant suggests for the *a priori* certainty of apperception.[35] Unfortunately, it is not a sound argument for this premise, for it is not in fact true that I must *know* that I have really had all of a putative series of representations through some period of my continued existence in order to investigate their possible empirical significance (where by "knowledge" at least belief with justification is meant). At the time of such an investigation it must certainly *seem* to me that I have had certain representations, or made certain observations, through such a period; but since there is no reason to assume *a priori* that one of the results of my investigation could not be precisely to reject the supposition that I actually had one or even several of the representations being investigated—for instance, there might be no other way to make the rest of my observations compatible with the empirical conclusions suggested by the overwhelming majority of my data—it cannot be the case that actual *knowledge* of my possession of any particular representations is presupposed by my empirical investigation of them. In other words, although the possibility of any empirical investigation at all may presuppose what we might call psychological possession of the relevant representations—the *belief* that I have had them all—it does not and even cannot presuppose actual *knowledge* of their possession by my single continuing self.[36] Thus the conditions of the possibility of conducting any empirical synthesis at all—what Kant ultimately appeals to in support of his argument from *a priori* apperception —do not include *a priori* certainty of the numerical identity of the self with regard to any representations it may consider.[37]

Why Kant's first premise would be open to this criticism can be made even clearer if we now consider the possible reasons for

Kant's adherence to (4), the supposition that knowledge that several different representations belong to my identical self requires a synthesis of these representations. Why should any such synthesis be required? Kant's basic reason for adherence to this supposition is apparently his agreement with Hume that there is nothing within the content of any given representation which represents its possession by a self, *a fortiori* a continuing self, coupled with the inference that Hume would not quite make, that such possession must be represented by some kind of combination among the several representations which are ascribed to such a self. Thus the *locus classicus*:

> . . . the empirical consciousness, which accompanies different representations, is in itself diverse and without relation to the identity of the subject. That relation comes about, not simply through my accompanying each representation with consciousness, but only in so far as I *conjoin* one representation with another, and am conscious of the synthesis of them. Only in so far, therefore, as I can unite a manifold of given representations in *one consciousness*, is it possible for me to represent to myself the *identity of the consciousness in these representations*. [B133]

In other words, only if I recognize some relation among my representations *other* than that of possession by my continuing self, or at least recognize that I perform some operation on them giving them such a relation (A108), can I recognize my common possession of them.

But this argument, plausible as it seems, is not in fact sufficient to account for Kant's assurance that different representations can be recognized as belonging to an identical self only in virtue of some synthesis performed upon them. For as far as any *single* and *present* representation is concerned, Kant seems quite willing to allow that the mere *occurrence* of the representation is sufficient for a recognition of its *possession* by an existent self. Thus he is happy to accept that "the 'I think' is . . . an empirical proposition" and yet to affirm that it "contains within itself the proposition 'I exist' " (B422n., cf. B418), and this seems to imply that my mere recognition of the occurrence of any current thought, whatever its content, is sufficient to entail that I exist as possessor of it, even though there is no feature of the content of this thought which actually furnishes what Hume wanted, an impression of the self. But if this is so, it would also seem that the mere occurrence of a *present manifold* of thoughts must be sufficient to allow me to recognize that I exist as the identical possessor of all of them. Why then should not the mere occurrence of a manifold of thoughts be sufficient to allow me to recognize that they all belong to my identical self without my performing any synthesis according to any specific rules on these thoughts?

The answer to this question lies once again in the underlying assumption accompanying the temporal version of the premise of the argument from apperception, namely, that there *is no* manifold of representation insofar as we think of our representation as "contained in a single moment" and that a manifold can be thought of *as a manifold* only if a "sequence of one impression upon another" is represented. In first deploying this premise, Kant emphasizes that the unity of a momentary representation requires that there be at least several moments of apprehension for a manifold of representations to be available for cognitive connection. But what his statement that "intuition . . . does indeed offer a manifold, but a manifold which can never be represented as a manifold, and as contained in a *single representation*" without a synthesis (A99) also implies is that at *any given time* my *representation of a manifold of representation* is not itself a *manifold of representations* but a *single representation* which must be *interpreted* or *judged* to *represent* a manifold of representations. And we can only provide such an interpretation by the use of a rule which tells us that a present manifold with a certain kind of content can be understood only as the representation of a sequence of previous representations. For if we assume that there is no *a priori* constraint upon the internal complexity of any representation regarded simply as a presently occurrent mental state, it will follow that the mere content of a present representation cannot itself dictate that it be interpreted as a representation of several temporally diverse representations—what we need in order to interpret it as representing a manifold of representations at all. And this means that it is only if we synthesize the content of the representation according to rules requiring us to interpret it as representing the "sequence of one impression upon another" that we can interpret it as a manifold at all. Thus it is that while the occurrence of intuitions is in itself sufficient to provide the material for a manifold of intuition, it cannot actually provide a recognition of a manifold, and *a fortiori* knowledge of the possession of this by an identical self, except when its present state is interpreted by some rules sufficient to introduce into it an interpretation of temporal diversity.

This now shows us why a synthesis according to rules should be necessary to represent the identity of the self in its manifold of representations, for it is necessary to represent even the diversity as well as the connection of the manifold of representations itself. But we must now realize that this very explanation of (4) undermines the assumed certainty of (1), for as soon as we see that my representation of a manifold requires the *interpretation* of my present representational state as representing a temporal diversity of states, we also see that there is no reason why an error should not occur in this interpretation, or some feature of my present state be interpreted to represent a past representation which never occurred or which at least was not mine. If I think of the manifold of representations as somehow all before me at once, there seems to be no possibility of error, and thus *a priori* certainty, in determining that they are all mine, but also no need for rules of synthesis to determine that they belong to my identical self. But if I must apply some such rules in order to interpret features of my present state as representing members of a temporally extended manifold of states, then there is no reason why it should not be possible for me to err in this application. What might otherwise appear to be just the curious fallibility of memory claims is in fact an intrinsic feature of any representations of a manifold whatsoever. And though the possibility of such an error is no reason to say that I never have knowledge of my numerical identity with respect to a given manifold of representations, it is sufficient reason to deny that I can ever have *a priori* certainty of such numerical identity. Thus the very reason why we should accept Kant's premise (4) is a reason why we should not accept his fundamental premise (1), and his argument from the *a priori* certainty of apperception to the *a priori* validity of the categories must fail.[38]

IIB

The very fact, however, which undermines the *a priori* certainty of apperception—namely, that the representation of a manifold is a representation of a temporal diversity of states which requires an act of interpretation of my present representational state—suggests the possibility of an alternative argument, that even the empirical judgments involved in determining that an identical self has had a diversity of representations are possible only if certain rules for time determination are applied to the contents of such representations. Such an argument—tactic IIB—might be sufficient to establish at least the conditional necessity of such rules, that is, to show that these rules must be employed if certain judgments are to be made, even if the latter are not themselves necessary or certain *a priori*. For even if it is not necessary that we do so, it is surely possible for us to make empirical judgments about the diversity of representations of our identical selves; thus IIB would be a strong argument even with an empirical premise.

The argument of IIB would thus be that even the empirical judgment that I have remained a single self through a period of diverse representations presupposes that I can judge that I have had a *manifold* of representations, and that in turn requires the determination that a *temporal succession* of representations is represented by my present representational state—and *that* in turn requires the use of certain rules for determining the temporal significance of representations, which rules can be associated with the categories. I will now show that Kant recognized that these connections hold, though he never fully argued such a claim in either version of the Deduction itself. Instead, he left the actual work of developing such an argument from the premise of A99 to a never completely explicit conjunction of the Analogies of Experience with the Refutation of Idealism, and indeed to a version of the latter which he developed only *after* 1787.

Thus we actually find no more than intimations of tactic IIB, but we do find these in a wide range of sources. One such hint is found in a letter to Marcus Herz written in May, 1789. There, discussing the need for rules in thinking of objects as well as intuitions for perceiving them, Kant emphasizes with regard to the former that

> only under these conditions, therefore, can we have experience of objects; and consequently, if intuition (of objects of appearance) did not agree with these conditions, objects would be nothing for us, that is, not objects of *knowledge* at all; we should have knowledge neither of ourselves nor of other things.[39]

Then, as if to make it clearer that he does mean what the last clause of this sentence implies, namely, that rules for the knowledge of objects are conditions for even the most minimal form of self-knowledge, that awareness of a manifold of subjective states required even by an empirical judgment of self-identity, Kant shortly adds:

> . . . all *data* of the senses for a possible cognition would never, without those conditions, represent objects. They would not even reach that unity of consciousness that is necessary for knowledge of myself (as object of inner sense). I would not even be able to know that I have [such data]; consequently for me, as a knowing

being, they would be absolutely nothing. They could still (if I imagine myself to be an animal) carry on their play in an orderly fashion, as representations connected according to empirical laws of association, and thus even have an influence on my feeling and desire, without my being aware of them (assuming that I am even conscious of each individual representation, but not of their relation to the unity of representation of their object, by means of the synthetic unity of their apperception). This might be so without my knowing the slightest thing thereby, not even what my own condition is.[40]

Thus Kant distinguishes the conditions for the mere occurrence of a multiplicity of representations from the conditions for recognizing that one has such data and suggests that the latter recognition, as minimal and empirical a form of self-knowledge as it may seem to be, requires the synthesis of the understanding.

But we do not have to rely only on such a late document for evidence of Kant's awareness of the possibility of tactic II*B*. In fact, we find hints of such a maneuver as early as the *Duisburg Nachlass*. Thus, we find the Kant of the 1770s writing that "apperception is the consciousness of thinking, that is, of representations, as they are positioned [*gesetzt*] in the mind. There are three exponents [of this position]: 1. the relationship to the subject; 2. the relation of succession to one another; 3. the synthesis [*Zusammennehmung*]" (*R*4674, Ak. 17, p. 647). By using the explicitly temporal term "succession" in 2 above, Kant implies that apperception involves an awareness of the temporal succession of representations and thus that the conditions for determining such a succession are necessary conditions for the consciousness of apperception itself. Another passage makes it even clearer both that such a determination involves the application of a rule and that it is a necessary condition of regarding even subjective states as belonging to a single subject: "Now since everything must be given in time, which therefore includes everything in itself, the [use of a rule] is an *actus* of apperception, namely the consciousness of the subject which apperceives [itself] as that which is given in the whole time, [and] is necessarily connected with [the use of a rule], for otherwise the sensation would not be represented as belonging to me" (*R*4674, Ak. 17, p. 656). Several points are crowded together here, but it seems to be Kant's view that both ascribing any particular sensation to a particular moment in even the subjective experience of the subject and representing the continuity of that experience— representing the subject as "that which is given in the whole time"

—require the use of certain rules. Finally, there are several passages which both link "apperception" with "self–perception" (*Selbstwahrnehmung*) and define "perception" as involving temporal position, thus implying that the "relations of apperception" which are to be determined by synthesis according to categories are precisely the determinate relations of subjective states in time: "Perception is position in inner sense in general and resolves into sensation according to relations of apperception of self-consciousness, according to which we become conscious of our own existence" (*R4677*, Ak. 17, pp. 658–59). The prose is dense but implies that the kind of consciousness of our own existence with which Kant is concerned is consciousness of the existence of our different states in time.

Remarks implying tactic II*B* also appear in sections 24 and 25 of the B Deduction. In section 25, Kant emphasizes that intuition as well as mere thought is required for self-knowledge:

> Now in order to *know* ourselves, there is required in addition to the act of thought, which brings the manifold of every possible intuition to the unity of apperception, a determinate mode of intuition, whereby this manifold is given; it therefore follows that . . . the determination of my existence can take place only in conformity with the form of inner sense, according to the special mode in which the manifold which I combine, is given in inner intuition. [B157–58]

But section 24 has just argued that, while intuition is a necessary condition of knowledge, its mere occurrence is not a sufficient condition thereof, precisely because intuition can only be made *determinate* in judgment:

> Inner sense . . . contains the mere form of intuition, but without combination of the manifold in it, and therefore so far contains no *determinate* intuition, which is possible only through the consciousness of the determination of the manifold by the transcendental act of imagination (synthetic influence of the understanding upon inner sense). [B154]

To make the intuition of time determinate, which is required to bring its manifold to the unity of apperception, judgment according to certain rules is required. For, Kant next asserts,

> . . . we cannot obtain for ourselves a representation of time, except under the image of a line, which we draw, and . . . by this mode of depicting it alone could we know the singleness of its dimension;

and similarly . . . for all inner perceptions we must derive the determination of lengths of time or of points of time from the changes which are exhibited to us in outer sense. . . . The determinations of inner sense have therefore to be arranged as appearances in time in precisely the same manner in which we arrange those of outer sense in space. [B156]

Thus Kant holds that in order to make determinate judgments about the temporal succession of subjective states at all, which is presupposed by even empirical knowledge that my continuing self actually has a manifold of representations, I must link those representations in some way to objects in space which are capable of both continued existence and yet determinate changes; only thus can I determine that my present state actually represents a "sequence of one impression upon another." Yet to make such connections requires precisely that we make judgments about the continued existence of objects regarded as distinct from mere modifications of inner sense and judge the changes of such objects. What can this be but to apply the concepts of inherence and subsistence to things regarded as objects in a strong sense and to apply to such objects the further dynamic categories of causality and dependence and perhaps even reciprocity of action? Thus making the temporal judgments presupposed by any self-knowledge requires the use of the categories, and it is at least necessary that *if* one makes the former then one must use the latter.

Yet although sections 24 and 25 of the B Deduction assert these connections, they hardly argue them; indeed, Kant seems to mention these connections only to prove that the temporal knowledge of subjective states, since it depends on knowledge of objects in space, must be, like the latter, knowledge of mere appearances rather than of things in themselves. And Kant is not as willing to suggest that apperception is actually equivalent to the "self-perception" of temporally successive states as he was in the *Duisburg Nachlass*; the opening line of section 25 still seems to insist that even the mere knowledge "that I am" already involves the "original synthetic unity of apperception" (B157) and its *a priori* rules, implying that the determinate self-knowledge discussed in section 24 must not be identical to transcendental apperception but only an addition to it. I think that both of these problems have the same source, however: that Kant was in fact persuaded by the argument from apperception that we have examined under II*A* and thus thought that an analysis of the conditions of merely empirical self-knowledge, though that of course involves the categories, and can thus furnish an additional proof of them, required basically only the application of a point already proved.

This also explains why Kant's discussion of the conditions of time determination in the Analogies of Experience, and even his argument in the Refutation of Idealism that any determination of the temporal relation of subjective states presupposes these objective time determinations, take the guise of the "schematism" or application of the results of the Transcendental Deduction instead of being presented as an independent argument free of the prior assumption of a priori knowledge. Nevertheless, in the several years after publishing the second edition of the Critique—the period in which he wrote the letter to Herz quoted above—Kant did in fact attempt to construct self-sufficient arguments demonstrating that even the representation of a merely subjective manifold as temporally successive requires the categorical concepts of substance and causation and thus did in fact attempt to execute IIB. Obviously, however, my discussion of those efforts must await another occasion.[41]

Since Kant's tactics IA, IB, and IIA failed, and since IIB cannot be fully discussed here, I cannot conclude this article with an assessment of the ultimate success of Kant's strategy for the transcendental deduction. One point, however, can be made now. Basically we have seen that Kant's strategy for deriving the necessity of a priori categories from the conditions presupposed by any empirical knowledge at all can be implemented only if we recognize that the synthesis which produces such knowledge presupposes a manifold, but that this manifold must be a temporally diverse one; yet as we are never actually in possession of such a manifold at any one moment, we can represent it only by interpreting our present representation as a representation of temporally diverse representations according to certain rules. Since reference to such a manifold is also presupposed by any informative reference to an identical self, the use of such rules is also a necessary condition of any judgment of the identity of the self. A moment's reflection, however, must persuade us that it cannot be synthesis according to such rules which first generates any consciousness of time at all or the condition in which it merely seems to us that we are aware of a succession of different representational states. For not only does the metaphysical conception of an understanding which does not itself act in time but which generates temporal order out of a diversity which is itself both atemporal and also preconscious verge on unintelligibility, or at least require the refuge of

194

transcendental idealism (B155–56), but, more important, the causal laws about the behavior of objects by which we actually make the temporal interpretation of our own experience according to B156 are themselves laws which must be inductively confirmed in time, and so cannot be first used to generate any consciousness of time at all. It is, however, perfectly intelligible to suppose that causal *beliefs*, like the *beliefs* about our own states which they can and must be used to confirm, can be transformed into knowledge *within* time; and so if we interpret Kant's theory not as a theory of the psychological genesis of temporal consciousness but as an epistemological theory of the confirmation of temporal knowledge, it is at least intelligible.

Thus, to borrow terms from the *Duisburg Nachlass*, the "principles of thought" which Kant's argument produces cannot be "foundations" (*Grundsätze*) of consciousness itself but can only be "restrictions" (*restrictionen*) on those cases of consciousness that are to count as cognitive judgments (cf. *R4678*, Ak. 17, p. 661). This means, of course, that Kant's theory cannot require us to postulate psychological processes which in every case of consciousness at all must employ or instantiate the rules we need for the synthesis of determinate temporal relations. But this presents no real objection to my interpretation of Kant's only plausible tactic, precisely because Kant's only argument for the view that there are transcendental syntheses which are actually "exercised" (*ausgeübt*: A99) *a priori* requires his assumption that apperception is *a priori*. Without that assumption we have no need to postulate transcendental syntheses taking place whether we know it or not, or before we know anything at all, but must claim only that when empirical judgments of apperception can in fact be justified certain rules must be employed.[42] On IIB, however, since we neither have an *a priori* guarantee for our judgments of self-knowledge nor need one in order to undertake empirical synthesis, the categories need not be supposed to be implemented in any act of synthesis except empirical synthesis itself. Kant's psychology and epistemology can at last be separated—but only when we reject the *a priori* certainty of apperception.[43]

NOTES

1. References to the *Critique of Pure Reason* will be given by the pagination of the first (A) and second (B) editions; I have generally followed the translation by Norman Kemp-Smith but have occasionally modified it. References to other Kantian works and materials are given by volume and page in the Berlin *Akademie* edition (cited as Ak.); the numbers of the individual Reflections in Kant's *Nachlass* are prefixed with an R. The translations of these are my own. I capitalize the word "Deduction" when I

mean to refer to the specific portion of the *Critique* to which that term usually refers; where I use the lower case I refer to Kant's argument itself.

2. My use of the metaphor of "strategy" and "tactics" obviously owes something to Lewis White Beck, "Kant's Strategy," now in his collection *Essays on Kant and Hume* (New Haven, 1978), pp. 3–19.

3. The suggestion that Kant offers four different kinds of argument in pursuit of his strategy for the deduction may well remind the reader of the interpretation of Robert Paul Wolff, in *Kant's Theory of Mental Activity* (Cambridge, Mass., 1963), pp. 116–62. It should be obvious, however, that my division has little to do with his. It owes far more to Dieter Henrich, *Identität und Objektivität* (Heidelberg, 1976), though the point of section II*A* below will be to reject a major premise of Henrich's reconstruction of Kant's argument.

4. Graham Bird, *Kant's Theory of Knowledge* (London, 1962); P. F. Strawson, *The Bounds of Sense* (London, 1966).

5. Norman Kemp-Smith, *A Commentary to Kant's Critique of Pure Reason*, 2d ed. (London, 1923); Henrich, *Identität und Objektivität*.

6. "Did the Sage of Königsberg Have No Dreams?" in Beck, *Essays on Kant and Hume*, p. 40.

7. On this passage, however, see note 38 below.

8. See *Metaphysical Foundations of Natural Science*, Ak. 4, p. 475n.

9. A comment on Karl Ameriks's "Kant's Transcendental Deduction as a Regressive Argument" (*Kant-Studien* 69 [1978]: 273–87) is in order here. Ameriks's view is that Kant's argument is not intended as a "proof of objectivity which will answer skepticism" from the mere concession of self-consciousness at all, but only as an answer to empiricism, by means of a regress "from the assumption that there is empirical knowledge to a proof of the precondition of that knowledge" (p. 273). This interpretation, however, depends upon taking section 18 in B's identification of transcendental with objective apperception as conclusive (p. 283) when, as I have already shown, that represents only one sense of an ambiguous term and one which is indeed reached in that context by a fallacious argument (see note 38 below). Thus Ameriks provides no reason for rejecting what he calls the "received interpretation" (that the deduction aims "to *establish* objectivity . . . from the minimal premise that one is self-conscious" (pp. 276–77)) as an interpretation of at least one of the two main ways in which Kant tries to execute the strategy of the deduction. I am, however, happy to accept his characterization of the deduction in *any* of its forms as "regressive," where a "regressive argument would show y is a necessary condition of knowledge x," where x is already assumed (pp. 282–83), for I will not argue that there is any characteristic difference in logical structure among Kant's arguments (fallacies in execution aside), but only some crucial differences in the content and strength of the premises assumed as "knowledge x."

10. In an interesting though misleadingly titled article called "Two Kinds of Transcendental Arguments in Kant" (*Kant-Studien* 67 [1976]: 1–19), Richard E. Aquila argues that the informativeness of Kant's transcendental deductions lies in the fact that they combine two different kinds of *premises* (not two different kinds of arguments at all), those which are transcendental with respect to *knowledge*, "necessary truths about the conditions for some object's being *known*," and those which are transcendental with respect to empirical *existence*, or "necessary conditions for something's existing in a 'phenomenalistically reduced' sense" (p. 3); it is from the ontological fact that empirical objects have been reduced to appearances, Aquila argues, that the further fact that the independent requirements of knowledge can be

196

satisfied only if categorical rules are applied to objects follows. Aquila is correct in seeing that the need for rules in order to cope with the separateness of representations is the key to Kant's argument but wrong in thinking that this must be a consequence of Kant's alleged phenomenalism. In fact, the deduction needs to assume only what may be called the atomism of Kant's theory of perception—that *representations* are given individually and must be connected by us—and not that empirical objects are nothing but representations. Of course, thinking that he has already proved his transcendental idealism in the Transcendental Aesthetic, Kant does sometimes *expound* the deduction as though the need for an act of combination followed from the distinction between appearances and things in themselves (e.g., A108–109), but passages like B129–30 make it clear that the need for combination is independent of that distinction, and other passages (e.g., A125ff., B164) make it clear that Kant wants transcendental idealism to be a *consequence* of the deduction as well as the Aesthetic, in which case it should be possible to state the deduction without presupposing it.

11. This is the argument suggested by section 26 of the B Deduction; cf. Dieter Henrich, "The Proof-Structure of Kant's Transcendental Deduction," *Review of Metaphysics* 22 [June, 1969]:640–59.

12. Ak. 4, p. 475n. From the translation by James Ellington (Indianapolis, 1970), p. 13.

13. It should be noted that the reference to the self in this passage functions only to explain the *separation* and not the *unification* of representations; this is some evidence for my division of Kant's arguments into those (II) in which the unity of apperception plays a role and those (I) in which it does not.

14. For the expression of this distinction as that between "logical" and "subjective" unity, see the *Critique of Judgment*, sec. 8.

15. The problem of whether judgments of perception are judgments at all obviously arises from conjoining the assumption that they are subjectively valid only with the definition of judgment as necessarily objectively valid. Subtle attempts have been made to solve this problem (notably by Gerold Prauss in *Erscheinung bei Kant* [Berlin, 1971]), but attempting to solve it is wasted effort if it can be shown that the argument for the necessity and universality of judgment both cannot be a persuasive version of Kant's deduction and need not be employed for its execution.

16. For further discussion of these passages, see note 38 below.

17. This is to ascribe to Kant a stronger conception of what an object is than Henrich does (*Identität und Objektivität*), e.g., pp. 43–47.

18. Such an understanding of the concept of an object would appear to be all that is required by the discussion of an object in *R*6350 (Ak. 18, p. 676), which is the basis of Henrich's account (*Identität und Objectivität*, p. 44).

19. Indeed, by an argument that may well have been intended to prepare the way for acceptance of the definition offered at A104.

20. Thus I am accusing Kant of committing the modal fallacy of confusing the necessity of a conditional with the necessity of its antecedent and of thus illicitly inferring the necessity of its consequent. The reader may find it hard to see Kant as capable of such an error, but it should be noted that Kant commits precisely the same kind of error when he argues that Descartes's *sum* cannot be the product of an inference from *cogito* through the premise " 'Everything which thinks, exists'; for then the property of thought would render all things which possess it necessary beings" (B422n.). But of course this premise does not have this consequence; it would have it only if, in addition to its being (1) necessary that if something thinks it exists, it

were also (2) necessary that the thing thinks, which is not implied by (1). Thus here too Kant is insensitive to the difference between the necessity of a conditional and the necessity of its antecedent. (In *Synthese* 47 [1981]:385–448) "Apperception and section 16 of the 1787 Transcendental Deduction," which is otherwise very careful, Robert Howell makes the rather casual assumption that Kant is content to show the categories to be necessary just in the "necessity-of-the-conditional sense," thus missing precisely this kind of difficulty.)

21. Such an argument is found in R5216, Ak. 18, p. 121 (from 1773–75). Criticism of such a line of thought, though without reference to this or any similar passage, is offered by Henrich in *Identität und Objektivität*, pp. 63–64.

22. E.g., Jonathan Bennett, *Kant's Analytic* (Cambridge, 1966), pp. 76–79.

23. The problem about the necessity of using all the functions of judgment is not, of course, original with me; and Arthur Melnick, for example, has raised the problem about the necessity of introducing any of the relational functions other than categorical judgment (*Kant's Analogies of Experience* (Chicago, 1973), pp. 52–53). He does not suggest, however, that the problem arises precisely because of the difference between atomic judgments linking nonjudgmental representations and higher-order judgments linking other judgments.

24. See Henrich, *Identität und Objektivität*, pp. 12–13.

25. R4674–84, Ak. 17, pp. 643–71.

26. See Henrich, *Identität und Objektivität*, pp. 55–57.

27. Ibid., p. 86.

28. To draw this conclusion is not to invade fallaciously an intensional context, that is, simply to assume that because in a given case some generic concept *F* is instantiated by some specific property *G* it must also be *known* that this is so, for since the only kind of argument Kant is concerned with is an argument from the existence of some knowledge, what is relevant to him is how it can be *known* that *F* is instantiated—and that is precisely by knowing that *G* is.

29. Cf. Henrich, *Identität und Objektivität*, e.g., pp. 86ff.

30. I here depart from Kemp-Smith, reading the original *einigen* instead of Vorländer's *einzigen*.

31. *An Essay Concerning Human Understanding*, bk. 1, chap. 2, sec. 5.

32. For a more elaborate discussion of this point, see my "Kant on Apperception and *A Priori* Synthesis," *American Philosophical Quarterly* 17 (July, 1980): 205–12.

33. This argument was overlooked in the article cited in note 32, which essentially criticized Kant on points (*a*) and (*b*).

34. Cf. B130, sec. 15. Note, however, that Kant's claim here that representation of the mere unity of the manifold as such precedes the use of the specific categories as "concepts of combination" actually undercuts his argument (as at A119) that those same categories are the necessary conditions of transcendental apperception itself.

35. It seems to be what Kemp-Smith thought was Kant's argument, as well; see his *Commentary*, p. 284.

36. In the article mentioned in note 20, Robert Howell argues that the main problem with Kant's deduction is its confusion of knowledge of the *de dicto* necessity that there is some single subject for all my representations with that of the *de re* necessity that *I* am in fact the entity that has such a feature, the former being acceptably *a priori* but the latter not. Surely, however, it is permissible for Kant to assume that I know the Cartesian (and *de re*) necessity that *I* am the subject of my present thought (cf. B418, p. 422n.), from which it does follow that I also know with equal necessity that *I* am the subject of whatever other thoughts I know to be

connected with that thought as thoughts of the same subject. The real problem with Kant's argument is precisely that this is true even if my knowledge that I have a multiplicity of connected thoughts is thoroughly empirical and that Kant has no ground for his assumption that I have *a priori knowledge* of both the diversity of my representations and my possession of them before I perform any empirical syntheses upon them.

37. Henrich too seems to find something problematic in this kind of argument but does not seem to realize that it is the only possible support for a synthetic interpretation of the "Cartesian certainty" which he thinks both must and can be employed in any successful reconstruction of Kant's deduction; cf. *Identität und Objektivität*, pp. 70–71.

38. At this point I want to observe that, while the unsoundness of this argument, which is the argument of sec. 16 in B, moots the validity of Kant's argument in section 17 to 20 insofar as it is meant to depend on sec. 16, there is another grave problem with Kant's argument in those sections. In sec. 17, Kant asserts that "an *object* is that in the concept of which the manifold of a given intuition is *united*" and then infers from this that, since "it is the unity of consciousness that alone constitutes the relation of representations to an object," knowledge of objects must be subject to whatever conditions constrain the unity of consciousness itself. The problem is that, while *this* inference is valid, it does not in fact entail the necessity of a strong conception of an object as in any way distinct from a unity of subjective states; but it is precisely such a conception which Kant assumes by sec. 19, where he *contrasts* objective and subjective validity of consciousness, implying that the former is required by the unity of apperception itself. The only explanation of the latter assumption, then, is that Kant has confused the thesis that the rules for objects depend on the rules for apperception—the proper interpretation of sec. 17—with the distinct claim that apperception itself depends upon knowledge of objects in a restrictive or strong sense (what is in fact asserted by sec. 18).

39. Letter 340, May 26, 1789; Ak. 11, p. 51 (translation from Arnulf Zweig, *Kant: Philosophical Correspondence 1759–1799* [Chicago, 1967], p. 152).

40. Ak. 11, p. 52, from Zweig, pp. 153–54. I have altered Zweig's translation somewhat, chiefly by replacing his potentially misleading "sense data" with a more literal rendition of Kant's phrase *data der Sinne* (*sic*).

41. The key document here is R6313 (Ak. 18, pp. 613–15), but also important are R5453–54, 6311–12, 6314–17.

42. Thus Kemp-Smith's apparent satisfaction with the conclusion that Kant's mature "phenomenalism," unlike his allegedly immature "subjectivism," requires that "mental processes, in so far as they are generative of experience, must fall outside the field of consciousness" (*Commentary*, p. 273) is possible only because he fails to see the problem in Kant's assumption that the principle of apperception is both synthetic and yet certain *a priori*.

43. Research for this article was begun during my tenure of a National Endowment for the Humanities Fellowship for Independent Study and Research in 1978–79, and I would like to acknowledge that support here. I would also like to thank all those, both colleagues and students, on whom I have tried out various of the arguments of this paper, especially Patricia Kitcher and Robert Howell, who allowed me prepublication access to some of their own work on the topic of this paper, and Carl Posy and Manley Thompson, for several particularly useful conversations.

Kant's Theory of Mathematics Revisited

JAAKKO HINTIKKA

In a number of earlier publications I have outlined an interpretation of Kant's theories of the mathematical method, space and time, and the analytic-synthetic distinction (at least insofar as this distinction applies within mathematics).[1] I have also tried to show how these views of Kant's entered into the structure of his philosophical thought. Since Kant held that the gist of the mathematical method lies in the use of constructions, i.e., in the use of intuitions to represent general concepts, I have also presented an analysis of the meaning of the term "intuition" (or, strictly speaking, of its counterparts *intuitus* and *Anschauung*) in Kant. This interpretation has prompted a few relatively detailed criticisms.[2] One of the purposes of this article is to return to my interpretation in the light of the criticisms. Naturally, one focal point of my paper will be a discussion of the main texts on which my critics base their allegations. Even more important is the view we have to take of the historical background of Kant's theory.

I cannot here recount adequately my interpretation but must be content with a summary.[3] The interpretational basis of my theory is, in a nutshell, as follows: By intuition (*Anschauung*), Kant meant a representative (*"Vorstellung"*) of a particular entity in the human mind. By *construction*, Kant meant the introduction of such a particular to instantiate a general concept. The gist of the mathematical method *apud* Kant was the use of such constructions (a modern logician would say "the use of rules of instantiation"). A mathematical argument is synthetic if it involves the use of "auxiliary constructions," i.e., the introduction of new particulars over and above those given in the conditions of the argument (sometimes given in the premises and sometimes given in the premises *or* in the purported conclusion). A mathematical truth is synthetic if it can be established only by such synthetic arguments.

Among the consequences of the interpretation are the following:

1. There is nothing "intuitive" in the basic force of the concept of intuition in Kant. Insofar as there is a reference to imagination or sensation contained in Kant's concept, it is supposed to be an

outcome of his arguments, not a *presupposition* of those arguments.

2. The immediacy of intuitions in relation to their objects is merely a corollary to their particularity.

3. This immediacy of intuitions has no bearing on their value as helping to establish any a priori truths, let alone on their alleged status as a source of such truths.

4. The use of constructions and intuitions in a mathematical, e.g., geometrical, argument does not mean appeal to what in our contemporary usage would be called mathematical (geometrical) "intuition." It merely means using particular representatives of general concepts, i.e., instantiation rules, in a mathematical argument.

5. What Kant says of mathematics pertains more to contemporary first-order logic, whose mainstays are precisely instantiation rules, than to what we twentieth-century philosophers would classify as specifically mathematical modes of reasoning.

6. What makes mathematical truths synthetic is brought out by the mode of argument used in establishing them.

7. More specifically, the intuitive (constructive, synthetical) steps of a mathematical argument are, according to Kant, firmly within the axiomatic and deductive proofs, not in collateral appeals to intuition (in our present-day sense) or in the nature of the axioms of a mathematical theory.

In spite of strong textual support for my interpretation, mistakes abound in the literature. For instance, the two latest major German encyclopedic dictionaries of philosophy botch up their respective articles on *Anschauung* as far as Kant is concerned.[4] Perhaps more important, several scholars are still reluctant to adopt my interpretation, as illustrated by the specific criticisms they have prompted. I will not try to present a detailed answer to all the criticisms. It seems to me more constructive to discuss further the direct problems of Kantian interpretation. In this respect I have found extant discussions of my views keenly disappointing, not to say frustrating. The discussions have centered on the interpretation of particular passages. Next to no attention has been paid to the overall picture of Kant's thinking about mathematics in its historical setting or to my view of the role of Kant's theory of space, time, and mathematics (including the whole of his transcendental aesthetics) within the structure of his philosophical system. It seems to me that this exemplifies a much more widespread fault with philosophers' discussions of historical matters. Whether a philosopher likes it or not, the way he interprets a major character in the history of philosophy depends crucially on the view he takes of that philosopher's historical position and problem situation. If these questions are not raised explicitly, the philosopher in question is in effect relying on unexamined and usually uncritically adopted received views, not to say prejudices. Yet all too frequently these questions are not even raised, and all of the discussion centers on the interpretation of particular passages taken out of context. If specific examples are needed, it seems to me that there is no hope whatever of understanding Aristotle's discussion of future contingents without first understanding his general assumptions concerning time, necessity, truth, and chance.[5]

Likewise, it may be interesting and important to compare Kant's philosophy of mathematics with such contemporary problems as intuitionism or formalism, but only if one realizes at the same time that such problems simply were not within his intellectual horizon. What paradigms of mathematical practice did Kant know? There is one overwhelming answer. If we look at what Kant read as a student and as a mature philosopher, what he thought, and what he dabbled in *qua* mathematical amateur, the answer is crystal clear. Kant's view on what mathematicians "really" do is modeled on Euclid's *Elements* and its eighteenth-century variants (one probable reason for the neglect of the role of Euclid in providing the paradigm of mathematics for Kant is philosophers' ignorance of the extent to which Euclid's *Elements* dominated elementary and secondary mathematics education in Kant's time).[6] Kant's only extensive attempts to do something on his own in mathematics were vain efforts to prove Euclid's fifth postulate.

Now Euclid's procedure offers an obvious and clear model of Kant's views on the mathematical method and on the concepts of intuition and construction. All the different features of Kant's philosophy of mathematics mentioned above as a part of my interpretation are strongly and immediately suggested by Euclid's procedure.[7] Hence my interpretation, unlike its rivals, is defensible by reference to the letter of Kantian texts. Moreover, when viewed in the right perspective, it turns out that my interpretation ascribes to Kant the most natural view of mathematics that anyone in Kant's historical situation (and with Kant's limitations) could possibly have adopted. However one is inclined to read individual passages in Kant's texts, in the last analysis they have to be judged against the whole of his historical situation. This is what my interpretation is calculated to do. I have not seen any similar attempt made on behalf of its competitors.

How is it that Euclid actually proceeds in presenting and establishing a proposition? He first presents a general proposition. To use Kant's favorite example as our illustration, he formulates proposition 32 of book 1 by saying that "in any triangle . . . the three interior angles of the triangle are equal to two right angles."

Euclid, however, never does anything directly on the basis of this general enunciation or *protasis*. He always goes on to apply (as we are tempted to say) the enunciation to a special case (some particular figure). In our example, he says: "Let *ABC* be a triangle. . . . I say that the three interior angles *ABC*, *BCA*, and *CAB* are equal to two right angles." This part of a Euclidean proposition was called the *ekthesis*. The same term was used by Aristotle in his logical work for what in modern terms is to all practical purposes instantiation. The received English terms for this part of an Euclidean proposition are *exposition* and *setting-out*.

If we look away from the sometime part of an Euclidean proposition called *diorismos*, we can say that *ekthesis* is followed by the *auxiliary construction* or *preparation*. In it some new geometrical objects are introduced into the argument. In proposition 32 this part reads, "For let *CE* be drawn through the point *C* parallel to the straight line *AB*." Such introductions of new geometrical objects are justified by the postulates of Euclid's system or by solutions to earlier problems, in our sample case by proposition 31 of book 1.

The auxiliary construction is followed by the proof (proof proper), the *apodeixis*. This is the only part in which an actual demonstrative argument is carried out. Its several steps are based on the assumptions Euclid calls *Common Notions*, theorems proved earlier, plus the properties ascribed to the geometrical objects in question on the basis of their "construction," i.e., on the basis of what general properties they were introduced to instantiate in the *ekthesis* and in the auxiliary construction. This is illustrated by proposition 32. In its *apodeixis* part, Euclid appeals to earlier theorems, to common notions, and to the general characteristics the different parts of the relevant diagram were introduced to instantiate ("Again, since *AB* is parallel to *CE* . . . ").

Here we can see what Kant's ideas of the mathematical method are modeled on and what they amount to. When he says that mathematics is based on the use of intuitions, after having defined intuitions as particular *Vorstellungen*, what he has in mind is Euclid's use of what looks like particular cases. Another variant of this

Kantian jargon is to say that the mathematical method is based on the use of *constructions*, which are defined by him as introductions of particular entities to instantiate general concepts. The role they play in Euclid's system of geometry is essentially that of the instantiating free symbols used in modern logic, especially in the so-called natural-deduction methods, notwithstanding the frequently repeated myth that Euclid needed them in order to appeal tacitly to geometrical "intuition" (in the twentieth-century sense of the term). Admittedly, Euclid occasionally takes steps in his arguments which can only be explained as being based on geometrical "intuition." In so doing, however, he was probably violating his own principles, and he was beyond any doubt violating Kant's principles. As he formulates them, if a geometer "is to know anything with a priori certainty he must not ascribe to the figure anything save what necessarily follows from what he has himself set into it in accordance with his concept" (*B*xiii). Can you rule out appeals to geometrical "intuition" more explicitly?

Why, then, does Kant think that the use of constructions (instantiations) is useful (indeed, indispensable) in mathematics? The reason is that he realized, without being at all clear about the logical basis of the phenomenon, that *certain arguments simply cannot be carried out without the use of auxiliary constructions*. This is the datum on which Kant bases his theories of mathematics, space, and time. In spite of the fact that Kant makes the point forcefully and unmistakably, especially in A712–27/B741—55, this fundamental feature of his overall argument has been completely missed by the philosophers who have recently discussed Kant's philosophy of mathematics. It was noted by C. S. Peirce and made the basis of one of the central tenets in the philosophy of logic, but Peirce's insight too was completely overlooked until I called attention to it.[8]

This observation has several important consequences. For one thing it means that the nontrivial (synthetic) element in geometrical reasoning lies in the auxiliary constructions. Accordingly, it is in those constructions that Kant locates the synthetic element in mathematical (for us, logical) reasoning. In contrast, the "common notions" on which *apodeixis* ultimately rests were taken by Kant to be analytic. As he puts it, "Some few fundamental propositions presupposed by the geometrician are, indeed, analytic, and rest on the principle of contradiction. But, as identical propositions, they serve only as links in the chain of method, and not as principles, for instance, $a = a$; the whole is equal to itself; or $(a + b) > a$, that is, the whole is greater than its part" (B16–17). The last of these examples is precisely Euclid's fifth Common Notion. Further evidence is found in A164/B204.

For another thing, we can now see that the *explanandum* of Kant's transcendental aesthetics contains no reference to any specially intimate relation between an intuition and its object. Nor is there any trace here of the idea that the reason an intuition in the Kantian sense can give us new information is its especially close relation to what it stands for (*vorstellt*). There was in Kant's background a very strong assumption that the intuitivity of a *Vorstellung* meant an immediacy in its representational role. Kant, we can now see, reinterpreted this immediacy so that it amounted completely to individuality (particularity). It is simply and solely the role of Kant's so-called intuitions *as instantiating terms* (and hence as particulars corresponding to a concept) that helps us gain information by their means in mathematical proofs.

But, it may be objected, surely the Euclidean paradigm covers only geometry, not arithmetic or algebra. Furthermore, limited though Kant's mathematical knowledge may have been, he could not have been oblivious of such developments as Descartes's "analytical" geometry.

In reality, Descartes's geometry offers crucial further evidence for my interpretation. If we note what Descartes emphasizes in his own new geometry, we see that it supplies to Kant the missing ingredient which enabled him to extend concepts based on the Euclidean model to other branches of mathematics. In Descartes's mind and in his readers' first impressions, the great novelty of his treatment of geometry was not the use of coordinates. They slip into his book only as helpmeets in dealing with specific problems. As is shown by the very first sentences of La Geometrie, Descartes sees the essence of his mathematical method in a systematic and comprehensive *analogy between geometrical constructions and algebraic operations.*[9] It was precisely by means of this analogy that Kant was able to think of the concepts he had first formulated by reference to geometrical constructions as being applicable to all mathematics. Indeed, it is in Kant's references to simple arithmetical equations like $7 + 5 = 12$, that his adherence to the Euclidean model becomes most conspicuously clear. He calls them "indemonstrable" and "immediately certain" (A163–64/B204–205). Yet he describes a process by means of which these equations are ascertained (B15–16) and even says that their syntheticity is seen more clearly if we take greater numbers.

It is nearly incredible that most interpreters of Kant still apparently maintain in the teeth of such passages that according to Kant the synthetic nature of mathematical reasoning is due to appeals to "intuition." Clearly it is not. But to what, then, is it due? What does Kant mean by calling $7 + 5 = 12$ "indemonstrable"? The Cartesian analogy supplies a ready answer. Such equations are "indemonstrable" in the literal sense that no counterpart to the Euclidean demonstration or *apodeixis* is needed, Kant thinks, in establishing them. It suffices to carry out *ekthesis* and the auxiliary construction, which for Kant means the addition of one number to the other unit by unit (cf. B15–16). And, of course, it is the use of auxiliary construction that makes an argument synthetic according to Kant, and, of course, the need of actually carrying out the addition is seen more keenly in larger numbers. As I have pointed out earlier, Kant to all practical purposes affirms this way of looking at what he is saying in his letter of November 25, 1788, to Johann Schultz. The reason he calls such equations as $7 + 5 = 12$ "immediately certain practical judgments" is that they need no "resolution" and no "proof," these being the current labels for standard parts of geometrical arguments. "Resolution" was in fact another name of the *diorismos* part (of problems rather than theorems) which was mentioned but not described above.

The evidence which I have briefly (and partly) surveyed shows convincingly that it was the use of auxiliary constructions (plus, possibly, of *ekthesis*—Kant is not clear on this subsidiary point) that makes many mathematical (for us, logical) arguments synthetic and that contains the gist of the mathematical method. It would be extremely interesting to see how Kant uses this idea in the rest of philosophy. This task is too large to be undertaken here, however.

Instead, let me simply sharpen the problem an interpreter is facing here. What we have found is (as was mentioned above) that the synthetic element in mathematical reasoning is squarely within the framework of the Euclidean axiomatic and deductive treatment of geometry (and mathematics more generally). It lies in the use of procedures which are closely related to the instantiation rules of modern logic. *This* is the *datum* which Kant's Transcendental Aesthetics is calculated to explain, not the alleged use of spatial and temporal imagination in mathematical arguments. Whoever does not appreciate this fact has not understood what Kant's Transcendental Aesthetics is all about.

Here I shall not analyze the ways in which Kant sought to account for this remarkable feature of the mathematical practice of his time and the logical practice of our days. Perhaps it is historically understandable that his thought took the turn it did even when this purely axiomatic character of Kantian use of intuitions is realized. After all, Alexander the Commentator had explained the use of instantiation or *ekthesis* in Aristotelian logic in a way distinctly reminiscent of the Transcendental Aesthetics. Such an *ekthesis* is according to Alexander comparable to an appeal to sense perception. Be this as it may, however, here I will merely try to clear the underbrush further and eliminate one more objection to locating the synthetic element in mathematical reasoning in *ekthesis* and in auxiliary constructions, i.e., in certain parts of mathematical *arguments*. As has been pointed out repeatedly by Ernst Cassirer, among others, and recently by Gordon Brittan,[10] there is a passage in Kant which prima facie suggests a different view, a view which these two scholars have in fact adopted. According to this view, what makes mathematical truths synthetic is not any feature of mathematical *arguments* but the nature of mathematical *axioms*. To defend my own interpretation, I must therefore discuss this passage. It runs as follows:

> *All mathematical judgments, without exception, are synthetic.* This fact . . . has hitherto escaped the notice of those who are engaged in the analysis of human reasons, and is, indeed, directly opposed to their conjectures. For as it was found that all mathematical inferences (*Schlüsse*) proceed in accordance with the principle of contradiction (which the nature of all apodeictic certainty requires), it was supposed that the fundamental propositions of the science can themselves be known to be true through that principle. This is an erroneous view. For though a synthetic proposition can indeed be discerned in accordance with the principle of contradiction, this can only be if another synthetic proposition is presupposed, and if it can then be apprehended as following from this other proposition; it can never be so discerned in and by itself. [B14]

The first thing to be noted about this passage is that Kant is *not* saying that mathematical truths *always* get their syntheticity from the syntheticity of earlier theorems (and ultimately from axioms or postulates) from which they can *always* be deduced analytically. All he is saying is that this *can* happen and that the only way in which a synthetic proposition can thus be deduced analytically is from another synthetic proposition. This possibility is emphasized by Kant as one of the reasons for his opponents' mistakes rather than as an ingredient of his own constructive theory. Moreover, Kant could not conceivably be saying in the quoted passage that the syntheticity of synthetic mathematical truths can in all parts of mathematics be traced to the syntheticity of its axioms, for the simple reason, that according to Kant, arithmetic has no axioms (A163–65/B204–205), only "fundamental propositions" which are established one by one without being reducible to any general axioms. From this it follows that not all the "fundamental propositions" (*Grundsätze*) Kant mentions in the quoted passage are axioms. This is confirmed in B16, where Kant says, after having discussed simple arithmetical equations like $7 + 5 = 12$, "just as little is any *fundamental proposition* [my italics] of pure geometry analytic." And, as we all know, Kant goes through a whole song and dance to spell out how it is that our way of establishing equations like $7 + 5 = 12$ makes these propositions of arithmetic synthetic.

Moreover, Kant's remarks are addressed not to the status of all and sundry mathematical truths but only to those fundamental propositions which earlier analysts of human reason had mistakenly thought they could prove analytically. All he is saying is that even these particular allegedly analytical *Grundsätze* are based on some more fundamental propositions, which are synthetic. The obvious candidates for this role of earlier analysts of mathematical foundations are Leibniz and Wolff. Indeed, Kant's comments on $7 + 5 = 12$ on the very following page can very well be thought of as his reply to Leibniz's claim that such arithmetical propositions can be proved logically. But if so, Kant's statements have no bearing on mathematical truths in general, more specifically, no bearing on the question whether the syntheticity of most mathematical truths is an inheritance from the syntheticity of mathematical axioms and postulates or whether it is due to the way they are proved. In sum, contrary to popular misconceptions, Kant never says that the syntheticity of all mathematical theorems is due to the syntheticity of mathematical axioms.

Here the roots of Kant's thoughts in Euclid come in especially handy. It is almost embarrassingly clear what he means when we recall the structure of an Euclidean proposition. What misled earlier philosophers, Kant says, is that mathematical *inferences* (*Schlüsse*) proceed in accordance with the principle of contradiction, i.e., analytically. Kant does not say mathematical *proofs*. Now what is the part of an Euclidean proposition in which *inferences* are drawn? The proof proper, the *apodeixis*, of course. Hence, what Kant is saying is that his predecessors have correctly realized that the *apodeixis* is analytical and from that have mistakenly concluded that the whole proposition can be established analytically. That this is his meaning is neatly verified by Kant's rider on the former of these two theses. The analyticity of all mathematical inferences is what "the nature of all *apodictic* [my italics] certainty requires." Kant is thus even verbally conforming to my reading. Moreover, from the first couple of lines of B17 it is seen that "the nature of all apodeictic certainty" did not, according to Kant, require that the whole argument for a proposition (or the proposition itself) be analytic. Hence, the requirement scarcely meant anything else but that the *apodeixis* part of a proof must proceed "in accordance with the principle of contradiction." This is supported by the remarkable contrast in the quoted passage between "mathematical inferences" and ways of coming to know the truth of basic mathematical propositions. This contrast alone should give pause to interpreters of the Cassirer-Brittan type.

Hence, what we find in the quoted passage is not a counterexample to my view but further evidence for it. It serves to confirm further that Kant located the analytical element of a geometrical proof in the *apodeixis* and the synthetic element in the *auxiliary construction* or *kataskeue*.

What I have said is connected with an exegetical and even textual problem. I have in effect been looking at what Kant says in the sentences I have quoted from B14 through the glasses offered to us by what he says in B17 (beginning with the words "Was uns hier" and ending with "hinzukommen muss, anhänge"):

What here causes us commonly to believe that the predicate of such apodeictic judgments is already contained in our concept, and that the judgment is therefore analytic, is merely the ambiguous character of the terms used. We are required to join in thought a certain predicate to a given concept, and this necessity is inherent in the concepts themselves. But the question is not what we *ought* to join in thought to a given concept, but what we *actually* think in it, even if only obscurely; and it is then manifest that, while the predicate is indeed attached necessarily to the concept, it is so in virtue of our intuition which must be added to the concept, not as thought in the concept itself.

This passage strongly supports my interpretation. The necessity of a synthetic proposition a priori is said to reside in the concepts involved and not to result from some special faculty called "intuition." The reason we do not actually think of the conclusion (predicate) when we think of the premise (subject) is that the necessary connection between them can be seen only by means of an intuition. By "intuition" Kant does not here mean a faculty or any other source of knowledge, for if it were that, the necessity of the connection could not be inherent in the concepts themselves. What he obviously means is precisely the use of "intuitions" (particular representatives of general concepts) which takes place in the *ekthesis* and in the auxiliary construction of a proposition in Euclid. And this use of intuitions (instantiations) explicitly excludes all appeals to outside sources of information like geometrical imagination ("intuition"). Indeed, Kant repeatedly rules out such appeals. Hence the quoted passage from B17 supports my interpretation.

There is an intriguing possibility that the latter passage was indeed intended by Kant as a comment on the former. The B17 passage is obviously out of place; in its present location it cannot be read as a meaningful comment on the immediately preceding passage. Vaihinger has suggested that it should be attached to the preceding paragraph ("Ebensowenig . . . möglich ist"),[11] but this would break the unity of Kant's discussion of the syntheticity of the *Grundsätze* of geometry. The apparently displaced comment is general; it pertains specifically neither to geometry nor to arithmetic (which Kant discusses in B15–16). Hence it follows naturally the initial paragraph of B14 which we have been discussing.

There is some evidence for this in the text. For instance, the reference to "apodictic judgments" (*apodiktische Urteile*) in B17 is naturally taken to pick up the reference to "apodictic certainty" (*apodiktische Gewissheit*) in B14. In the B17 passage Kant discusses certain unnamed but previously mentioned judgments ("*solche Urteile*"). The closest earlier mention of judgments (as distinguished from the *Grundsätze* which Kant discusses in the preceding three paragraphs) is in B14. Moreover, in the B17 passage Kant is discussing the reasons for certain unspecified mistakes, viz., mistaken classifications of some judgments or others as analytic rather than synthetic. Now the closest mention of such mistakes (*any* mistakes) in Kant's text is precisely in the originally quoted passage.

Furthermore, if the passage in B17 were attached to the second paragraph of B16, as Vaihinger suggests, it would be repetitious: the need of intuition would be asserted twice over. In the second paragraph (the famous 7 + 5 = 12 discussion) of B15, Kant mentions repeatedly what is actually *thought of* (*gedacht*) at different stages in the process of establishing this equation. These references

211

presuppose the criteria of syntheticity given by Kant in B17, according to which the real question is not what we have to think in connection with certain concepts but what we actually think in them. All this suggests that the B17 passage really belongs immediately after the B14 passage.

In any case, whatever the purely textual situation is or may be, interpretationally it has to be taken to pertain primarily to the passage from B14 that we have been considering. If so, my interpretation receives strong support.

The way of summing up my interpretation is therefore to compare what we have found about B14–17 by comparing it with what Kant says in Bxi–xii. It is instructive here to set parts of the two passages side by side (with transpositions):

B14, 17	Bxi–xii
But the question [in attributing analyticity] is not what we *ought* to join in thought to the given concept but what we *actually* think in it. . . . Intuitions, therefore, must be called in.	The true method [of geometry is] not to inspect what [one] discerned in the figure, or in the bare concept of it, and from this, as it were, read off its properties . . . .

B14, 17	Bxi–xii
We are required to join in thought a certain predicate to a given concept, and this necessity is inherent in the concepts themselves.	. . . but to bring out what was necessarily implied in the concepts that he had himself formed a priori. . . .
It is manifest that, while the predicate is indeed necessarily attached to the concept, it is so in virtue of an intuition which must be added to the concept.	. . . and had put into the figure by which he presented it to himself.
[As] the nature of all apodictic certainty requires	If he is to know anything with a priori certainty, he must ascribe nothing to the figure
. . . all mathematical inferences must proceed in accordance with the principle of contradiction	. . . save what necessarily follows from what he has himself set into it in accordance with his concept.

This comparison shows unequivocally that Kant located the intuitive and synthetic elements in geometrical and other mathematical arguments within the explicit proofs themselves, not in their premises, not in some nondiscursive appeal to our geometrical (or temporal) intuition. In fact, such appeals are ruled out in so many words in Bxii.

The mistake of the line of thought I am criticizing may be partly based on another error. Because scholars like Cassirer believe that by the use of intuitions Kant meant appeal to our geometrical imagination, they cannot locate the intuitive and constructive element in geometry within an actual argumentative structure of, say, Euclidean propositions. As soon as we clearly see that by the use of intuitions in geometry Kant meant nothing more or less than the use of instantiation, such as those employed in Euclidean *ekthesis* and auxiliary construction, we can happily locate the intuitive and synthetic element right in the middle of axiomatic and deductive arguments and need not pursue the rainbow of syntheticity back to the axioms.

Even if Kant had departed from the spirit of his own basic ideas and mistakenly thought that somehow the syntheticity of mathematical truths can be traced back to that of the axioms and postulates, even so my interpretation would not be invalidated. For the all-important question remains *how* precisely the synthetic axioms and postulates enter into the proof of a mathematical theorem. As every historian of geometry knows, so-called postulates entered into geometrical arguments in Euclid as justifying the auxiliary constructions needed in most geometrical proofs. If so, the dependence of the syntheticity of a geometrical theorem on the status of the so-called postulates is compatible with my thesis. The syntheticity of a geometrical theorem is on my account recognized from the use of auxiliary constructions in its proof. Now we might equally well have said that it is recognized from the need of using so-called postulates as premises in its proof. There is hence no incompatibility whatsoever between tracing the syntheticity of a mathematical theorem back to its premises among the axioms and postulates of the branch of mathematics in question and saying that it is the use of auxiliary individuals in its proof that makes it synthetic.

Moreover, even if the likes of Cassirer and Brittan are correct and Kant thinks that the syntheticity of mathematical truths is due simply and solely to the syntheticity of those mathematical axioms from which they can be analytically derived, even then they face a formidable exegetical task which none of them has ever shouldered. If we do not lift the quoted passage from context, we find a truly remarkable thing. Instead of considering how the axioms of mathematics are intuited, Kant actually discusses in most of the section in question the actual arguments by means of which sundry particular truths of arithmetic and geometry can be established. What the rationale of this procedure—this sudden change of logic—could conceivably be has never been explained by the adherents of the Cassirer-Brittan interpretation.

All told, my interpretation thus receives strong support both from the examination of Kant's historical background and from the analysis of particular Kantian texts—and especially from both of them combined.

NOTES

1. Most of my work on Kant has been collected in my *Logic, Language-Games, and Information: Kantian Themes in the Philosophy of Logic*, (Oxford: Clarendon Press, 1973, chaps. 5–10; or in my *Knowledge and the Known*) Dordrecht: D. Reidel, 1974, chaps. 6–10. See also my papers "On Kant's Notion of Intuition (*Anschauung*)" in Terence Penelhum and J. J. MacIntosh, eds., *The First Critique: Reflections on Kant's "Critique of Pure Reason"* (Belmont, Calif.: Wadsworth, 1969), pp. 38–53; and "Kantian Intuitions," *Inquiry* 15 (1972): 341–45.

2. See Charles Parsons, "Kant's Philosophy of Arithmetic," in Sidney Morgenbesser *et al.*, ed., *Philosophy, Science, and Method: Essays in Honor of Ernest Nagel* (New York: St. Martin's Press, 1969), pp. 568–94; Manley Thompson, "Singular Terms and Intuitions in Kant's Epistemology," *Review of Metaphysics* 26 (1972): 314–43; and Gordon G. Brittan, Jr., *Kant's Theory of Science*, (Princeton, N.J.: Princeton University Press, 1978), pp. 49–56. All these criticisms are marred by total mistakes. As I pointed out in "Kantian Intuitions" (note 1 above), Parsons misunderstands the force of the Kantian concept of intuition. Thompson likewise misunderstands completely the idea that Kantian intuitions have an immediate relation to their objects. He writes: "To refer immediately, then [sic], is to refer to an object by means of marks or characteristics that it alone possesses." This is diametrically opposed to what Kant intends. For him the immediacy of intuition representation lies precisely in that it does *not* take place by means of "marks or characteristics." This is brought out clearly in Kant's definition of intuition in A320/B376–77 and in his *Logic*. Brittan misunderstands Kant's comments on his predecessors in B14, as I shall argue below.

3. For details and for evidence see the literature referred to in note 1 above.

4. See F. Kaulbach, entry on "Anschauung" in Joachim Ritter, ed., *Historisches Wörterbuch der Philosophie* (Basel, Schwabe & Co., 1971), 1:340–47; entry on "Anschauung" in Jürgen Mittelstrass, ed., *Enzyklopedie der Philosophie und Wissenschaftstheorie*, (Mannheim: Bibliographisches Institut, 1980) 1:120–21.

5. At attempt to do so is made in Jaakko Hintikka et al., *Aristotle on Modality and Determinism*, North Holland, Amsterdam, 1976.

6. Wolff's influence tended to strengthen, not to weaken, Euclid's dominance in this respect.

7. A philosophical reader will find a statement of this procedure in Leibniz's *Nouveaux Essais*, book 4, chap. 17, sec. 3.

8. See my "C. S. Peirce's 'First Real Discovery' and Its Contemporary Relevance," *Monist* 63 (1980): pp. 304–15.

9. The second sentence of *La Geometrie* spells out this analogy explicitly: "Just as arithemetic consists of only four or five operations, namely, addition, subtraction,

multiplication, division, and the extraction of roots . . . , so in geometry, to find required lines it is merely necessary to add or to subtract other lines; or else, taking one line which I shall call unity in order to relate it as closely as possible to numbers, and which can in general be chosen arbitrarily, and having given two other lines, to find a fourth line which shall be to one of the given lines as the other is to unity (which is the same as multiplication); or, again, to find a fourth line which is to one of the given lines as unity is to other (which is equivalent to division); or, finally, to find one, two, or several mean proportionals between unity and some other line (which is the same as extracting the square root, cube root, etc., of the given line. And I shall not hesitate to introduce these arithmetical terms into geometry, for the sake of greater clarity."

10. Ernst Cassirer, "Kant und die moderne Mathematik," *Kant-Studien* 12 (1907): 1–40; Brittan, *Kant's Theory of Science*, pp. 55–58.

11. H. Vaihinger, *Commentar zu Kants Kritik der reinen Vernunft* (Stuttgart: W. Spemann) 1881, 1:303–304.

How Kant Almost Wrote
"Two Dogmas of Empiricism"*

PHILIP KITCHER
University of Vermont

I

In the preface to the first edition of the *Critique of Pure Reason*, Kant characterizes his project as one of investigating the extent of the province of pure reason. He offers an apparently straightforward account of his enterprise: "I do not mean by this a critique of books and systems, but of the faculty of reason in general, in respect of all knowledge after which it may strive *independently of all experience*" (Axii).[1] Kant's description encourages us to think that the *Critique* will specify the sciences whose propositions may be known a priori and will explain why they and they alone enjoy this special epistemological status. This simple view of Kant's goals is supported further by the quartet of questions about the possibility of pure mathematics, pure natural science, and metaphysics (as natural disposition and as science) which Kant poses in the introduction to the *Critique* (B20–22) and in the *Prolegomena*. My general aim in this paper is to disentangle some of the very different projects which are covered by Kant's deceptively simple description of his intentions. Specifically, I shall suggest that Kant's anticipation of some Quinean themes leads him from the questions announced in the prefaces to the enterprises of the Transcendental Analytic.

Anyone who has advanced beyond the Transcendental Aesthetic will have learned that Kant's discussions resist assimilation into the framework which the prefaces and the introduction appear to promise. Although we might be content to interpret the Aesthetic, at least in part, as providing an explanation of the possibility of a priori knowledge, the Analytic seems much more remotely connected with Kant's opening questions. The lack of connection is reflected in a broadened usage of the notion of apriority which Kant initially uses to characterize his project. Although 'a priori' enters the *Critique* as an epistemological predicate, attaching primarily to items of knowledge, it quickly becomes applied to almost everything in sight: judgments, concepts, intuitions, faculties,

*And Why He Didn't.

syntheses are all labeled 'a priori.' If we can understand how and why Kant broadens the usage of one of his key terms in this way, then we shall be able to discern more clearly the goals which are set in the Analytic. So at least I shall suggest.

I shall begin by tracing a route from Kant's conception of a priori knowledge to the idea of an a priori concept. Because Kant appreciated an important point about a priori knowledge, a point which is crystallized in the famous final section of Quine's "Two Dogmas of Empiricism,"[2] he saw that a priori knowledge is not possible unless certain concepts are privileged. Believing, unlike Quine, that a priori knowledge is possible, he set out to show that some concepts which are employed throughout human inquiry have the requisite privileged character. I shall support this interpretation by showing how it can be used to make sense of Kant's many-sided treatment of mathematics, and I shall indicate briefly how it can shed some light on features of the Analytic which are prima facie puzzling.

II

The starting point for my investigation will be the notion of a priori knowledge which is explicitly characterized early in the introduction: "In what follows, therefore, we shall understand by *a priori* knowledge, not knowledge independent of this or that experience, but knowledge absolutely independent of all experience" (B2–3). Since I have elaborated and defended an interpretation of this definition elsewhere,[3] I shall rest content with a brief and dogmatic explication. To a first approximation, a priori knowledge is knowledge which we could have had in the same way no matter what our experience. If we are to be more exact, then we shall need two important notions. Let us call the total sequence of experiences which a subject X has had up to time t, X's *life at t*, and say that a life e is *sufficient for X for p* just in case, given exactly e, X could have acquired sufficient understanding to entertain the thought that p. Second, we shall adopt a *psychologistic* approach to knowledge, taking states of knowledge to be states of belief in true propositions, states which are (causally) produced "in the right way." Introducing the term 'warrant' for those processes which engender items of knowledge and leaving the notion of warrant unanalyzed for purposes of this paper, we can now unpack the Kantian conception of a priori knowledge as follows. To say that X knows a priori that p is to say that X knows that p and that X's knowledge that p was produced by a process which is an *a priori warrant* for it. The distinction between a priori warrants and other warrants is given by the following conditions:

1. α is an a priori warrant for X's belief that p if and only if α is a process such that, given any life e, sufficient for X for p, then

   a some process of the same type could produce in X a belief that p.
   b if a process of the same type were to produce in X a belief that p then it would warrant X in believing that p.
   c if a process of the same type were to produce in X a belief that p then p.

Thus a priori knowledge is knowledge produced by a special type of process, one which would have been *available* whatever (sufficiently rich) experience the subject had had and which would have produced *warranted true* belief whatever (sufficiently rich) experience the subject had had. I think that the discussions of pure intuition and its role in generating mathematical knowledge in the Aesthetic and the Transcendental Methodology show clearly that Kant was concerned to describe processes with these special characteristics.

Given the notion of a priori knowledge, it is easy to introduce a derivative notion of a priori proposition. A proposition is a priori just in case human beings could know it a priori. Waiving doubts about how we are to understand the type of modality which is appropriate here, we could use this equivalence to unpack many of Kant's remarks. When Kant contends that a proposition (judgment) is a priori, he would be read as maintaining that there is some special type of process which could serve as an a priori warrant for our belief in that proposition. Unfortunately, matters are not so simple. Very early in the *Critique*, Kant yokes the concept of apriority to two further notions: "Necessity and strict universality are thus sure criteria of *a priori* knowledge, and are inseparable from one another" (B4). For the purposes of this paper I am going to ignore Kant's concept of universality and the claims he makes which involve it. The connection between necessity and apriority is problematic enough to justify us in focusing on it, independently of the further tie to universality.

One of the most obvious consequences of Kant's linkage of apriority to necessity is that he is led to advance the thesis that a proposition is a priori for a number of different reasons. Sometimes he is concerned to argue that the proposition can be known a priori and to explain how it can be known a priori. On other occasions he wants to show that the proposition is necessary and to explain why it is necessary. Occasionally he engages in both projects at once. I shall now suggest that *some* of the complications of Kant's investigations of the "province of pure reason" stem from his oscillation between epistemological and metaphysical enterprises.

Kant's approach to necessity involves problems of its own. It is helpful to understand Kant's conception(s) by introducing the familiar idiom of possible worlds semantics for modal logic—an idiom which descends, of course, from Leibniz—taking necessary truths to be propositions true in all possible worlds. Kant has a distinctive approach to necessity because he takes a possible world to be a totality of possible appearances—that is, a totality of appearances which could constitute the experience of a subject. There are two loci of vagueness in this formulation. First, different conceptions of the nature of the subject can give rise to distinct conceptions of possible worlds (and, derivatively, to alternative doctrines about necessity and possibility). Throughout the *Critique*, Kant's primary usage holds fixed the cognitive constitution of the human subject, so that possible worlds are taken as totalities of appearances for subjects with the types of faculties found among *Homo sapiens*. One of the most obvious occurrences of this usage is Kant's attribution of necessity to certain statements about space and time, where the notion of possible experience is clearly subjected to the conditions of spatiotemporal (Euclidean) experience. There are also, however, indications of "higher" types of necessity, generated by relaxing the constraints on possible worlds so as to allow for the experiences of nonhuman but rational subjects. The second locus of vagueness alluded to above lies in the term 'experience'. Notoriously, Kant sometimes uses 'experience' in a very strong sense, so that for something to count as a total possible experience for a subject it would have to involve (in some way) judgments, or even particular kinds of judgments, by the subject. At other times, for example, in the Aesthetic, Kant's conception of experience is much weaker, and a total experience can be taken as a sequence of sensory states. I shall not attempt to fix a determinate Kantian notion of possible world (or of necessity or possibility) which can then be used to analyze the central theses of the *Critique*. For the reasons just indicated, it seems to me to be a mistake to try to find *one* notion which will answer to all Kant's claims, and I suggest that the general view that a possible world is a totality of appearances which could constitute the experience of a subject should be filled out in different ways for application to different parts of the *Critique*.

One might think that by recognizing a number of different interpretations of the notion of necessity we could ascribe to Kant some true thesis asserting the equivalence of necessity and apriority. This hope is unfounded. As several writers have argued, the doctrine that necessity and apriority are equivalent fails in both directions: there are contingent truths which are knowable a priori and necessary truths (including knowable necessary truths) which are not knowable a priori.[4] The counterexamples are equally applicable to the versions of the equivalence thesis which employ Kantian conceptions of necessity. Hence Kant's claims to the effect that particular propositions are a priori are dangerously ambiguous.

Yet even if we were to grant Kant's equivalence between apriority and necessity, we would still have to separate two distinct enterprises which he sets for himself. In justifying the thesis that a proposition is necessary (or a priori), the equivalence might prove useful: from a premise asserting the apriority (necessity) of the proposition we could employ the equivalence to reach the conclusion that it is necessary (a priori). However, Kant does not simply want to argue that certain favored propositions are necessary (a priori). In many cases his principal interest lies in explaining why they are necessary (a priori). To grant the equivalence thesis would not ipso facto allow for the transmutation of explanations of the necessity of propositions into explanations of the apriority of those propositions or vice versa. Indeed, the account I have offered of Kant's notions of apriority and necessity enables us to see what explanations of the necessity and apriority of propositions will be like and why those explanations will be different. To understand why a proposition is a priori, we shall need a specification of a process which could warrant belief in it, independently of experience. By contrast, to explain the necessity of a proposition, we shall show why that proposition holds at any possible world. The general Kantian conception of a possible world points to the way in which the story will go: we may show either that the proposition owes its truth to some feature with which our minds inevitably structure appearances or that it states some condition on the possibility of a particular kind of experience (the former style of explanation is prominent in the Aesthetic; the latter, in the Analytic). Quite evidently, we may put forward explanations of the necessity of propositions without offering a specification of processes through which we could arrive at a priori knowledge of those propositions. Thus the task of accounting for the apriority of a proposition is not accomplished simply by showing why that proposition is necessary.

Although we have already seen how Kant's terminology allows him to include quite different projects under one rubric, this is only the first stage in separating Kantian themes. I now want to show how consideration of the *epistemological* a priori—reflection on the conditions which a priori warrants must meet—could prompt new distinctions and new enterprises.

III

Kant believes that the fundamental problem of a priori knowledge is the problem of *synthetic* a priori knowledge. His belief reflects the judgment that analyticity is not the solution to the problem of apriority. Here he agrees with Quine. My goal is to explain how Kant could come close to advocating the celebrated Quinean dictum "Any statement can be held true come what may. . . . Conversely, by the same token, no statement is immune to revision"[5] and how his partial appreciation of the point could lead him to an interesting articulation of the problem of a priori knowledge.

Let us begin with an important connection. Standardly, apriority is linked to unrevisability. If someone knows a proposition a priori, then, it seems, that proposition is immune to revision. It is not hard to begin to explicate the notion of immunity to revision which is involved here. We can say that a proposition is unrevisable for a person at a time just in case there is no possible continuation of that person's experience after that time which would make it reasonable for her to change her attitude to the proposition. The explication makes it apparent why one might think that propositions which a person knows a priori are unrevisable for that person. If you have a priori knowledge that p, then you have an a priori warrant for belief that p. Assuming that the warrant is available independently of time, then, given any continuation of your experience, you would have available to you a warrant which would continue to support belief. Hence it would never be reasonable for you to abandon p in favor of its negation. Whatever trickery your experience may devise for you, you will always be able to undergo a process which will sustain the belief.

It will facilitate our discussion to abstract from one weakness of this argument. A priori warrants are not generally available independently of time. To see this, we need only consider our knowledge of our own existence. I have argued elsewhere that, at each moment of our lives, each of us can have a priori knowledge of our own existence.[6] Given any (sufficiently rich) experience which we might have had at the time in question, there is available to us at that time a process which will warrant belief in the proposition expressed by our uttering "I exist" at that time. But at subsequent times there may not be any process available to us which would warrant belief in *that* proposition; *similar* processes will warrant belief in the propositions we *then* express by tokening "I exist," but those are different propositions. Our a priori knowledge is evanescent, giving way to a different item of a priori knowledge.

I shall henceforth ignore this complication, focusing on another difficulty with the argument connecting apriority and unrevisability. The trouble results from the fact that the argument adopts an overly simple view of the relevant changes in attitude. We take it for granted that the only changes of attitude which might occur are those in which the person passes from belief in the proposition to belief in its negation (or, perhaps, to suspension of belief). Let us call cases in which a belief that *p* is replaced by a belief in the negation of *p strong revisions of p*. Let us also suppose, for the sake of simplicity, that in cases where experience could lead us from belief to rational suspension of belief even more recalcitrant experience could engender rational denial of belief. Even with this simplification the strong revisions of propositions are not the only changes of attitude which should concern us. There are also cases in which we abandon a proposition by giving up the *concepts* which it involves. In such cases we do not come to think of the proposition which we formerly believed as false, nor do we hesitate between that proposition and its negation. Instead we may grudgingly acknowledge the proposition as true, hastening to qualify our endorsement by pointing out that it is vacuous or that it embodies a wrongheaded conception of things. I shall call cases in which we acquire an attitude like this toward propositions which we formerly believed *weak revisions* of those propositions.

An example may help us recognize the possibility of weak revision. I think it is plausible to think that the referent of the term 'mermaid' is fixed so that it follows that mermaids are female inhabitants of the sea whose heads and upper bodies are structured like those of human females but whose lower extremities consist of scaly tails. (If you disagree that this is the way that the referent of 'mermaid' is fixed for us, then you ought at least to concede that it *might* have been fixed in that way. If that is so, then you should replace my account of changes in our attitudes with a parallel story about changes in the attitudes of hypothetical speakers who do fix the referent in the way I take us to have done.) Once our attitude to the proposition expressed by "Mermaids are female" was one of straightforward belief. From nautical reports we, or more exactly our ancestors, would have supposed that there are mermaids and that all of them are female. Had we been asked to justify our belief, we would have appealed to our concept of a mermaid, insisting that the manner in which the class of mermaids is determined ensures that all its members will be female. Now we no longer maintain the same attitude toward the proposition. Although we might continue to insist that the concept of a mermaid determines that the proposition is true, we would hasten to add that scientific research has convinced us that the concept is useless, that it is inapplicable and that it plays no role in what, by our current lights, is the best description and explanation of the world. The proposition has not suffered strong revision. Instead it has undergone weak revision and has been demoted from a role in our cognitive endeavors. If the concept of a mermaid lingers on, it does so only because we sometimes use it in storytelling or in intellectual history.

In distinguishing between strong and weak revisions, I have, of course, appealed to a distinction which Quineans regard as anathema, namely, the distinction between changing one's concepts and changing one's beliefs.[7] Let me note an obvious point. Unlike Quine, Kant does not repudiate the notion of analytic truth. His agreement with Quine is restricted to the view that appeals to analyticity fail to achieve a certain purpose. To understand the nature of this agreement, we shall have to make use of a distinction which Quine ultimately rejects.

I shall now use the distinction between strong and weak revision to generate a derivative distinction between *complete* and *incomplete* unrevisability. Let us say that a proposition is *completely unrevisable* for a person if it is impossible that experience should continue in such a way that it would be rational for the person to undergo either a strong or a weak revision with respect to it. A proposition will be *incompletely unrevisable* for a person if it is impossible that experience should continue in such a way that it would be rational for the person to undergo strong revisions with respect to it. Our previous argument from apriority to unrevisability can now be interpreted as an attempt to show that propositions which can be known a priori are incompletely unrevisable. If we have an a priori warrant for belief that p, then, provided that the warrant is available to us independently of time, we can continue to use it to turn back the suggestions of experience against p. Can we argue, in similar fashion, that apriority should entail complete unrevisability?

Kant's answer is "Yes," and it is this answer which embodies part of his agreement with Quine and which also generates some of the projects of the *Critique*. I suggest that Kant believes that propositions which we know a priori should not even be subject to weak revisions, that he has good reasons for maintaining this belief, and that his downplaying of the role of analytic judgments in the *Critique* stems from an (implicit) recognition that the analyticity of a proposition does not entail that that proposition is not vulnerable to weak revision. Up to this point he agrees with Quine. The differences between Kant and Quine consist, first of all, in Kant's allowance for a distinctive source of knowledge based on recognizing conceptual relations, and, more significantly, in his reaction to the failure of analyticity to secure complete unrevisability. Whereas for Quine this failure dooms the project of apriorism, Kant views it as imposing more stringent demands on a priori knowledge and sets out resolutely to see whether those demands can be met.

Later in this paper I shall offer textual evidence for supposing that Kant held that a priori propositions must be completely unrevisable. One major source of support for this supposition will reside in the fact that it can be used to illuminate Kant's philosophy of mathematics. For the moment I shall concentrate on the reasons Kant might have for maintaining that a priori propositions should not even be subject to weak revisions. This issue is best confronted by considering an argument against the traditional connection between analyticity and apriority.

Kant believes that there is a distinctive class of truths, analytic truths, which can be known by means of processes of a type in which we disclose relations among our concepts. Let us grant him this idea. Do processes of this type count as a priori warrants? I would claim that they can be shown to meet conditions 1*a* and 1*c* of the analysis given above.[8] Where trouble arises is with condition 1*b*. Given an experience which enables us to acquire certain concepts which are involved in an analytic proposition but which calls into doubt the applicability of those concepts, the power of the process of conceptual disclosure to warrant belief in the analytic truth is undermined. Once we appreciate this point, two of the theses I have attributed to Kant will follow. First, the failure of the process to serve as an a priori warrant results from the possibility that experience might exhibit to us the futility of certain concepts, so that

225

we should infer that a priori propositions must not be vulnerable even to weak revisions. Hence (given the usual assumption about the time independence of the relevant warrants) apriority should entail complete unrevisability. Second, the argument shows directly that analyticity cannot be the key to the problem of a priori knowledge. Demonstrating that a proposition is analytic does not suffice to explain why that proposition is a priori.

The crucial claim in the argument of the previous paragraph is the thesis that experiences which would call into question the applicability of a concept would deprive of their warranting power processes in which we disclosed the relations of that concept to other concepts. This claim can be defended by canvassing intuitions about particular cases and by appealing to general considerations about the goals of inquiry. Discussion of examples will lead us naturally to the general points.

Do we know that mermaids are female? The question is an awkward one: it seems misleading to say either "Yes" or "No." I suggest that the awkwardness should be taken seriously. We no longer retain belief in the proposition that mermaids are female—at least we no longer believe that proposition in a way which allows for it to count as an item of our knowledge. We are prepared to assert "Mermaids are female" only in a limited range of contexts—when we are telling stories, for example—and this distinguishes us from our predecessors who preceded the Nautical Enlightenment. Were someone to have continued the old attitude of believing wholeheartedly that mermaids are female and of asserting "Mermaids are female" within the wider range of contexts embracing contexts of serious scientific discussion, we would characterize the belief as unwarranted. We should not credit an appeal to the concept of mermaid as warranting belief. Instead we should point out that use of that concept is unreasonable, given our experience, so that the process of disclosing the relations between the concept of mermaid and other concepts fails to warrant belief.

So far my discussion may have suggested that the only way in which experience can undermine concepts is by showing that those concepts are not instantiated. That is far too simple a view of the matter. Our right to use a concept may be called into question by experiences which convince us that the concept carves up reality in an inappropriate way (conversely, some concepts—idealizations in science—do an excellent job of carving up reality but are not instantiated). The intuitive point that experience can deprive one of a right to use a concept—even of a concept which is instantiated

—and so undermine one's beliefs is well made by a historical case introduced by Mill.[9] Chemists of the early eighteenth century conceived of acids as substances which contain oxygen, and, given that we are prepared to allow the analysis of concepts as a source of knowledge, it is plausible to suppose that their knowledge of the proposition that (what they called) acids contain oxygen was based on processes through which they disclosed conceptual relations to themselves. With the discovery that a substance which bears numerous resemblances to other acids (the substance which they called muriatic acid and which we call hydrochloric acid) does not contain oxygen, the definition of 'acid' was revised. Now if there were people who had continued to employ the old concept, maintaining that acids contain oxygen on the basis of the process of conceptual analysis, we should not suppose that they had retained a distinctive item of knowledge. Rather we should view the experiences involving the discovery of the composition of hydrochloric acid as undermining the old concept of acid and as depriving the process of analyzing the old concept of acid of its power to warrant belief.

The general point about inquiry which these examples suggest is that our goal is not simply to utter truths but to utter truths which employ appropriate concepts. Those who persist in using concepts which experience has shown to be inadequate may continue to assert the truth, but we do not credit them with knowledge of propositions involving the outworn concepts. Thus the process of conceptual analysis, which Kant envisages us as using to acquire knowledge of analytic truths, does not warrant belief if experience reveals to us that concepts which we are analyzing are inappropriate. Those who cling to outworn distinctions are not guilty of the same error as that made by those who adhere to beliefs which have been falsified, but they are equally deficient in aiming at the goals of inquiry and, as a result, equally deficient in having knowledge.

The kinds of considerations I have been advancing form *part* of Quine's attack on the notion of analyticity. Of course, the most obvious Quinean point is that we cannot separate out a class of analytic truths—or, to put the issue in the terms I have used (which are, I think, closest to Kant's way of approaching it), we cannot distinguish a special source of knowledge which consists of the analysis of concepts. However, in the final section of "Two Dogmas of Empiricism," as well as in the earlier essay "Truth by Convention," Quine can easily be understood as arguing that analyticity, even if it were to exist, would not solve the problem of apriority. Indeed, we can sharpen the point I have been making by adapting the main argument of "Truth by Convention," an argument which underlies the famous later claim that "any statement can be held true, come what may."[10] Suppose that we were to allow that appeal to concepts suffices to engender a priori knowledge and that the process of disclosing conceptual relations will continue to warrant belief even when experience calls our concepts into question. Then it would be easy for us to increase our store of a priori knowledge. We could tailor our scientific concepts, stipulating that the scientific statements we currently accept are to be regarded as constitutive of the concepts involved. In the wake of these stipulations we could defend our science by analyzing the concepts we have constructed, so that, *ex hypothesi*, we have a priori knowledge. Of course, we might want to deny that we now have a priori knowledge of exactly those truths which previously made up our empirical science, but we could claim to have replaced empirical science with a different corpus of truths known a priori. Hence if we accept the thesis against which I have been arguing, we are led to conclude that we do not need *empirical* science at all.

To suppose that analyticity entails apriority is thus to make a priori knowledge come too cheap. Kant seems to have appreciated the point. There is a revealing passage written by Kant's disciple Schultz in response to Eberhard's objections to the emphasis on the *synthetic* a priori which dominates the *Critique*. Eberhard had suggested that Kant's favored propositions could be replaced by analytic judgments if one expanded the subject concept. Schultz replied as follows:

> Let one put into the concept of the subject just so many attributes that the predicate which one wishes to prove of the subject can be derived from its concept merely by the law of contradiction. The critical philosophy permits him to make this kind of analytic judgment, but raises a question about the concept of the subject itself. It asks: how did you come to include in this concept the different attributes so that it [now analytically] entails synthetic propositions? First prove the objective reality of your concept, i.e. first prove that any one of its attributes really belongs to a possible object, and when you have done that, then prove that the other attributes belong to the same thing that the first one belongs to, without themselves belonging to the first attribute.[11]

Schultz's words can reasonably be taken to express Kant's thoughts.

228

We cannot account for the apriority of propositions by simply finding analytic surrogates for them. There are constraints on our concepts,[12] and an analytic judgment is a priori only if it accords with these constraints. To put it another way, the Kantian enterprise is as concerned with the applicability—"objective validity"—of our concepts as it is with the truth of our judgments.

I have suggested that Kant and Quine agree that analyticity does not (would not) solve the problem of a priori knowledge. But at this point they part company. The thrust of the final section of "Two Dogmas of Empiricism" is that there is no a priori knowledge. Kant, convinced that we *do* have some a priori knowledge but recognizing that that knowledge cannot simply be attributed to our ability to analyze our concepts, attempts to show that some concepts and some judgments are privileged. I shall now use this construal to explain the types of enterprise into which Kant is led by his quest for the a priori.

IV

If a priori propositions are to be completely unrevisable, then they must contain special concepts. Appropriately we can call these concepts *a priori concepts*. What features distinguish a priori concepts? For reasons which will shortly become evident, I shall not try to give a full answer to this question. Instead I shall indicate two approaches which Kant seems to have taken in response to it.

Two notions of a priori concept play a role in the *Critique*. The first, which I shall call the "objective validity" construal, identifies a priori concepts as those which must find application in our experience. The simplest way to explicate this idea is to suggest that the concept expressed by the predicate F is an a priori concept just in case $\ulcorner (\exists x) \urcorner Fx$ holds at any (Kantian) possible world. Many of Kant's remarks in the *Critique* seem to be directed at proving that particular concepts are necessarily instantiated. Nevertheless, there are two reasons for not adopting so simple a reading of his endeavors to demonstrate that concepts are "objectively valid." In the first place, the issue of whether a concept has instantiations is not necessarily relevant to the question of whether that concept is legitimately employed in attempts to describe and explain the world. We sometimes reject concepts which are instantiated because they do not lend themselves to a simple theory of the phenomena. Similarly, we sometimes continue to employ concepts which we recognize as not being instantiated: idealizations play an important role in our science. Second, even though a concept is necessarily instantiated and even though we concede that having instantiations suffices to make it correct to employ the concept, that would not solve the problem for which I have supposed the notion of an a priori concept to be designed. Weak revision of propositions involving concepts which are necessarily instantiated might still be rational, for it might be possible, given certain kinds of recalcitrant experience, that we should mistakenly, but justifiably, believe that those concepts were not instantiated.

Hence I shall propose a different way of explicating the "objectively valid" construal of a priori concepts. Kant would maintain that there are some concepts which it must be rational to employ in the description of any experience sufficient to enable one to acquire those concepts. It is not just that these concepts are inevitably instantiated but that anyone whose experience suffices for the acquisition of the concepts could not be justified in doubting that they are instantiated. If one makes a minimally rational response to one's experience, then one will be able to turn back any challenge that the concept in question is inapplicable. To anticipate the mathematical example which I shall use in later sections, there is no room for reasonable doubt about the applicability of quantitative concepts, given even the most recalcitrant of experiences, because, provided a subject makes minimally rational use of the experience, he must come to recognize that quantitative concepts are applicable to it. No trickery can deprive him of the equipment he needs to turn back any challenge.

This proposal is not a completely satisfactory explication even of one Kantian notion of a priori concept, for it fails to respond to the first point I made two paragraphs back. I have continued to use the property of having instantiations as a necessary condition for conceptual adequacy, adding as a further constraint on a priori concepts that it not be possible for experience to generate a reasonable doubt that they are instantiated. Evidently, a complete account of the notion of an a priori concept would be more complicated, but I suggest that my simple first approximation shows the *types* of conditions which such concepts would have to meet to serve Kant's turn. As we shall see below, it is also refined enough to shed some light on the *Critique*.

Let me now turn to the second construal of a priori concepts which I promised above. Sometimes Kant is interested not in those concepts which have to be recognized as being instantiated by any rational subject who has had a sufficiently rich experience but in those concepts which have to be used by anybody who would count as a subject of experience. A priori concepts, in this sense, are those which have to figure in propositions which the subject believes if she is to qualify as having experience at all. Let us call this the "subjectively necessary" interpretation of a priori concepts. It is relatively easy to see how this notion of a priori concept might be thought to resolve the problem posed by the threat of weak revisions. One who jettisons an a priori concept in the light of experience has, on this interpretation, ceased to be a subject of experience. Hence, it might be suggested, repudiating propositions by rejecting the concepts they contain must be irrational if the concepts in question are a priori concepts.

I shall not try to decide here whether this argument is ultimately successful. I believe that the notion of an a priori concept deserves careful scrutiny and that there are interesting questions connected with it. Is it possible to respond to the Quinean insight about revisability by arguing that some concepts cannot rationally be given up? What would be the distinctive features of such concepts? Are the two ways of developing the notion of an a priori concept which I have attributed to Kant equivalent? Detailed answers to these questions must await another occasion. My project in this paper is simply to sketch two Kantian notions of an a priori concept, to show that they are plausible responses to the Quinean insight which, I claim, Kant achieved and to interpret some apparently puzzling parts of the *Critique* from this perspective.

With this last aim in mind, let us return to Kant's own initial characterization of his intentions. Given the conception of a priori knowledge presented in the introduction, we might understand Kant's promise to explain how various kinds of synthetic a priori knowledge are possible as prefiguring a sequence of specifications of special processes meeting conditions 1a–1c. Once we appreciate Kant's connection of metaphysical and epistemological issues in his doctrine of the equivalence of necessity and apriority, the picture becomes more complicated. Now we see that the task of explaining the synthetic a priori may be an epistemological endeavor, a metaphysical endeavor, or both. The chief claim of this paper is that the complications do not stop there. Because Kant anticipated the Quinean point that mere analyticity cannot guarantee apriority, he was led to view the epistemological project as committing him to showing that certain concepts have special properties. Part of the task of explaining how a particular type of process can serve as an a priori warrant for a particular type of belief consists in demonstrating that the concepts involved in that type of belief cannot rationally be repudiated in the light of experience, no matter how recalcitrant the experience may be. Hence we may see the enterprises of showing that certain concepts must be employed if experience is to be possible, or of showing that these concepts must be instantiated, and recognizably instantiated, in any experience, as unfolding the project which Kant originally sets for himself.

In attempting to delineate the complex structure of Kant's project, without linking my discussion to specific passages in the *Critique*, I have courted the objection that the preceding interpretation is altogether too fanciful. Apart from the brief response to Eberhard, which was written by Schultz in any case, what evidence do we have for thinking that Kant achieved the insight I have attributed to him? In the rest of this paper I shall try to show that there is substantial evidence. By using the interpretation I have offered, we can understand what Kant is about in parts of the *Critique* whose apparent purposes are utterly mysterious. As my principal example I shall take Kant's discussions of the nature of mathematics, arguing that, from the perspective I have adopted, they form a coherent whole.

V

Kant discusses the nature of mathematics at a number of places in the *Critique*. His initial treatment, extending from the introduction through the Transcendental Aesthetic, dovetails with a section of the Transcendental Methodology to yield an account of mathematical truth and mathematical knowledge which can be summarized as follows. True mathematical propositions owe their truth to the structure which our mental faculties impose on experience. Those propositions can be known through acts of pure intuition, processes in which we disclose to ourselves that structure which informs experience. (This crude summary will serve our immediate purposes; I shall refine it below.) Here we seem to have an answer to the fundamental Kantian question about mathematics, an explanation of how mathematics as a body of synthetic a priori knowledge is possible.

The trouble is that Kant has more to say. Between the Aesthetic and the Methodology there occur some cryptic remarks in the Transcendental Deduction which are developed in the Axioms of Intuition. What shall we make of these remarks? One approach is to ignore them. Another is to turn away from the official aim of the Axioms of Intuition, namely, that of showing that all appearances are extensive magnitudes, and to concentrate on Kant's notion of extensive magnitude.[13] Both of these strategies refuse to take seriously Kant's own assessment of the Axioms section, and for that reason I shall not consider them. Let us begin instead by asking what the Axioms section is supposed to do for us.

In his prefatory explanation of the role of the Axioms, Kant promises that he will "include those . . . principles upon which the possibility and *a priori* objective validity of mathematics are grounded" (A160/B199). Retrospectively he claims that the principle established in the Axioms section "alone can make pure mathematics, in its complete precision, applicable to objects of experience" (A165/B206). In these passages and elsewhere Kant's specification of his aims seems to set a goal which was already achieved in the Aesthetic. After all, the theory of mathematics, space, and time which I have summarized above was defended on the grounds that the accounts of Kant's rivals must fail "since they are unable to appeal to a true and objectively valid *a priori* mathematical knowledge, nor bring the propositions of experience into necessary agreement with it" (A40–41/B57–58). The comparison with other approaches to mathematics suggests that Kant has succeeded on this score, that he takes himself to have explained how a priori mathematical knowledge is possible. But in this case it seems that the Aesthetic and the Axioms address a common goal. Thus it is hardly surprising that many commentators have adopted one of two construals, claiming either that the Axioms section recapitulates the doctrine of the Aesthetic or that it contradicts it and sets out to solve the old problem in a new way.[14]

Neither of these interpretations is very satisfactory. If we suggest that Kant became dissatisfied with the account of the apriority of mathematics which appears in the Aesthetic and decided to offer something different, then we must explain why the prior effort remains in the *Critique* and how it can be used to support the transcendental ideality of space and time. On the other hand, if we assume that Kant is simply recapitulating earlier doctrine, then it is unclear why he reposes the old problem, offering new observations without referring back to the earlier discussion.

The interpretation offered above provides a way out. Although in both cases Kant talks of explaining the a priori validity of mathematics, there are two different *explananda*. The task of the Aesthetic is to show that there is a process, pure intuition, which will be available to us independently of experience and which will warrant mathematical beliefs under a wide range of experiences. However, the Aesthetic does not consider the possibility that the power of that process to yield mathematical knowledge might be undermined by experiences which would question our right to use the concepts which figure in mathematical propositions. The task of the Axioms is to show that the apparent possibility is not genuine. Because "all intuitions are extensive magnitudes," experience could not make it reasonable to jettison the quantitative concepts which the mathematician employs. The possibility of a priori mathematical knowledge rests on the existence of pure intuitions and on the apriority of mathematical (quantitative) concepts.

To develop this resolution of the problem of understanding the role of the Axioms, we shall need a slightly fuller account of the theory of mathematics presented in the Aesthetic.[15] In the introduction Kant argues (in passages not noted for their cogency) that mathematical truths are synthetic a priori. His conclusion covers two claims: the metaphysical claim is that, although mathematical truths do not owe their truth to the nature of our concepts, they are nonetheless necessary; the epistemological claim is that, although mathematical truths cannot be known simply by analyzing our concepts, they are nonetheless knowable a priori. These claims serve as starting points for the arguments of the Aesthetic. Kant advances theses about space and time, contending that they must be accepted if we are to explain the conclusions of the introduction. Most of Kant's discussion concerns space and geometry, which provide him with his clearest example. The metaphysical doctrine about space is that our minds inevitably stamp the appearances with Euclidean spatial structure, and this doctrine is alleged to be the only explanation for the status of geometry as a body of synthetic necessary truths. The epistemological doctrine about space is that, by drawing geometrical figures in thought and inspecting them with the mind's eye, we can disclose to ourselves those spatial features with which our mind informs experience. This doctrine—Kant's theory of the process of pure intuition—is supposed to be forced on us if we are to explain how geometry is a body of synthetic truths which are knowable a priori.

To focus our discussion more precisely, it will help to use a very simple analogy. Imagine that our experience consists in looking toward a surface which is normally unlit, onto which pictures are periodically flashed. If we knew the geometrical properties of the surface, that knowledge would help us discern regularities and patterns among the pictures. A way of doing this, independently of the presence of any pictures, would be to draw luminous figures on

234

the surface. To do that would be, in Kant's terms, to make the surface an object of intuition, and by following the procedure, we would be able to bring out clearly the structural features of the surface which determine the properties of the pictures. This story appears to parallel Kant's view of pure intuition. Space, as form of intuition, is analogous to the surface in its role of determining the properties of the pictures; space, as object of intuition, is analogous to the surface as represented in the drawing of the luminous figures.

Let us now take the analogy one step further. Suppose that two subjects engage in the process of drawing figures. They draw different types of figures. One, the lucky one, produces figures which are regularly found among the objects depicted in the images which periodically appear on the surface. The other is less fortunate, constructing figures which are not found in the pictures which appear and learning geometrical features of the surface which are not applicable to the sequence of images which makes up the perceptual experience. Now from the perspective of the Aesthetic, each of these predicaments mirrors an apparent possibility for the aspiring geometer. As I see it, the role of the Axioms is to show that the employment of a certain type of concept will inevitably secure for us a fate analogous to that of the lucky subject, and the notion of pure intuition will then be restricted to cover only processes which involve the construction of concepts of the privileged class.

Although I think that the analogy of the last paragraph is useful in showing what Kant is trying to do, we must be careful that it does not mislead us. The root issue is not whether geometry will prove applicable to experience if we concentrate on constructing circles rather than triangles but whether the use of *quantitative* concepts will generate items of knowledge which can be applied to objects of perceptual experience. Euclidean geometry employs the concept of distance—indeed, the concepts of such figures as circle, square, and equilateral triangle involve the notion of distance. Kant's question is whether the concept of distance—and other quantitative concepts—must necessarily be applicable to our experience. Might we find ourselves in possession of a body of truths about metric relations, statements owing their truth to the structure of space, which were completely incidental to the objects of experience, in that the objects of experience failed to manifest the structural features described in our corpus? To put the issue in its starkest form, might we find ourselves asserting true statements of the form "(x) $(Ax \rightarrow Bx)$"—statements owing their truth to the structure imposed by the mind upon the appearances—but discovering that these truths are entirely useless for describing and explaining our experience, in that we encounter no objects which are (even approximately) *A*'s? Kant believes that it is possible to show that this predicament cannot be ours. It is a necessary feature of our perceptual experience that its objects fall under those concepts, quantitative concepts, which mathematicians employ in their constructions. The Book of Nature is inevitably written in the language of mathematics.

Let us now examine some passages in which Kant modifies the account of our mathematical knowledge presented in the Aesthetic. The first hint that the Aesthetic does not tell us the whole story about mathematics, space, and time comes in the Transcendental Deduction. The version given in the second edition makes it especially clear that Kant is troubled by an apparent tension between his thesis that knowledge involves both concepts and intuitions (and, specifically, that all knowledge involves the categories) and the treatment of the Aesthetic in which no mention of the role of the categories was made. The worry comes to the surface in two places. Initially Kant appears concerned that someone may respond to his claim that the categories must find application to objects of experience by alleging that it was sufficient for the concepts of pure mathematics that they be exemplified in *pure* intuition. I interpret the following passage as an attempt to disarm this imagined response:

> Through the determination of pure intuition we can acquire *a priori* knowledge of objects, as in mathematics, but only in regard to their form, as appearances; whether there can be things which must be intuited in this form, is still left undecided. Mathematical concepts are not, therefore, by themselves knowledge, except on the supposition that there are things which allow of being presented to us only in accordance with the form of that pure sensible intuition. Now *things in space and time* are given only in so far as they are perceptions (that is, representations accompanied by sensation)—therefore only through empirical representation. Consequently, the pure concepts of understanding, even when they are applied to *a priori* intuitions as in mathematics, yield knowledge only in so far as these intuitions—and therefore indirectly by their means the pure concepts also—can be applied to empirical intuitions. [B147]

The primary aim of this passage is, of course, to explain and defend

Kant's general claim about the application of the categories to objects of sensory experience. For our purposes, however, its interest lies in the suggestion that the account of mathematical knowledge provided in the Aesthetic may be incomplete in certain respects. What Kant appears to be saying is that the construction of an object corresponding to a concept in an act of pure intuition may not suffice for the generation of knowledge, that there is an *apparent* possibility that the construction might not correspond to the objects which are actually presented to us in sensory experience. Hence there will remain for him a task of showing how in the acts of pure intuition which generate our mathematical knowledge this seemingly possible threat does not arise. This, of course, is the task which I have interpreted the Axioms as undertaking.

The second puzzling passage, in which Kant also intimates that the doctrines of the Aesthetic are incomplete, occurs toward the end of the Deduction. Kant confesses that the approach to the intuition of space provided in the Aesthetic was one-sided in its emphasis on the sensible and concomitant neglect of the conceptual. The confession occurs in a cryptic footnote:

> Space, represented as *object* (as we are required to do in geometry), contains more than mere form of intuition; it also contains *combination* of the manifold, given according to the form of sensibility, in an *intuitive* representation, so that the *form of intuition* gives only a manifold, the *formal intuition* gives unity of representation. In the Aesthetic I have treated this unity as belonging merely to sensibility, simply in order to emphasize that it precedes any concept, although, as a matter of fact, it presupposes a synthesis which does not belong to the senses but through which all concepts of space and time first become possible. [Footnote to B160]

Without attempting to delineate Kant's doctrine of the "transcendental synthesis of imagination"—to which he refers in the closing sentence of this footnote[16]—I shall simply point out that the picture of pure intuition which is present in this passage brings to the fore elements which were not prominent in the Aesthetic. The explicit accounts of our geometrical knowledge provided in the early parts of the *Critique* emphasize the *perceptual* side of the process of pure intuition. Kant is at pains to point out that we can obtain geometrical knowledge by looking at mental pictures, that this is the way geometers proceed, and he tries to explain how a priori knowledge can result from this activity (see, for example,

A47–49/B64–66). But to leave matters there is to overlook the *constructive* aspect of the process. To represent the spatial structure which we impose on the appearances, we shall have to make space an *object* of intuition, and to do this will require the construction of an object according to some concept. Typically, Kant puts the point in the most abstract way, referring in the footnote I have cited to "combination of the manifold" and in a previous passage which anticipates it to "an action of the understanding on the sensibility" (B152). What he is aiming at is the same incompleteness of the Aesthetic which we have already discerned. If the representation of space as object of pure intuition must proceed by the construction of objects according to concepts what guarantees that the concepts thus presented should find application in our ordinary (empirical) perceptions?

The double-sided character of the process of pure intuition becomes explicit in the Transcendental Methodology. In the Methodology, Kant's principal aim is to warn philosophers against trying to emulate the method of the mathematician. To this end he notes two significant features of mathematical method. First, although mathematical concepts are, in a sense, arbitrary, the mathematician is able to construct the object corresponding to the concept and thus recognize a priori that the concept is exemplified. Second, by inspecting the constructed object with the mind's eye, the mathematician is able to gain knowledge of that object which outruns what is determined by the concept. Now the second of these points is a recapitulation of the themes of the Aesthetic. However, in developing the first, Kant introduces a point which is not anticipated in the Aesthetic. Attacking an obvious suggestion about the differences between mathematics and philosophy, he writes:

> Those who propose to distinguish philosophy from mathematics by saying that the former has as its object *quality* only and the latter *quantity* only, have mistaken the effect for the cause. The form of mathematical knowledge is the cause why it is limited exclusively to quantities. For it is the concept of quantities only that allows of being constructed, that is, exhibited *a priori* in intuition; whereas qualities cannot be presented in any intuition that is not empirical. [A714–15/B742–43]

This should strike us as puzzling. Given the idea of geometrical pure intuition which is presented in the Aesthetic, we are not prepared for the restriction introduced here: pure intuition seemed to consist in looking at mental pictures, and although it is true that geometers actually proceed by inspecting circles, triangles, lines, and so forth, there is no reason to think that we could not do something similar with patches of color. Perhaps the analogous enterprise with color patches would not lead anywhere, in that we would not be able to learn any synthetic truth by following the suggested procedure, but that does not seem to be Kant's point. His claim is that quality cannot be exhibited a priori in intuition, not that its exhibition a priori in intuition will not acquaint us with any synthetic truths. What we can draw from the passage I have quoted is the proposal that there is an important distinction between mathematical —quantitative—concepts and qualitative concepts, sufficient to motivate a restriction of the process of pure intuition to allow for it only to involve the construction of the former concepts.

We can make sense of all the passages I have cited if we take Kant to be haunted by the worry that, for all that he has said in the Aesthetic, it is possible that mathematical statements are vulnerable to weak revision. The first passage cited from the Deduction (B147) is explicitly concerned with the possibility that the concepts represented in acts of pure mathematical intuition might not apply to objects of empirical intuition; the second passage from the Deduction and the passage from the Methodology indicate that the process of pure intuition must draw on special concepts. So Kant faces the task of demonstrating that mathematical concepts have a privileged status. Consider in this light his specification of the project of the Axioms:

. . . there are pure *a priori* principles that we may not properly ascribe to the pure understanding, which is the faculty of concepts. For though they are mediated by the understanding, they are not derived from pure concepts but from pure intuitions. We find such principles in mathematics. The question, however, of their application to experience, that is of their objective validity, nay, even the deduction of the possibility of such synthetic *a priori* knowledge, must always carry us back to the pure understanding.

While, therefore, I leave aside the principles of mathematics, I shall none the less include those [more fundamental] principles upon which the possibility and *a priori* objective validity of mathematics are grounded. These latter must be regarded as the foundation of all mathematical principles. They proceed from concepts to intuition, not from intuition to concepts. [A159–60/B198–99]

We can understand this passage without the desperate suggestion that Kant is either recapitulating the ideas of the Aesthetic or contradicting them.

Here is my construal. The first three sentences remind us of the view of mathematical knowledge advanced in the Aesthetic. We gain a priori mathematical knowledge by undergoing a process of pure intuition. But Kant introduces a new point. The process of intuition is itself "mediated by the understanding." This draws our attention to the role of concepts in the activity of construction which makes space (in the case of geometry) an object of representation for us. At this point we must face up to the question whether the concepts by means of which we reveal the structure of space (and presumably of time) are applicable to the objects of perceptual experience. Kant asserts, in the last sentence of the first paragraph, that a full defense of the possibility of obtaining a priori knowledge by means of processes of pure intuition must rest on a demonstration of the applicability of mathematical concepts. More precisely, as the opening sentence of the second paragraph makes clear, we need to recognize the principles which guarantee that mathematical truths necessarily apply to experience. These principles will explain why mathematical concepts are privileged and thus show why the construction of concepts in pure intuition engenders a priori knowledge.

VI

If my interpretation of the role of the Axioms section is correct, then we should be able not only to understand its main thesis and how that thesis relates to Kant's general project, but also to obtain a clearer view of its argument. Let us begin by sharpening Kant's intended conclusion. The groundwork for the argument of the Axioms section is laid in the Schematism, where the three categories of quantity collapse into one schema: unity, plurality, and totality are transmuted into *number* (A142–43/B182). At the same time Kant offers an account of numerical representation. In representing numbers, we represent to ourselves wholes composed out of qualitatively homogeneous parts. This view of numerical representation explains the initially mysterious reduction of three categories to one schema. Number representations are formed by considering *totalities* of *many* objects each of which is thought of as a *unit* (thus numerical representation involves all three categorial concepts: we view plurality of units as totality). The purpose of the Axioms is to prove that appearances must submit to numerical representation. Let us again use geometry as a model. The thesis that the quantitative concepts, which the geometer constructs in pure intuition and employs to disclose the structure of space, must apply to objects of experience is recast as the thesis that spatially presented objects must submit to numerical representation. As we shall see below, one way of understanding this claim is to read it as asserting that the objects of outer experience must be measurable.

Kant's approach to the concept of number is a very natural one. Suppose that we are looking at a collection of physical objects—the fingers of a hand, let us say. Then to achieve a numerical representation of the objects is to abstract from the differences among them, adopting the perspective that they are homogeneous ("units"). In taking this perspective, we might view ourselves as constructing a new object, a concrete or "impure" number. Abstracting further from the particular character of the principle of individuation—that is, in the present case, the property of being a finger—we achieve a new construction which we might represent to ourselves by using stroke symbols ('/////'). The idea that numbers are constructed objects, generated in this twofold abstractive process, is popular with several eighteenth- and nineteenth-century writers. Despite Frege's objections to abstractive approaches to number, I think that the view I have attributed to Kant can be defended.[17] My purpose here, however, is not to defend the view but to show how it functions in the argument of the Axioms.

So far we have been concerned with *natural* numbers. In the Axioms, Kant is concerned to show that intuitions are extensive magnitudes. Hence it appears that his task will be to prove that the objects of experience must submit to *measurement*, so that a theory of *real* numbers will be needed. Kant has no theory of real numbers, and indeed, given the state of mathematics at his time, we should hardly expect him to have such a theory. This does not invalidate his project for the simple reason that he does not try to argue that a common system of measurement for all magnitudes must be applicable to objects of experience. Instead he conceives of measurement in its simplest terms. To measure an object is to represent it as a totality built up of standard units, where it is assumed that object and unit are so related that the former consists of integral multiples of the latter. Such simple measurements are comprehensible using the notion of natural number. Concentrating, as before, on the geometrical case, we may now formulate the goal of the Axioms as that of demonstrating the necessary applicability of the concept of number in simple measurement. The objects of experience must be such that it would be possible for us to abstract from their specific characteristics and to construct the numbers, specifically by representing perceptual objects as built up through the juxtaposition of homogeneous parts. Hence I interpret the principle of the Axioms as claiming that the concept of natural number is objectively valid, in the sense that the objects of experience must be amenable to that abstractive process whereby the numbers are generated. The possibility that experience might challenge our right to use the concept of natural number is blocked because, given any possible experience, we would be presented with objects which would serve as material for numerical construction, and, by carrying out the construction, we would come to recognize the applicability of the concept of number.

We are now ready to examine Kant's argument. This is presented in the opening paragraph of the section (Kant's subsequent remarks elucidate and develop particular points):

> Appearances, in their formal aspect, contain an intuition in space and time, which conditions them, one and all, *a priori*. They cannot be apprehended, that is, taken up into empirical consciousness, save through that synthesis of the manifold whereby the representations of a determinate space or time are generated, that is, through combination of the homogeneous manifold and consciousness of its synthetic unity. Consciousness of the synthetic unity of the manifold [and] homogeneous in intuition in general, in so far as the representation of an object first becomes possible by means of it, is, however, the concept of a magnitude (*quantum*). Thus even the perception of an object, as appearance, is only possible through the same synthetic unity of the manifold of the given sensible intuition as that whereby the unity of the combination of the manifold [and] homogeneous is thought in the concept of a *magnitude*. In other words, appearances are all without exception *magnitudes*, indeed *extensive magnitudes*. As intuitions in space or time, they must be represented through the same synthesis whereby space and time in general are determined. [A162/B202–203]

This is hardly pellucid. Nevertheless, I hope that my previous interpretative remarks will help us see the direction of argument. Kant's central idea seems to be that the recognition of objects in perception requires us to represent them as occupying space and time, that this recognition requires the representation of a "determinate space and time," and that this, in turn, requires us to

242

view (or to be able to view) these objects as complexes of homogeneous parts. As before, I shall restrict my discussion to the spatial case. The opening premise of the argument appears to be the claim that we must necessarily recognize the objects of experience as being in space. Kant then proposes that, in order for us to think of an object as spatial, we must form a conception of it as occupying a determinate space, and to think of it in this way is to abstract from the qualities it has and to see it as composed of homogeneous parts. So when one sees an object, and recognizes it as an occupant of space, one must be able to abstract from the diversity of its parts, adopting the perspective of regarding it as an aggregate of homogeneous fragments.

If this is correct, then the argument of the Axioms would run as follows:

1. Any object of outer experience must be recognized as occupying space.

2. To recognize an object as occupying space, the subject must be able to represent the space which it occupies.

3. If the subject can represent the space which the object occupies, then the subject must be able to conceive of the object as composed of homogeneous parts.

∴ 4. Any object of outer experience must be such as to enable the subject to conceive of it as composed of homogeneous parts (that is, as a magnitude).

I take it that 1 above is allegedly obtained from the Aesthetic and that the first sentence of Kant's proof (quoted above) is ambiguous between 1 and the conclusion of the Aesthetic. Kant's formulation that appearances are conditioned by "an intuition in space" is neatly equivocal. It might mean that appearances are necessarily informed with spatial structure, that the propositions of geometry are necessarily true, which is, as we have seen, the metaphysical version of the thesis of the Transcendental Ideality of space. Alternatively, it could be read as 1, that is, as the thesis that we necessarily represent objects as in space. The next sentence of Kant's proof makes it clear that the latter construal is needed for his argument. The first half of that sentence asserts 2; the second announces 3. In both cases Kant is recapitulating points made in the Transcendental Deduction. As he notes, representation of an object in space requires the construction of a "determinate space"—we do not have any capacity for seeing space as some perceptible containing medium whose parts can be perceived before the perception of objects which occupy them (see B138, B154, B160–61). His idea here is, I think, both more straightforward and more defensible than it initially sounds. To represent the objects in one's perceptual field as occupying space is to place over them a grid which screens out such qualities as their colors—as if we viewed them through a sheet of graph paper. Perhaps this, as it stands, is too crude, but Kant's claim is that some such filtering and partitioning of the visual appearances will be needed if we are to represent objects spatially.

On this reconstruction I claim that we not only obtain a version of the argument of the Axioms which fits Kant's text but we also achieve something of philosophical interest. Let me briefly enumerate some of the issues which are raised by my interpretation. First, I think it is clear that the argument of the Axioms oscillates between the two notions of a priori concept which I indicated in section IV. Although the principle of the Axioms (and the passages which announce the project of the Axioms) seems (seem) to be addressing the issue of whether the concept of number is objectively valid, Kant's argument comes close to the claim that this concept is subjectively necessary. If we were to amend 3 and 4 slightly— demanding not that the subject *must be able* to conceive of objects as composed of homogeneous parts but that the subject *must* so conceive them—then the argument I have attributed to Kant would defend the doctrine that mathematical concepts must be used by any subject of experience. Of course, this possibility raises again a question set aside in section IV, the question of the relation between the two Kantian approaches to a priori concepts. Second, there are interesting issues generated by the principles I have ascribed to Kant. Does Kant accept 1 simply because he formulates ambiguously the conclusion of the Aesthetic, or is there some Kantian route to 1?[18] How are the principles 2 and 3 supported by the remarks about spatial representation offered in the Transcendental Deduction?

The third topic, which may be the most important, concerns Kant's goal and his strategy for achieving it. Kant brings to the fore a point which is appreciated by other writers on mathematics but which is often confused with other issues. Why is an unarithmetical world impossible? Why is it that truths about numbers must apply to all worlds? An appeal to the analyticity of arithmetic would explain why arithmetical truths are necessary, but it would not answer these questions. Aficionados of analyticity want to hold that "All cats are animals" is analytic, but they do not usually insist that

244

the concept of cat must find application. On the other hand, a Platonist construal of arithmetic would raise the question of why certain abstract objects—the numbers—have to exist at all worlds. I suggest that Kant's discussion in the Axioms attacks a genuine philosophical problem about mathematics, a problem which has been largely neglected by his successors. In treating that problem, however, we may want to reject Kant's own strategy, and, in particular, we may wish to abandon the close connection which he makes among number, space, and time.[19]

VII

In the previous two sections I have attempted to redeem my promise that, by understanding how Kant's quest for a priori knowledge leads him from a priori warrants to a priori concepts, we could achieve a clearer view of his philosophy of mathematics. In conclusion I want to defend my claim about Kant's Quinean insight by looking at a more general issue. If the announced goal of the *Critique* is to explain the possibility of a priori knowledge, then what is Kant's account of the apriority of the principles of the Analytic?

Although Kant explicitly claims that the principles advanced in the Analytic are a priori, he tells us very little about how we can (or do) know them a priori. Only in two places does Kant address this issue, and on both occasions his remarks are cryptic. Before the systematic exposition of the principles of pure understanding, he claims that "conditions of possible experience" represent the "third thing" whereby we are able to go beyond the subject concept to the predicate concept (see A155–58/B194–97). At the end of the *Analogies* the same idea recurs:

> . . . through mere concepts of things, analyse them as we may, we can never advance from one object and its existence to the existence of another or to its mode of existence. But there is an alternative method, namely, to investigate the possibility of experience as a knowledge wherein all objects—if their representation is to have objective reality for us—must finally be capable of being given to us. [A217/B264]

Kant's discussion suggests that there are two fundamentally different types of synthetic a priori judgment. We can best explain the distinction by focusing on a particular form of judgment—say, judgments of form "All *A*'s are *B*'s." *Intuitive* synthetic a priori propositions of this form are those for which I can represent *A*'s to myself in pure intuition, thus coming to see that they are *B*'s.

Conceptual synthetic a priori propositions of the form are known by employing the procedure of conceptual analysis to show that all *A*'s *which can be objects of experience* are *B*'s and inferring that all *A*'s are *B*'s. Analysis of the conditions of possible experience is the distinctive way in which conceptual synthetic a priori propositions are known. I take it that this analysis is *displayed* (not described) in the Analytic, while the process of pure intuition is *described* (not displayed) in the Aesthetic and the Methodology. If this is a correct account of Kant's idea that the conditions of the possibility of experience are the mediating factor for some of our synthetic a priori knowledge, then we must conclude that the way in which we know a priori the principles of the Analytic (if we do) is by following the type of reasoning which the Analytic contains.

My reconstruction invites Eberhard's criticism. For it seems that we have found a place for synthetic a priori propositions beyond those knowable via pure intuition only by restricting the subject concepts of analytic truths. If "All *A*'s and *B*'s" is a conceptual synthetic a priori truth, then "All *A*'s which are objects of possible experience are *B*'s" is analytic. It is here that the notion of an a priori concept enters the discussion. Kant would respond that epistemological prizes are not automatically gained by inflating subject concepts; we need to ensure the "objective validity" of our concepts. Thus, in the case of the principles of the Analytic, the important feature is not whether we can convert them into analytic truths by amending the subject concepts but whether the concepts they contain are a priori concepts. Hence the major enterprise of the Analytic is to defend the apriority of particular concepts, and this enterprise is continuous with Kant's original plan of accounting for a priori knowledge.

A simple example of Kant's strategy occurs in the First Analogy. Halfway through his discussion, Kant casually admits that the principle of the Analogy (that substance is permanent) is tautological. How can we account for this remark? On the interpretation I suggest, there should be no surprise. Distinguish two conceptions of substance. The first concept, $substance_1$, does not contain the characteristic of permanence, while the second, $substance_2$, does. Kant will argue that any $substances_1$ which can be objects of possible experience must be $substances_2$ and that the concept of $substance_1$ must find application in experience. This will complete his account of the a priori status of "Substances are permanent" by doing all of the following: (1) showing that the conditions of possible experience determine that any substance we encounter is permanent, (2) displaying a route to the knowledge that all substances are permanent through analysis of the conditions of possible experience, and (3) demonstrating that experience cannot lead us to abandon the concept of substance. Depending on whether we read "Substances are permanent" as "Substances$_1$ are permanent" or as "Substances$_2$ are permanent," we can divide our labors among the three tasks—the more we pack into the concept of substance$_1$ the easier we make (1) and (2) and the harder we make (3)—but we do not save any work by glossing the principle so that it becomes analytic. Thus, with the Analytic in general, as with the Axioms in particular, interpreting Kant as achieving a Quinean insight enables us to make sense of some of his most mystifying remarks.[20]

NOTES

1. Throughout this paper I shall follow the standard practice of referring to passages from the *Critique* by citing the pagination of the first and second editions. All quoted translations are from the Norman Kemp Smith translation.

2. W. V. Quine, *From a Logical Point of View*, 2d ed.(Harvard University Press, 1961, 1980), pp. 20–46.

3. "A Priori Knowledge," *Philosophical Review* 89 (1980): 3–23.

4. Saul Kripke, "Naming and Necessity," in D. Davidson and G. Harman, eds., *Semantics of Natural Language* (D. Reidel, 1972), pp. 253–355, 763–69; and Edward Erwin, "Are the Notions 'A Priori Truth' and 'Necessary Truth' Extensionally Equivalent?" *Canadian Journal of Philosophy* 3 (1974): 591–602. In "Apriority and Necessity," *Australasian Journal of Philosophy* 58 (1980): 89–101, I apply my analysis of a priori knowledge to argue that the traditional equivalence is flawed beyond repair.

5. Quine, *From a Logical Point of View*, p. 43.

6. See "A Priori Knowledge," Sec. 5, "Apriority and Necessity," sec. 3.

7. Interestingly enough, Hilary Putnam has used something similar to this distinction to evaluate Quine's doctrines about apriority and unrevisability. See the postscripts to "There Is at Least One A Priori Truth," *Erkenntnis* 13 (1978): 153–70. Putnam's assessment of the significance of Quine's famous essay is also akin to my own: see "Two Dogmas Revisited," in G. Ryle ed., *Contemporary Aspects of Philosophy* (Oriel, 1978).

8. There are complications in defending the view that such processes will meet *1a*. Defenders of the approach to reference which has been advanced by Kripke and Putnam may try to claim that it is possible to entertain a proposition without having any very full conception of the objects with which the proposition is concerned, so that some lives which are sufficient for allegedly analytic truths would not permit the subject to undergo the process of conceptual disclosure. If this point is correct, then it multiplies the troubles of the traditional connection between analyticity and apriority. Despite its initial plausibility, however, I believe that the challenge based on the Kripke-Putnam approach to reference can be turned back.

9. John Stuart Mill, *A System of Logic* (Longmans, 1970), p. 91. I have discussed Mill's use of this example in "Arithmetic for the Millian," *Philosophical Studies* 37 (1980): 215–36.

10. W. V. Quine, "Truth by Convention," in *The Ways of Paradox*, 2d ed., (Harvard University Press, 1975), pp. 77–106. The passage on pp 101–102 is especially close to some Kantian themes.

11. See H. E. Allison, ed., *The Kant-Eberhard Controversy* (Johns Hopkins, 1973) p. 175. My attention was originally drawn to this passage through its citation in L. W. Beck, "Can Kant's Synthetic Judgments be Made Analytic?" in R. P. Wolff, ed., *Kant*, pp. 3–22. I concur with Beck's judgment that the passage reflects Kant's ideas, even though it was written by Schultz "under Kant's supervision." There are a number of places in the *Critique* where the same thought is expressed, although perhaps never so forthrightly. See, for example, footnote *a* to A242, A252–4/B308–10.

12. Kant's commitment to this idea is especially clear from the lectures on logic. See R. Hartman and W. Schwartz, trans., *Logic* (Bobbs-Merrill, 1974), pp. 68–72, 141–44.

13. This approach is adopted by Jonathan Bennett in *Kant's Analytic* (Cambridge, 1966) pp. 167–70. Bennett makes some very insightful observations about Kant's notion of an extensive magnitude, but I think that he fails to see how the Axioms section makes any contribution to Kant's account of mathematics.

14. As one might expect, Kemp Smith defends the view that the approaches of the Axioms and Aesthetic are incompatible (*A Commentary to Kant's "Critique of Pure Reason"* [Macmillan, 1929], pp. 345–47). For the opposite view, briskly stated and defended, see A. C. Ewing, *A Short Commentary on Kant's "Critique of Pure Reason"* (Chicago, 1938), p. 148. The inconsistency of the Aesthetic and Axioms is argued by Robert Paul Wolff (*Kant's Theory of Mental Activity* [Harvard, 1963], pp. 18, 228–31) and is taken as a serious problem by Arthur Melnick (*Kant's Analogies of Experience* [Chicago, 1973], pp. 18–22). Ralph Walker seems to believe that the Axioms section is superfluous (*Kant* [Routledge and Kegan Paul, 1978], p. 94), and H. J. Paton struggles (unsuccessfully) to make it both compatible with the Aesthetic and nonredundant (*Kant's Metaphysic of Experience* [Allen and Unwin, 1936], 2:119ff.). Perhaps the most revealing discussion of the role of the Axioms is given by W. H. Walsh (*Kant's Criticism of Metaphysics* [Edinburgh, 1975], secs. 20–21). Like Paton, Walsh believes that the Aesthetic and the Axioms are compatible, but he does not have a sufficiently precise account of Kant's framework notions or of the views on mathematical knowledge advanced in the Aesthetic to articulate a defense of this idea.

15. More detail about Kant's views on mathematics can be found in my "Kant and the Foundations of Mathematics," *Philosophical Review* 84 (1975): 23–50.

16. I have not quoted the final sentence of the footnote in which the notion of 'synthesis' which figures in the penultimate sentence (i.e., the last sentence cited) is identified as the transcendental synthesis of imagination.

17. For Frege's criticisms see *The Foundations of Arithmetic* (Blackwell, 1950), secs. 34–44. Frege's citations reveal the popularity of the view among his predecessors and contemporaries.

18. I take it that one highly influential line of Kantian interpretation would suppose that there is an alternative route. Several writers, most notably P. F. Strawson (*Individuals* [Methuen, 1959], chap. 2), Jonathan Bennett (*Kant's Analytic*, chap. 3), and Onora O'Neill, "Space and Objects" (*Journal of Philosophy* 73 [1976]: pp. 29–45), try to show that, if certain types of judgments are to be possible, the subject must have a capacity for (some type of) spatial representation. I have three reasons for thinking that this approach is misguided. First, there is no textual support for ascribing any such argument to Kant. Second, to suppose that Kant might have advanced this type of argument is to convict him of confusion: before the Axioms, Kant discusses space in the Aesthetic and (briefly) in the Deductions; the latter

passages are concerned with the conditions under which the employment of spatial concepts are possible (that is, they already presuppose 1), while the Aesthetic explicitly abstracts from consideration of the *concepts* which we must use. Third, the arguments advanced on Kant's behalf presuppose a concept of space which he himself rejected. "Master sounds" and "perceptual contexts" are introduced as surrogates for space and places, and it is supposed that perception of these will enable the subject to make certain kinds of discriminations. Given Kant's emphasis on our inability to perceive space without prior constructive activity, this will hardly recommend itself as an interpretative approach, even if we waive philosophical difficulties about the necessity and sufficiency of appeals to the master sound.

19. In a celebrated passage Frege claims that "the truths of arithmetic govern all that is numerable. This is the widest domain of all; for to it belongs not only the actual, not only the intuitable, but everything thinkable" (*Foundations of Arithmetic*, p. 21). If we accept Frege's claim, then we must see Kant's attempt to explain the necessary applicability of the concept of number as failing to reach the root of the problem, since the most Kant could defend would be the necessity of applying arithmetical concepts to a proper subset of their appropriate objects. Interestingly, Frege's contemporary, Dedekind, did attempt to show that arithmetical concepts must necessarily apply to all objects of thought, using the kind of constructivist approach to numbers which Kant employed but liberating it from the connection to space and time. See R. Dedekind, *The Nature and Meaning of Numbers*, in W. Beman, ed., *Dedekind's Essays on the Theory of Numbers* (Dover, 1963), pp. 31–34.

20. I am grateful to Patricia Kitcher for her helpful comments.

Two Kinds of Transcendental Objectivity: Their Differentiation

CHARLES M. SHEROVER
Hunter College, CUNY

Why, two hundred years after the event, should a paper be written that seeks to clarify Kant's use of two of his own technical terms? Already in its first two hundred years, the first *Critique* has revolutionized the development of philosophic thinking; yet standard translations—like the commentaries and disputes based upon them—almost universally ignore key distinctions which the German text suggests Kant was decidedly careful to make. Before one can discuss the import of some key concepts, he must first repair the damage wrought by translations which collapse key distinctions into a lowest common denominator. That later German may have coalesced them does not mean that Kant had used them interchangably in 1781; that they may indeed be synonymous, as translations suggest, is something to be proved by textual exegesis, not to be presumed without even notice.

What is termed in English as 'the transcendental object' is one of these translation reductions; much of the dispute concerning its meaning seems to derive from the fact that this English term coalesces two very different German words which Kant was seemingly careful to keep apart. Norman Kemp Smith himself admonished us: "It is always safer to take Kant quite literally. He nearly always means exactly what he says at the time when he says it."[1] If Kant used two distinctive terms for what the English terms 'transcendental object'—*der transzendentale Gegenstand* and *das transzendentale Objekt*—he must have intended some difference between them. Notwithstanding the valued service that the Smith translation has rendered to Kant scholarship, it is crucial, at least with reference to these two terms, to take Smith's admonition more seriously than he himself did.[2]

Clarification is crucial for any consideration of the speculative implications of the Critical philosophy for that metaphysical thinking which Kant had held to be congenital to the human mind. It is equally crucial for understanding the first *Critique* itself, for Kant uses at least one of these two German terms in virtually every section of the work, and he did *not* delete them from the second edition. Kant was not noted as a literary stylist, and he generally

251

made technical distinctions between associated words.[3] His German does not accord with subsequent English (and French) practice of collapsing the two distinctive German words for 'object' into one. Use of both proximately to each other suggests the hypothesis that a differentiation of meaning was intended, a differentiation too long ignored.

The question of this article is whether Kant's usages in each of the sections in which they appear present a distinction of meaning. Because the paucity of the English vocabulary offers only one word for Kant's two, it would be necessary to create distinguishing English neologisms for them; rather than do that, I will restrict here the use of (1) 'transcendental object(ivity)' to that of an umbrella term, and (2) bring the German *Gegenstand* and *Objekt* directly into the English.

This paper is, then, divided into two main parts: first, a brief overview of what seems to be suggested by an examination of the Kantian text of the 1781 edition, and, second, a section-by-section examination of the 1781 edition itself to note each use of 'Transcendental *Gegenstand*' or 'Transcendental *Objekt*.'[4] In view of Kant's continued use of these distinctive terms, it would seem that clarification of this most obscure yet central of Critical doctrines should help throw light on the meaning of that enterprise which Kant unveiled in 1781.

I

Although the use of 'Transcendental *Gegenstand*' and 'Transcendental *Objekt*' is not always marked by a stringent consistency, it does seem that Kant was struggling to differentiate distinctive meanings between them. As the text develops, the differentiation between them appears to become increasingly clear; if one then reads the developed differentiation back into the earlier sections (which I do *not* propose to do here), the earlier uses of these two different terms become clearer in intent.

Through the first *Critique*, Kant seems to be struggling with the question of the possibility of objectivity in the light of his Copernican Revolution, the question of how the human mind, functioning in terms of its own interpretative canons, capabilities, and limitations, is able to achieve some definable degree of objectivity—first, in cognition of a world perceived as consisting of separable objects, and, second, in the reach of speculative thought about the nature of that world.

Generally speaking, Kant has used the term '*Gegenstand*',

whether on an empirical or on a transcendental level, to refer to what is conceived by us to be external to us and/or to be independent in its being of the cognitive or intellectual processes wherein an awareness of it becomes an ingredient of our own conscious thought. Thus 'Gegenstand' seems to refer to a possible specifiable object of experience to which a cognitive act claims to refer, and 'Transcendental Gegenstand' generally seems to refer to those characteristics—as counterparts of our categorial intellect—which those specifiable objects must be understood to 'incorporate' in order to be able to become referential objects of our cognitive experiences. This externality and existent independence seems to be buttressed by Kant's use, in the Dialectic, of 'Transcendental Gegenstand' to refer to God—taken as a transcendent being, the ground or primal source of the world of nature that is taken to exist quite aside from our inherently finite knowledge of objects comprising it.

If we are to have any knowledge of an 'external' object, we must have a concept of it in our thinking that is itself separable in thought from the object of which it claims to be a concept. I cannot think without thinking something, some concept which is the grammatical accusative of the declaration 'I think . . .' This seems to be the meaning of the word 'Objekt'—internal to the act of thinking itself in an essential grammatical sense.[5] If this is so, then cognitive objectivity would depend on the compatibility of the conceptual 'Objekt' of an act of thinking with the 'Gegenstand' that is what the thinking claims to be about. If we do in fact have knowledge of empirical objects, and if we are able to think the general (categorial) requirements which any object must offer to meet our requisites for understanding it, we must be able to do so. Hence, just like 'Gegenstand', the word 'Objekt' must have both empirical and transcendental significance. And, further, if both 'Gegenstand' and 'Objekt' must, on either level, correlate with each other, it would seem that any Critical doctrine of cognitive objectivity depends on the central import of the "Highest Principle of All Synthetic Judgments" (A154–58) as the fulcrum on which it rests.

II

To determine whether this reading is fair, one must consult the text itself. What I propose to do in this inquiry is to examine each of the sections of the Critique in which some aspect of the doctrine of transcendental objectivity is presented.

This first main section begins with the famous sentences:

> Of whatever kind and through whatever means a cognition may relate to *Gegenstand*s, it is intuition⁶ through which it is immediately related to them and onto which all thinking as means is aimed. This transpires however only so far as the *Gegenstand* is given to us. [A19]

Knowledge, we are told, in the passages which follow, is dependent on our capacity to have representations, the manner in which *Gegenstand*s affect us so that we may become aware of them.

After presenting the theses concerning the nature of time and space as the two forms of intuition, he turns, in his "General Remarks" to the first mention of transcendental objectivity. He does so by means of an example, the experience of rain. The transcendental distinction is lost if we treat an empirical representation as not rooted in some thing (*Sache*) in itself: we then take a rainbow as a mere appearance and rain as a thing itself. Taken in a merely physical sense, this is fine; but we must ask whether, in its general character, it represents a *Gegenstand* in itself, "not the raindrops, for they are already, as appearances, empirical *Objekts*"; it is the question of the relationship "of the representation to the *Gegenstand*" that is transcendental. For appearances include not only the raindrops "but also their rounded form, indeed even the space in which they fall"; these are "but mere modifications, or foundations of our sensible intuition; the Transcendental *Objekt* remains however to us unknown" (A45–46).

The question is now posed. If we attend to Kant's language, we seem to have three levels of discrimination: (1) the empirical *Objekt*s, i.e., the raindrops, (2) the phenomenon of raining in its most general sense, appearing to sensible intuition as the *Gegenstand* itself; and (3) the Transcendental *Objekt* seemingly undergirding the entire experiential event: the particular in the appearance, the empirical event in which it appears, and that unknown ground of that appearing to human sensible intuition which is a manifestation.

Kant is here emphasizing the point that appearances are not self–sustaining; they are not hallucinatory but are modifications of human sensibility by things–themselves (sometimes referred to as *Sache* and sometimes as *Ding*), which are not distinct from the thing-as-appearing, but yet the appearing thing itself insofar as the forms of human sensibility (and thought) can deal with it. Whether this suggested tripartite distinction finally holds, whether the

254

Gegenstand itself is not perhaps more than I have here taken it to be, it seems clear that Kant is suggesting some kind of distinction between the *Gegenstand*–itself and the Transcendental *Objekt*.

The Transcendental Deduction

In the Aesthetic we were presented with the Transcendental *Objekt*. In the Deduction, in contrast, Kant discusses only the Transcendental *Gegenstand*. The few references to the *Objekt–überhaupt* possibly suggest confusion of any clearcut differentiation; however, if we quickly follow the passages, some possible clarification may result.

1. Before we proceed to the Deduction itself, it is fruitful to look at Kant's use of *Gegenstand* and *Objekt* in the "Transition" (section 14). In its first two paragraphs (A92–94) he uses the word *Gegenstand* fifteen times and the word *Objekt* only twice.

The problematic is set out in the famous second sentence: "Either the *Gegenstand* makes the representation, or this [representation] alone makes the *Gegenstand* possible." Knowledge is of a *Gegenstand* presented by sensory intuition; but that *Gegenstand* must also be thought conceptually—as *Gegenstand* as such (= *überhaupt*), for "Concepts of *Gegenstands* as such, as a priori conditions, ground all empirical knowledge." But this is possible only if empirical cognitions conform to such concepts, just because "without their presupposition, nothing is possible as *Objekt of experience*" (Kant's italics). Finally, "Without this original relation to possible experience, in which all *Gegenstands* of cognition come forth, the relation to any one *Objekt* could not be conceived."

Transcendental logic has been described as that "which should contain merely the rules of pure thought of a *Gegenstand*" (A55); we have been told that "the difference between the transcendental and the empirical belongs only to the critique of cognitions and does not concern their relation to their *Gegenstand*" (A57); therefore, it becomes clear that, in the "Transition," Kant seeks to lay the ground for justifying empirical knowledge. Such knowledge depends upon the integration of sensibility and conceptual thought in the awareness of any known entity. When a chair is seen as a chair, both perceptual receptivity and conceptualization are already integrated (synthesized) in the apprehending awareness of consciousness. A cognition is of a particular *Gegenstand*; to be apprehended it must have met the intuitive requirement of temporal and spatial perceptibility and of the conceptual structure of descriptive thinking. Our idea of the chair determines the character of that chair as we are aware of it, just because it is only through that idea that it can be known as a real and concrete thing in the experience of it. In preparing to justify the role of pure concepts (categories) in cognitional activity (i.e., forming empirical concepts integrated with temporal–spatial perception), Kant suggests the prior necessity of being able to think the character of any *Gegenstand* as such in order to recognize the appearing chair as an example. *Gegenstand* then seems to be the particular entity that is known, and *Gegenstand* as such, those characteristics of an object as such which *any* particular *Gegenstand* must embody in order to be recognized as a particular *Gegenstand* by us. Such characteristics will turn out to be the categories of understanding exemplified in any empirical concept.

Noteworthy is the last sentence of this first long paragraph: "the objective validity of the categories" ("according to the form of thinking") yields the conclusion that "they relate necessarily and a priori to the *Gegenstand*s of experience, since only by means of them as such can any particular *Gegenstand* of experience be thought"(A93).

Throughout this discussion Kant's use of *Gegenstand* is sometimes singular and sometimes plural. But the italicized *Objekt of experience* is singular, has no precedent article, and so may be construed as a more abstract term. In the second use of *Objekt* it is indeed particularized, but contrasted to the pluralization of *Gegenstand*.

At this point we can begin to see the differentiation of the two terms: our empirical knowledge of particular *Gegenstand*s must conform to the conditions of thinking (as to the conditions of sensibility); such conditions of cognitive thinking define the conceptual structure of any possible *Gegenstand* of awareness as such regardless of its particularity; only so can it as such have met our cognitional requirements and thus enter into the class of *Objekt of experience* as this *Gegenstand* of a particular cognitive activity. Despite the particularization of the second usage of *Objekt*, this would seem to hold.

2. It is in explicating the "Synthesis of Recognition in the Concept" that the Transcendental *Gegenstand* is first introduced (A109). In this section *Gegenstand* is used twenty-nine times, and *Objekt* only once.

Beginning in A104, Kant seeks to clarify what is meant by "a *Gegenstand* of my representations." Kant's concern here is clearly with the conceptual structure we must be able to think regarding any appearance that becomes a *Gegenstand* of knowledge. Insofar as appearances are not to be taken as *Gegenstands* "outside of the power of representation," and yet must be thought as both corresponding to, while different from, cognition, "it is easy to see that this *Gegenstand* must be thought only as something as such = *x*"; it is that unity "which constitutes [*ausmacht*] the concept of a *Gegenstand*" (A105); this unity, "which the *Gegenstand* makes necessary, could be nothing other than the formal unity of consciousness in the synthesis of the manifold of the representations." Insofar as all cognitions require a concept, and a concept is, in its form, universal [*allgemeines*] and serves as a rule, the concept of a *Gegenstand* as such is a rule for intuition as it represents in given appearances "the synthesis of the manifold of representations." We can then say that "we know the *Gegenstand*, if we have effected synthetic unity in the manifold of intuition."

Arguing that the transcendental unity of apperception grounds the unity of consciousness (A106), Kant then considers it possible "to determine our concept of a *Gegenstand* as such more accurately" (A108). Insofar as appearances presented in intuition are not things themselves but only representations which, again, have their object (that itself cannot be intuited), such a *Gegenstand* is not empirical; it may thereby "be named Transcendental *Gegenstand* = *X*" (A109). And then:

The pure concept of this Transcendental *Gegenstand* (which actually is always one and the same for all our knowledge = *X*) is that which, in all our empirical concepts, can generally bring about a relation to a *Gegenstand*, i.e., objective reality [*objektive Realität*].

The Transcendental *Gegenstand*—"always one and the same"— cannot be things themselves; what is one and the same for all cognitions is precisely the conceptual structure, the categorial unity, which must be present in our cognitive thinking, thereby in any cognitive concept if that concept is to have cognitive relation to appearances, i.e., truly to serve as rule for cognitive accomplishment; by defining the characteristics of any 'something' which can appear as a particular thing in our cognitive consciousness. Derived not from things but from our own mode of cognitive competence, such concept is thereby a priori; only as such can it define in advance of any presentation just what categorial characters that presentation must enable us to read from it, that enables that presentation to be a *Gegenstand* of our experience. A generalized 'something' is not intuitable, only specific things are;

the characteristics of 'somethingness' are, however, the conceptual elements of our conceptual structure which any particular must be able to meet if it is to be known by us. The Transcendental *Gegenstand*, then, seems to be not something 'out there' to be encountered, but as *'Gegenständlichkeit'* (i.e., the conceptual form which must be met by any possible candidate for cognition by us).

This interpretation is supported by Kant's presentation of Transcendental Apperception as the correlate of the Transcendental *Gegenstand*. As he initiates that separable (but not separate) discussion:

All necessity at any time is grounded by a transcendental condition. Therefore, a transcendental ground of the unity of consciousness must be met in the synthesis of the manifold of all our intuitions, and consequently as well, the concepts of *Objekt*s generally, hence also of all *Gegenstand*s of experience; without this it would be impossible to think any one *Gegenstand* for our intuitions; for this *Gegenstand* is nothing more than the Something [*Etwas*] of which the concept expresses such a necessity of the synthesis. [A106]

Kant's epistemological dualism is at work here. Transcendental Apperception, the unity of consciousness, is the correlate that also grounds our outer representations, the unity of which it projects from 'the identity of its own activity' (A108). *Objekt*, then, is the internal correlate to the *Gegenstand* apprehended as in outer sense; the pure concept of Transcendental *Gegenstand* then seems to be the categorial description of 'somethingness' which meets the internal requirements of objectivity. Tentatively, then, I suggest that *Gegenstand* is used as the mind's intentional referentiality to outer experience, while *Objekt* seems to be Transcendental Apperception's ground for such projection onto and receptivity from that which is apprehended in intuition. Insofar as Kant is concerned to establish that experience of external *Gegenstand*s is grounded in a subjective condition, it would seem that the notion of *Objekt* as such is the internal (and thereby mediating) ground of the *Gegenstand* as such or Transcendental *Gegenstand*.

3. In the fourth subsection, "Preliminary Explanation of the Possibility of the Categories as Cognitions A Priori," *Gegenstand* is used twice and *Objekt* three times. Kant is here primarily concerned to justify the thesis of the *"affinity* of manifolds"(A113).

In a passage which virtually duplicates the famous passage in the section entitled "Highest Principle of All Synthetic Judgments,"

Kant asserts: "The a priori conditions of a possible experience as such are at the same time conditions of the possibility of the *Gegenstand*s of experience" (A111; cf. A158 and below). If the categories, as conditions of thinking, and space and time as conditions of intuition, must join together as conditions of any experience, then "they are each also ground concepts to think *Objekt*s as such for appearances" (A111). Experience rests on employing an "empirical rule of association" (A112), and "The ground of the possibility of the association of the manifold, so far as it [with Erdmann: *er*] lies in the *Objekt* is called the *affinity* of the manifold" (A113).

Even nature itself is to be conceived not as a thing itself but as "merely a collection of representations of the mind" (A114), and its conceived unity is to be found in the source of all our knowledge, that radical faculty entitled Transcendental Apperception just "because of which alone it can be called *Objekt* of all possible experience, i.e., Nature" (A114). The unity in terms of which we then see what we call nature is a priori just because it originates in the nature of our minds as modes of thinking, not as "borrowed from the *Gegenstand*s of nature itself." (A114).

4. In the "Summary Representation" at the end of the systematic version of the Deduction, *Gegenstand* is used eight times and *Objekt* only twice, and both times in the singular. In each case, *Gegenstand* refers to that which is the intentional referent of a cognitive claim. In the line before A129, *Objekt* could conceivably be taken as synonymous. The second instance is, perhaps, more problematic:

In this unity of possible consciousness, however, the form of all cognition of *Gegenstand*s is also to be found (through which the manifold as belonging to a Single *Objekt* is thought). Therefore the mode of how the manifold of sensible representation (intuition) belongs to consciousness, precedes all knowledge of *Gegenstand*s, as its prior intellectual form, and itself constitutes a formal knowledge of all *Gegenstand*s a priori, so far as they are thought (categories). [A129–30]

Here there is little doubt concerning the meaning of *Gegenstand* as the intentional reference of cognitive acts and, in a formal sense, the intellectual (categorial) form in which *Gegenstand*s must be thought in order to be known as particular referents of cognitive activity. The word '*Objekt*' here could be interpreted either (1) as a synonym for any particular referent, or (2) as previously suggested, as that in Transcendental Apperception which is the subjective grounding correlate of what is claimed to be known in the appearance of an external x, the *Gegenstand* of experience being the empirical consequent.[7]

The Analytic of Principles

Insofar as this major segment seeks to found the possibility and nature of empirical knowledge, we should not anticipate much discussion of transcendental objectivity. Only five passages need be cited before we move on to more explicitly fruitful ground.

1. The chapter on the Schematism, concerned with the temporalization of the categories requisite for their cognitive employment, is replete with references to *Gegenstand*s. The word *Objekt* appears only once where the emerging distinction seems clear. In A147 we find the following sentence:

> In fact, a meaning certainly remains in the pure concepts of understanding, after the separation of all sensible conditions, but it is only a logical meaning of the mere unity of representations; to such representations however no *Gegenstand* and thereby no meaning is given, which only could be given to a concept of an *Objekt*.

Cognitive meaning requires a referential *Gegenstand*, not merely an *Objekt* of thinking.

2. In "The Highest Principle of All Analytic Judgments" (A150), the first sentence buttresses the emerging distinction: *Objekt* is used as the referent of purely logical, not cognitive thinking. (In this connection it must be remembered that the point of this entire section is to restrict the utility of the principle of contradiction to a merely negative function with no authority as a sign of cognitive truth.)

3. In "The Highest Principle of All Synthetic Judgments" (A157), prefatory to the Principles of Pure Understanding, in which the possibility of cognition is finally grounded, the distinction between *Objekt* and *Gegenstand* is invoked. *Objekt* is the referent of logical thought—truth is defined as "agreement with the *Objekt*"—but only so far as "it contains nothing further than what is necessary to the synthetic unity of experience as such." *Gegenstand*, as the referent of cognition under the conditions of the intuitive manifold, is the only one of these words used in the last two paragraphs (A158) restating the Principle; in the last paragraph (in language picked up from A111), we are clearly told: "The conditions of the *possibility of*

260

experience as such are at the same time conditions of the *possibility of the Gegenstands* of experience."

4. In "The Anticipations of Perception" (A166), *Gegenstand* is identified, in the statement of the Principle as "*(realitas phenomenon)*," i.e., the phenomenally real; this fully accords with preceding uses, whether in a sensible sense as the empirical *Gegenstand* or in the transcendental sense as the categorial constitution of any possible appearing entity. (Only in the B version is the distinction possibly obscured by the use of *Objekt*, not in the statement of the Principle, be it noted, but in the new explanatory paragraph.)

5. Perhaps more directly to this inquiry than any other separate passage so far, the first paragraph of the Second Analogy (A189–91) speaks directly to the differentiation of *Gegenstand* and *Objekt*; in doing so it specifies at least one meaning of Transcendental *Gegenstand*. This paragraph is clearly prefatory —Kant's next paragraph begins with the sentence: "Now let us proceed to our task." It is a short essay in definition and is prefatory to explication of the "Principle of Production," Kant's name for the rule governing the necessary sequentiality of appearances.[8]

Kant opens by noting that the "apprehension of the manifold of appearances is always successive," but this is *not* to say that the successiveness is also "in the *Gegenstand*." Appearances, as representations, are the *Gegenstands* of consciousness; they are the objects of cognitive activity as the power of imagination has presented them in the synthesis of apprehension. Just what they may be, as things themselves, is beyond the "sphere of our knowledge."

He cites the example of a house which in the successiveness of apprehension appears itself successive, even if we do not believe that the house itself might also be. This does not create a real problem, however, for "as soon as I raise my concept from a *Gegenstand* [of experience] to the transcendental meaning, the house is certainly no thing–itself but only an appearance, i.e., a representation, whose Transcendental *Gegenstand* is unknown." The appearance, successively appearing as representation, is nothing–itself, for "the content of this representation is considered as the *Gegenstand*, with which my concept, which I extract from the representation of apprehension, shall agree."

Conceivably, Kant points out, one could use the word *Objekt* for that which is represented in consciousness, but such usage could not signify anything beyond the *Gegenstands* of experience. *If* appearances were things–themselves, we still would be unable to explain just how the succession of representation of the manifold is to be joined in such *Objekt*. The word *Objekt* points in a direction different from that of *Gegenstand*: it denotes something more, for truth is "the agreement of knowledge with the *Objekt*"—not with the *Gegenstand*. The word *Objekt* denotes the "formal conditions of empirical truth," clearly distinguished here from the representation of apprehension; for truth "can be represented only through the *Objekt* different from them" if there is a rule, different from all apprehensions, which necessitates the unification of the manifold. "That in the appearance, which contains the condition of this necessary rule of apprehension, is the *Objekt*."

Here *Gegenstand* is clearly used as the empirical entity, the appearing appearance, that to which cognition claims reference; and Transcendental *Gegenstand*, as the thing–itself, the ground (= *Ursache*: we should be more than cautious in saying 'cause' in any efficacious sense) of that which appears to us. In this instance, the Transcendental *Gegenstand* seems to be the house–itself, that which appears to us as 'this house' in the succession of imaginative apprehension.

Objekt, on the other hand, clearly refers *to us*, to our 'transcendental machinery', to the "formal conditions" which we must impose, the requisite agreement of a cognitive claim with our own cognitive requirements. The term "formal conditions" has a very clear meaning for Kant, however; its referent = the forms of space and time in which all appearances must appear in order for us to become aware of them. If we recall the statement of the Highest Principle of All Synthetic Judgments: the possibility of the *Gegenstand*s of experience are equally the conditions of our possibility of experiencing them; if we remember the principle of the Schematism—only by entering into the form of time can categorial concepts achieve empirical cognitive employment—then the meaning of *Objekt* here seems clear: the *Objekt*, agreement with which defines truth, is the form of time in us, the form of inner sense, in which all consciousness functions, to whose requirements all application of categorial concepts must be conformed. The *Objekt* to which truth claims refer is the temporal form of cognitive truth itself, the form of schematic temporalization of otherwise abstract categories. It seems entirely appropriate that Kant, seeking to explicate the rule of sequentiality in experience, prefaces his discussion by identifying it not only with the form of time but underlines this identification by tying it to Apprehension, the most explicitly temporal 'moment' of the threefold synthesis presented in the Deduction.

In contrast to the *Gegenstand* which is seen as outside of us, whether empirically cognized or transcendentally presupposed, *Objekt* is the correlate within cognitive subjectivity, that subjective form which grounds our capacity to have knowledge and delineates the finite kinds of knowledge we may have.

Phenomena and Noumena

This suggested distinction between *Gegenstand* and *Objekt* seems to hold generally through the rest of the Analytic.[9] The capstone chapter of the Analytic is entitled "Of the Ground of the Distinction of All *Gegenstand*s as Such into Phenomena and Noumena." We may then expect the discussion to focus on *Gegenstand*s, some of which may be seen as noumenal; just how *Objekt* enters into this differentiation of different kinds of *Gegenstand*s should be instructive.

In A246 we read the phrases "*Gegenstand*s of the senses" and "*Gegenstand*s of experience," while *Objekt* seems to be used only as the referent of possible self–contained thinking.

In A247 the two words are thus juxtaposed:

Thinking is the activity to relate a given intuition to a *Gegenstand*. If this kind of intuition is in no way given, the *Gegenstand* is merely transcendental, and the concept of understanding has nothing other than transcendental use, namely the unity of the thinking of a manifold as such. Through a pure category in which every condition of sensible intuition (the only kind possible for us) is abstracted, no *Objekt* is determined, but only the thought of an *Objekt* as such, expressed in different modes. Now there belongs to the use of a concept a function of the power of judgment, which subsumes a *Gegenstand* under it, and thereby at least the formal condition under which something in intuition can be given.

A crucial passage (A249) distinguishes *Gegenstand*s—as phenomenal or as conceivably noumenal—from *Objekt*. Significantly, it is rooted in the Aesthetic: " . . . the limited concept of appearances through the Transcendental Aesthetic already by itself gives us the objective reality of Noumena, and the division of *Gegenstand*s into Phenomena and Noumena." When appearances are thought as *Gegenstand*s "according to the unity of the categories," they are called Phenomena. If, however, I presume a thing, as "the mere *Gegenstand* of the understanding," and equally, an "intuition" of a nonsensible kind, such things are called Noumena or Intelligibles. Accordant with the definition of *Gegenstand* as *realitas phenomenon* (A166), the distinction between phenomenal and noumenal *Gegenstand*s revolves around the question whether they are possible referential contents of sensible intuition (cf. A249).

In trying to elucidate this, Kant makes his first use of Transcendental *Objekt* since the Aesthetic (A46):

> All our representations are in fact related through the understanding to some *Objekt*, and, since appearances are nothing but representations, so the understanding relates them to a Something, as the *Gegenstand* of sensible intuition; however, this Something is so far only the Transcendental *Objekt*. This means, however, a Something = X, of which we certainly know nothing . . . but only as a correlate of the unity of apperception to the unity of a manifold in sensible intuition . . . through which the understanding secures the unity of the same [correlation] in the concept of a *Gegenstand*. This Transcendental *Objekt* does not permit itself to be separated from the sensible data, since then nothing remains through which it might be thought. It is therefore no *Gegenstand* of knowledge in itself but only the representation of appearances under the concept of a *Gegenstand* as such through which the manifold of these appearances is determinable. [A250–51]

At first blush this might seem to be compounding distinctions only to identify them. The Principle of Synthetic Judgments must be borne in mind, however. The cognitive principles of empirical *Gegenstand*s are the principles of my possibility of experiencing them. Although the intentional directions of *Gegenstand* and *Objekt* are in opposite directions, they must, on this principle, look very much alike in the outlook of the experiencing subject. Thus the categorial description of any possible empirical referent, i.e., the Transcendental *Objekt*, must be the same as the modes which describe the appearing *Gegenstand*. This dual perspectival consideration seems to undergird Kant's differentiation. This reading seems borne out in A253: "The *Objekt* to which I relate the appearance as such is the Transcendental *Gegenstand*, i.e., the wholly undetermined thought of Something as such. This cannot be called Noumenon . . . [for I only know it as] the *Gegenstand* of a sensible intuition as such" and nothing of it as it is in itself.[10]

It is clear from this citation that, at least in this discussion, neither

264

the Transcendental *Gegenstand* nor the Transcendental *Objekt* can be identified as thing–itself. On my reading, the latter certainly cannot be; the former could perhaps be so identified only if it is not particularized but is taken as the generalized categorial description of any entity which, as particularized appearance, can enter into the awareness of human consciousness. From the point of outlook of the human subject, the *Objekt* of thought is here perhaps akin to a general intellectual receptivity for external *Gegenstands* in their generality so as to become particularized referents of our cognitive activity.

Concepts of Reflection

Appended to the end of the Analytic is a critical examination of central Leibnizian concepts, in a discussion clarifying essential similarities to the monadological idealism from which the Critical philosophy developed. This discussion has its own intrinsic interest; but the note which follows it can be read as an essay differentiating *Gegenstand* from *Objekt*. Both terms are repeatedly used, but differentiation is evident; 'Transcendental *Gegenstand*' does not appear, though '*intelligible Gegenstands*' appears once (A286); Transcendental *Objekt* appears twice (A277 and A288).

Leibniz did not differentiate as concepts the *Gegenstands* of the senses in the understanding alone, without a separate consideration of their "place in intuition in which only the *Gegenstands* can be given"; therefore, he could not consider the "transcendental place of these concepts (whether the *Objekt* should be counted under appearances or under things themselves)" (A271). Consequently, he is criticized for extending the principle of the Identity of Indiscernibles to the *Gegenstands* of sense. *Objekt* is used as purely conceptual, as an entity of the Understanding alone; *Gegenstand*, as is increasingly usual, is used as a sense referent.

After criticizing Leibniz's thesis that things cannot logically conflict, Kant suggests the proper function of the monadology to be to distinguish inner from outer; finally he criticizes Leibniz for intellectualizing time and space instead of recognizing them as forms of sensibility; Kant reminds us of his own thesis: "What things as such may be I do not know and also need not know, since a thing can never occur for me except in the appearance" (A277).

In similar fashion matter is to be understood as a *substantia phenomenon*. What its interiority may be for pure understanding is a "mere whim, for this is throughout no *Gegenstand* for pure understanding; the Transcendental *Objekt*, however, may be the ground of this appearance which we name matter, and is a mere Something, of which we would be able to understand nothing, [even] what it may be, even if someone should tell us" (A277). The inner nature of the things we experience are beyond all possible human understanding; "transcendental questions which go beyond nature" cannot be answered by human reason because all observation, even of our own minds, is by means of the only mode of outlook we have, the form of inner sense. "The relation [of our sensibility] to an *Objekt*, and what the transcendental ground of this unity may be, lies without doubt too deeply hidden" (A278).

"Outside of appearances," Kant insists, "we cannot assume *Gegenstand*s of pure thinking, i.e., Noumena, since they have no positive meaning to offer" (A287). Thinking, however, is not in itself a product of the senses and thus is not limited by them; yet it does not follow that it has a pure "use of its own without being accompanied by sensibility, since it is then without *Objekt*" (A287). "One cannot name the Noumenon such an *Objekt* because this signifies the problematic concept of a *Gegenstand for* a wholly different intuition and a wholly different understanding from ours" (A287). The question of noumenality is a matter not of an *Objekt* but of the limitation of human sensibility. Insofar as sensible intuition does not extend to all things, there "remains for us a place for additional and other *Gegenstand*s" (A288), and therefore the question of noumenality cannot be decided by us and must remain open:

> Understanding limits sensibility accordingly without widening its own fields; as it warns sensibility that it may not pretend to go to things themselves, but merely to appearances, so it thinks for itself a *Gegenstand* as such but only as Transcendental *Objekt*, which is the prime source [*Ursache*] of the appearance (thereby not itself appearance). [A288]

and to which categorial concepts cannot be applicable. "We will name this *Objekt* Noumenon, since the representation of it is not sensible, so it leaves us free to do so" (A288). Although we think something generally, not only do we determine it according to the laws of sensibility, but also we represent it generally as *Gegenstand in abstracto*, by thought alone; this is "a mere logical form without content . . . as the *Objekt* exists in itself (Noumenon) without regard for the intuition which is limited to our senses" (A289).[11]

In the Aesthetic, the one use of Transcendental *Objekt* (A46) could have been taken as either thing–itself or referent of the thinking act. Insofar as the nature of thinking is developed only in the Analytic, thus leaving the Aesthetic as an introductory chapter which sets up the problematic, that ambiguity may be excusable. In the Analytic a distinction has generally been made between *Gegenstand* as the cognitive referent and *Objekt* that is thought. As each is raised to transcendental status, each comes to look like a correlate of the other; on the basis of the Highest Principle of Synthetic Judgments this is as it should be, for the *Objekt* of cognitive thinking must present the same delineations as the generalized predicates of the *Gegenstand* that can be known, if cognition is to take place.

The differentiation seems clear. Roughly speaking, *Gegenstand* is taken in the sense of thing–ness; in contrast, *Objekt* is usually taken as the product (and necessary instrument) of the imaginative intellect, mediating between knowing subject and *Gegenstand* that is to be known; in its cognitive functioning, the notion of *Objekt* thus correlates with that of *Gegenstand*. As suggested toward the end, however, as the intellect's activity becomes more speculative, it is in terms of *Objekt*s of imaginative thought, not 'external' *Gegenstand*s, that the mind finds its own movement.

If it is, indeed, true that the Dialectic is the obverse (and thereby the confirmation) of the cognitive limits pronounced in the Analytic, the use of these terms, as transcendental, should be illuminating. Transcendental *Gegenstand* and Transcendental *Objekt* are used with some frequency in three sections of the Dialectic—in the Paralogisms, in sections of the Antinomies, and, finally, in Kant's attempts, in discussing arguments concerning divine being, to treat of the Natural Dialectic of Human Reason. For the sake of brevity, I merely direct attention to these passages.

The Paralogisms of Pure Reason

In this discussion of transcendental subjectivity (already presented in the Synthesis of Recognition in the Deduction) Transcendental *Gegenstand* appears five times and Transcendental *Objekt* only twice:

1. Under the Second Paralogism: Of Simplicity:
  a. In A358 we are told that outer sense is directed to external *Gegenstand*s, but not to those internal states which ground external appearances and permit us to be affected by them; "this Something, considered, as Noumenon (or better, as Transcendental

Gegenstand)" can still be thought by us, even if we cannot ascribe categorial predicates to it as an *Objekt*. The Transcendental *Gegenstand*, described as noumenally real, apparently is the personal subject as such. *Objekt* is left unexplained as perhaps the imaginative act of thought which is self–affecting in its working.

b. In A361 we accept the notion of the soul or thinking 'I' as possibly a simple substance, while refusing to concede that doing so implies any extension of knowledge; still we might claim "the thinking *I*, the soul (a name for the Transcendental *Gegenstand* of inner sense) is simple." Although externality has now been left behind, the meaning is accordant, as Transcendental *Gegenstand* is here identified as a real entity, which underlies its own appearances to inner sense and is not merely the referent of thinking.

2. Under the Third Paralogism: Of Personality (A365–66):
The complexities of this section preclude elucidation in this brief compass. A contrast is drawn between the belief in matter and the personal self: "What matter may be for a thing itself (Transcendental *Objekt*) is completely unknown." Although we can observe its persistence as something outer, the only way in which I can observe my own 'I' is "by changes of representations, [for] I have no other correlate of my comparison than once again myself with the general determinations of my consciousness." All aspects of the concept of myself and the unity of its qualities "belong to myself as *Objekt*." The *idea* of the self, confined in thought, is not a *Gegenstand*, because it represents no externality but is an *Objekt* to its own thinking.

3. Under the Fourth Paralogism: Of Ideality:
a. In A372–73, Kant identifies transcendental idealism with the Cartesian 'cogito, ergo sum' and reminds us that even if we presume the source of appearances to be in external somethings taken as transcendental, the *Gegenstands* to which we refer our representations are to be met with only in consciousness. "The Transcendental *Gegenstand* is, in the outlook of inner as of outer intuition, equally unknown."

b. In A379–80, Kant continues discussion of the ideality of outer appearances, a doctrine "already demonstrated in the Transcendental Aesthetic independently of these consequences which we could not at that time foresee"; his entire discussion is in terms of *Gegenstands* until he comes back to the question of the 'I':

I, represented through inner sense in time and *Gegenstand*s in space outside of me are wholly different appearances, but they are not thereby thought as different things. The Transcendental

Objekt, which lies at the ground of outer appearances, equally that of inner intuition, is neither matter nor a thinking entity in itself, but a ground, to us unknown, of appearances which give to hand the empirical concept of the first as of the second kind.

Again, *Objekt* is given to us, somehow, from within ourselves as thinking constituted by the limits of possible experience, while the *Gegenstand*s of the senses are external entities. The Transcendental *Objekt* is used here just because the ground of possible experience of both inner and outer appearances is grounded *in us*, in our capacity to have experiential concepts of experiential *Gegenstand*s, even if we cannot push our inquiry beyond the bounds of sensibility to ask why.

c. In A390, Kant discusses the source [*Ursache*] of our experiences; all the passages refer to empirical *Gegenstand*s. In a polemical passage he writes: "What the true (Transcendental) *Gegenstand* of our outer senses is cannot be the source of those representations (appearances)." The source of our experience is, again, in us.

d. In A393–94 he asks how outer intuition, i.e., space, can be possible for a thinking subject: "This gap in our knowledge can never be filled, but indicates only that one ascribes outer appearances to a Transcendental *Gegenstand*, which is the source of the kind of representation." Indeed, in experience, we treat appearances as though they were *Gegenstand*s in themselves without concerning ourselves about their possibility. But if we would go "beyond that boundary, the concept of a Transcendental *Gegenstand* is necessary." In the paragraph that follows, the phrase "Transcendental *Gegenstand*" is used twice in the same way.

The Antinomies

After presenting the four Antinomies, Kant seeks a transcendental solution to the problem they pose. In that discussion the concept of the Transcendental *Gegenstand* is invoked seven times, and that of the Transcendental *Objekt* twice.

1. Under "Of the Transcendental Problems of Pure Reason Insofar as They Absolutely Can Be Soluble," A478–79:

Insofar as any question of ours may be answered, it must "arise from the same source" as the question to which it responds. Transcendental philosophy thus asks whether any question concerning an *Objekt* presented through pure reason may be answerable. At least moral questions are exempt from any disclaimer, for we can have no moral obligation to right and wrong that is beyond our knowledge. But with regard to the natural order, the *Gegenstand* must be given empirically, and if "the *Gegenstand* is Transcendental and thereby itself unknown, e.g., whether the Something whose appearance (in us) is thought (soul), to be a simple being in itself, whether it provides in itself a source of all things together, which is absolutely necessary, etc.," we must seek a *Gegenstand* for the idea; even if the Transcendental *Gegenstand* is unknown to us, it is not thereby impossible.

The Transcendental Subject, Kant adds in a long note, is not itself appearance and "is therefore not *given* as a *Gegenstand*"; that is, the categories do not meet the requirement of sensible intuition for their application. It is with regard to the categories "to which the question is really set." Our answerable questions, therefore, are always concerned with a thing, an entity, not as itself but only as a *Gegenstand* of possible experience.

Two points should be noted: first, the sole use of '*Objekt*' concerns that which is presented to pure reason out of itself, almost as the grammatical referent of a thinking; second, *Gegenstand*, empirical or transcendental, is conceived as outside the process of thought, that *to which* thought refers; the Transcendental *Gegenstand* is thus implicitly distinguished from the thing–itself (cf. A479, last three lines) and seems to be (as the note indicates) the categorial description of that which can be presented through sense intuition.

2. Under the heading "Transcendental Idealism as the Key to the Unraveling of the Cosmological Dialectic":

a. In A494: A sharp distinction is here offered between the two terms. *Gegenstand* is specifically defined as "representations . . . insofar as they are connected . . . in space and time, and are determinable according to the laws of the unity of experience." *Objekt*, however, in the following sentence, is "the nonsensible source of those representations which is wholly unknown . . . and cannot be intuited." A *Gegenstand* would have to be representable in the forms of space and time; however, "the Transcendental *Objekt* we may call the merely intelligible source of appearances as such"; it is to such "Transcendental *Objekt* that we can ascribe the whole extent and connection of our possible perceptions and say that it is given in itself prior to all appearances." If these appearances are to be ascribed to "an actual *Gegenstand*," it must be within the limits of the rules of the unity of experience.

b. In A495: If perception, under the rules of the unity of experience, is to mark out the actual *Gegenstand*s to which it refers, perception always takes place as a present experience applying (instantiating) the conditions of possible experience. But present perception is taken to imply a continuity with that which preceded it. For us, then, to say that the "*Gegenstand*s of past time are actual" means that "the actual things of past time are given in the Transcendental *Gegenstand* of experience." By thinking a regressive series, with the guidance of either history or laws of sequential connection, present empirical perception leads back to a past succession as conditions leading to what is presently seen.

If the Transcendental *Gegenstand* is the way in which we must conceive, beyond present knowledge, the ground of those *Gegenstand*s which appear as the constituents of experience, the Transcendental *Gegenstand* becomes necessary for the construction of a regressive time series from which the presently appearing *Gegenstand*s arise. Because experience consists in what appears as present, it also consists in a certain continuity with the past; the presence of the past in current presentations is represented to us in the understanding of any apprehensive act.

In the Aesthetic, Kant set up the problem to which, in large measure, the balance of the *Critique* responds.[12] Kant is here using the Transcendental *Gegenstand* as a conceptual instrument prerequisite to any notion of sequential causality; with it we can integrate our continually changing current representations into a sequential continuity so that the persistence [*Beharrlichkeit*] of substance, the sequential relations of causal efficacy (the 'principle of production' in A), and the continuity of the reciprocity of influence and effect permit a rational comprehension of the systematic relations which the appearances of things suggest as they enter into our representational schema. Used in this way, the Transcendental *Gegenstand* shows that our conception of the ground of our representations is independent of the existence of our perceptual acts.

3. Under "Possibility of Causality Through Freedom":

a. A538: This section starts with a definition of 'intelligible': "I name that in a *Gegenstand* of the senses, which is itself not appearance, *intelligible*." All appearances, we are now told, rest on a Transcendental *Gegenstand*, since they are not things but representations; this Transcendental *Gegenstand* may have ascribed to it a double character: first, that of appearing as a basis or source which is not an appearance although its effect is met in appearance, and, second, also its "intelligible character through which it is indeed the source of each act as appearance." In the first case we call it the "thing in the appearance"; in the second, "the thing itself."

As intelligible, it does not, Kant tells us, stand under "time determinations" just because time "is only the condition of appearances, not of things–themselves." Such intelligible ground cannot be representable in an empirical series; it cannot be known (for it cannot be perceived); but we can think it just "as we must place a Transcendental *Gegenstand* at the ground of appearances" in our thinking about them.

In contrast to other moves, the Transcendental *Gegenstand* is here identified as the thing–itself in one of the two ways in which it is to be understood. But again, it refers to what underlies those 'external' 'things' appearing to us as representations, and it is a conceptual instrument for thinking coherently in a unity of possible experience.

b. A545: As we ascend from the empirical *Gegenstand* to the Transcendental *Gegenstand* the acting subject may be seen first as phenomenal source bound up with nature, and then as noumenal and thereby purely intelligible. Admonishing us not to seek explanation of empirical representations on this higher level, the intelligible character of the acting subject is yet that "transcendental source of the empirical [character]" which "serves as its sensible sign" but which remains unknown (A546).

What occurs here is reiteration of identification (cf. A361)—of the Transcendental *Gegenstand* as noumenal and also as the Transcendental Subject, whose reality is necessarily presupposed in its empirical manifestations.

c. A557: After an excursus on the freedom of moral reason which manifests itself in empirical happenings, Kant concludes by saying that the causality of freedom permits us to reason to an intelligible cause but not beyond it. And the Transcendental *Gegenstand* is again described as the "Transcendental *Gegenstand* of our outer sensible intuition" which affords us intuitions in space.

4. Under the heading "Closing Remark on the Whole Antinomy of Pure Reason" (A565):

This last paragraph seeks to effect the transition from the Antinomies to the next chapter of the Dialectic, "The Ideal of Pure Reason," or God. We have here one more use of the term Transcendental *Objekt*.

When reason views the totality of the conditions of the sensible world and considers its *Gegenstand*s, Kant tells us, our ideas are transcendental or cosmological; but when the unconditioned ("with which we are really concerned") is posited as wholly outside the sense world, and thereby beyond all possible experience, Ideas become *transcendent*. As such they detach themselves from experience and "make *Gegenstand*s for themselves" which cannot be derived from experience but which rest completely on a priori concepts. "Such transcendent Ideas have a merely intelligible *Gegenstand*, which, as Transcendental *Objekt*, of which one knows nothing . . . [is] a mere thing of thought [*Gedankending*]." It cannot establish the possibility of any particular *Gegenstand*.[13]

The Ideal of Pure Reason

In discussing the traditional attempts to prove the existence of God, as the 'ideal of Pure Reason,' Kant uses Transcendental *Gegenstand* three times and the term Transcendental *Objekt* once. Perhaps more clearly than in any previous section, this final chapter of the Dialectic delineates the distinction between the two terms.

1. Under the heading "Of the Transcendental Ideal" (A579):

a. Kant begins the section in which the discussion takes place by offering a definition of 'ideal'. It is two steps beyond the categories in dealing with 'objective reality'; the first step beyond are the 'Ideas' which are to be distinguished from categories in that "no appearance can be found permitting them to be represented as such *in concreto*" (A567). But the 'ideal' claims to represent not merely concretely but also as individual: "Still further removed from objective reality then the Idea is that which I call the Ideal by which I understand the Idea, not merely *in concreto*, but *in individuo*, i.e., as an individual thing determinable or even determined through the Idea alone" (A568). An ideal, he tells us, was for Plato "an *Idea of the divine understanding*, an individual *Gegenstand* in the pure intuition of the same [*Gegenstand*] . . . and the basic ground [*Urgrund*] of all imitations in the appearance" (A568).

Unlike Plato, Kant claims that human reason has ideas and ideals which do not have creative power but do have practical power (as regulative). Thus the Ideal of pure reason, "much more the highest reality, underlies the possibility of all things as a ground, and not as their content or summary [*Inbegriff*]" (A579); "consequently, the manifoldness of the possibility of things" rests not on the limitation of the prime being [*Urwesen*] but on its complete issue or result [*Folge*]." "The concept of one such being is the concept of *God*, thought in transcendental understanding, and so the Ideal of pure reason is the *Gegenstand* of a transcendental theology" (A580).

In the passages which follow, Kant repeatedly refers to the *Gegenstand*s of the senses, which are all that can be given to us. Thus nothing can be a "*Gegenstand* for us" unless it presupposes the summary [*Inbegriff*] of all "empirical reality."

Such empirical *Gegenstand*s, Kant argues, must be presumed by us to rest on a Transcendental *Gegenstand* which is conceived by pure reason as the Ideal of pure reason, as the ground of things appearing to us in our representations. Conceived as a primal necessary being, it is beyond investigation but presumed as binding the ground of all possible experiences together (cf. A585).

Clearly, whether it is conceived as an empirical referent of representation or as the ultimate presupposition of a priori reason serving as the ground of that with which understanding is qualified to deal, this *Gegenstand* is conceived as an 'outside–of–us' referent whose being is not dependent on being thought by us, though it is by virtue of being thought that it is conceived as thinkable by us.

b. A591: Although the term Transcendental *Gegenstand* is not used in this concluding–section paragraph, the concept of God is described as "the *transcendental concept*" which is the goal of all of reason's endeavors.

2. Under the heading "Of the Impossibility of the Cosmological Proof of God's Existence" (A613):

The one use here of Transcendental *Objekt* refers not to what is given in appearances but to what we bring to the apprehension of those things that and as they appear:

The Transcendental *Objekt*—lying at the ground of appearances, and with it the reason why our sensibility has much more applicability to these rather than other higher conditions—is and remains for us inscrutable even though the fact [*Sache*] itself is indeed given but is just not comprehended.

An ideal of pure reason, however, given from our reason alone, can be investigated as such, for it is not given as a thinkable *Gegenstand*, but as Transcendental *Objekt*, "as mere idea" (A614).

3. Under the heading "Of the Final Purpose of the Natural Dialectic of Human Reason" (A678–79):

a. The transcendental idea of God, Kant tells us, cannot determine the validity of the concept; it merely provides us with that whereof "all empirical reality grounds its highest and necessary unity" (A675). As the ground of the fundamental concepts by which experience is organized, such a being would have to be outside the world; such concepts "can indeed be used for the explanation of the possibility of the things in the sense world, but not the possibility of the world as a whole as such, since this ground of explanation must be outside the world and thus no *Gegenstand* of experience" (A677). As such, "I in no way require, and am also not warranted to require, that I know this *Gegenstand* of my idea as to what it may be in itself."

"If we cast our glance now at the Transcendental *Gegenstand* of our Idea, we see that we cannot presuppose its actuality [*Wirklichkeit*] according to the concepts of reality, substance, causality, etc.," since these concepts have application only to the world of sensibility. "Therefore, the supposition of reason of a highest being [*höchsten Wesen*] as the supreme source [*oberster Ursache*] is a merely relative thought with regard to the systematic unity of the sense world and is a mere Something in the Idea of which we have no concept as to what it might be in itself." (A679).

God is then conceived by us as a Transcendental *Gegenstand*, ultimate, self–subsistent, the source of all we may know as appearances through sense by use of the understanding. God is conceived not only outside our own thinking but outside the world in which we are and about which we think. True to Kant's now–developed usage, Transcendental *Gegenstand* is used as refering to the external intentional referent of an idea, rather than to the accusative (grammatical) referent of thinking as such. As on the empirical, so on this supremely transcendental (and transcendent), level, God is conceived as existent, independent of thought, and as necessarily presupposed even if no concept we may have may be adequate to what that supreme *Gegenstand* may be. All then that my representations may accomplish is to establish connections "*as if* they were arrangements of a highest reason, of which ours is a weak imitation" (A678).

   b. A698: Again, approaching the end of the section, Kant identifies God as necessarily presupposed by us as the ground of the world of things, as of the things–themselves; God is then a Transcendental *Gegenstand* for human reason in its quest to unify in experience its world of possible experience:

> . . . can we still assume (one will continue to ask) one single, wise, and supreme originator of the world [*Welturheber*]? *Without all doubt*; and not this alone, but we must presuppose such an originating being. But do we then extend our knowledge over the field of possible experience? *No way.* For we have only presupposed a Something, of which we have no concept as to what it may be in itself (a merely Transcendental *Gegenstand*) . . .

which, in relation to systems of purposive order of the structure of the world, we have to think according to analogies from empirical concepts and which, thus, as far as knowledge is concerned, remains a necessarily presupposed but nevertheless unknown being.

III

In the preceding pages, I have tried, by textual examination, to discover what Kant might have intended as he worked out his developing distinction between Transcendental *Gegenstand* and Transcendental *Objekt*. I stated my conclusion at the outset so that the reader could be alerted to test it as the evidence was then presented. If it is agreed that the reading is correct—that Kant managed to establish, despite an occasional lapse, some clearcut distinction between these two concepts—this would have some far–reaching implications for the reinterpretation of the Critical philosophy and would also have much to say to the speculative interests of the Critical thinker. Neither of these consequents can be pursued here, but at least a discussion may have been provoked, and the way may have been prepared.[14]

NOTES

1. Norman Kemp Smith, *A Commentary to Kant's 'Critique of Pure Reason'* (New York: Humanities Press, 1950), p. 89.
2. Some other terms—but by no means a complete list—which have been similarly confounded in translations and commentaries, but which Kant's text seems generally to have kept apart are *Existenz* and *Dasein*, *Princip* and *Grundsatz*, *Beharrlichkeit* and *Beständlichkeit*, *Sache* and *Ding*, and *Etwas* and *etwas*.
3. Cf., e.g., Smith, *A Commentary*, pp. 79–88.
4. Because of the need for greater terminological exactness than the English translations provide, all the quotations herein are directly translated from the edition of the first *Critique* published by Verlag von Felix Meiner. N.B.: To aid visual identification, the initial 't' in both Transcendental *Gegenstand* and Transcendental *Objekt* has been capitalized; no inference of reification should be drawn from this.
5. Cf. entries under *"Object, Objekt"* and *"Objectiv, Objectivisch"* in Jacob Grimm and Wilhelm Grimm, *Deutsches Wörterbuch* (Leipzig: S. Hirzel, 1897), p. 1109.
6. Although I have reluctantly retained the standard English rendering of *Anschauung* as 'intuition', Kant's meaning might be more clearly conveyed in most passages by taking it in the more literal sense of 'outlook'.
7. Three passages in the B Deduction augment the differentiation (though without explicit statement of transcendental objectivity): (1) in section 22 (B146), *Gegenstand* is used twice to refer to objects of experience; (2) in section 23 (B149), Kant speaks of *Objekt* as the referent of a nonsensible intuition: even if we suppose it given and represent it to ourselves as sharing no characteristics of a *Gegenstand* of sensible intuition—i.e., it is not extended as spatial, its "duration is no time," and is without change (defined as "succession of determinations in time")—no authentic

knowledge is to be had; (3) in the postscript to section 24 (B154), proceeding from a discussion of the thesis that inner sense represents our own selves to consciousness not as we are in ourselves but as we appear to ourselves, Kant says: "Apperception and its synthetic unity are indeed not one with inner sense; the first, as the source of all unification, goes to the manifold of intuitions as such under the name of the categories, before all sensible intuition goes to *Objekt*s as such." Whereas *Gegenstand* is used to refer to what can be presented through intuitive sensibility, *Objekt* is a different term referring to the act of thinking itself (presumably God's thinking, empowered by nonsensible intuition as Kant held, would concern itself with *Objekt*s, not with the *Gegenstand*s of our sensible referential thinking). N. B.: The phrase "duration is no time" above is no casual phrase; for Kant clearly distinguished *Dauer* ("duration") as a kind of temporal dimension of noumena, from the *Zeit* ("time") which is the form of inner sense. This ascription of *Dauer* to *Objekt*s of a nonsensible intuition, would seem to buttress my reading here of the emerging differentiation of Transcendental *Gegenstand* and Transcendental *Objekt*; cf. note 12.

8. Smith's translation renders both *Gegenstand* and *Objekt* by the word 'object' thus making it useless insofar as this essay in definition is concerned to differentiate them.

9. For example, the thesis of the "Refutation of Idealism" in the second edition (B275) claims to prove "the existence of *Gegenstand*s in space outside of me."

10. In closing the chapter, Kant speaks of the problematic nature of "*intelligible Gegenstand*s" (A259), i.e., *Gegenstand*s of a possibly nonsensible intuition. The concept of such is for us "completely empty" just because our cognitive principles have meaning only as applied to empirical *Gegenstand*s, i.e., appearances in the form of sensible intuition.

11. The Analytic ends with a postscript seeking to divide "the concept of a *Gegenstand* generally [as the] highest concept" without deciding "whether it is Something or Nothing" (A290). Working from the concept of *Nichts* ("Nothing") in the order of the categories, he discriminates four meanings with the observation that an equivalent division of the concept of Something would follow from it. He concludes with the sentence "Negation and the mere form of intuition are, without a real, no *Objekt*s." (A292).

12. N. B.: But *if* time is merely the form of inner sense in which representations of external *Gegenstand*s must be represented for consciousness in order for us to be aware of them, it seems clear that a more 'real' durational order is presumed so that we may make rational sense of the momentary presentations in the sequentialities we comprehend in terms of the Analogies. That this is truly Kant's view can be seen by examining sections of the second *Critique* where duration [*Dauer*] seems treated as noumenal in contrast to the time [*Zeit*] of the human outlook. Cf. A771 and my "The Question of Noumenal Time," *Man and World* 10 (1977): 411–34.

13. The fourth antinomy, however, yields the task of assuming —beyond possible knowledge—a self–subsistent reality, wholly beyond sensibility. The reason is that only in such an intelligible *Gegenstand* may the regressive steps be terminated. Appearances can be seen by us as "contingent kinds of representations of intelligible *Gegenstand*s by such beings which themselves are intelligences." In order to form concepts of such intelligible things—"of which we do not have the slightest knowledge as they are in themselves but yet have to form some concept about them"—we must proceed from empirical temporal concepts by way of analogic reasoning. This step beyond the world of experience is the inquiry into that of any absolutely necessary being.

14. I am deeply indebted to Joseph Doherty, formerly of the University of Munich, for his persistent interest and good counsel, both of which were crucial to the completion of this article. I am also deeply grateful to Wilhelm Würzer, of Duquesne University, for his kindness in reviewing my translations from the German text.

NOTES ON CONTRIBUTORS

RICHARD E. AQUILA is Professor of Philosophy at the University of Tennessee. He has taught at Northwestern University, Duke University and the University of Iowa. His publications include *Intentionality: A Study of Mental Acts, Rhyme or Reason: A Limerick History of Philosophy*, and numerous articles appearing in *Nous, Kant–Studien, Journal of the History of Philosophy* and elsewhere.

GERD BUCHDAHL is Reader in History and Philosophy of Science at the University of Cambridge. He is former chairman of the Department of History and Philosophy of Science, Cambridge, and founder and first chairman of the Department of History and Philosophy of Science at Melbourne University, Australia. Among his several books are *Metaphysics and the Philosophy of Science: The Original Sources, from Descartes to Kant* and *The Image of Newton and Locke in the Age of Reason*. Buchdahl's articles, which have appeared in various books and journals, include several studies in the philosophy of Kant, especially as it bears on the philosophy of science and the light shed thereby on the thought of such diverse figures as Kepler, Newton, Hegel, Schleiden, et al. He is also editor of *Studies in History and Philosophy of Science*.

A. C. GENOVA is Professor of Philosophy and Chairman of the Department of Philosophy at the University of Kansas. He has been awarded research grants from the Ford Foundation, the Council for Philosophical Studies, and the National Endowment for the Arts and Humanities. He publishes widely in national and international journals and is currently at work on a book manuscript on Kant's *Critique of Judgment*.

MOLTKE S. GRAM is Professor of Philosophy at the University of Iowa. He has also held positions at Indiana University and Northwestern University. His publications include *Kant: Disputed Questions, Kant, Ontology and the Apriori*, and *The Ontological Turn*. Currently in press are *The Kantian Heritage, Direct Realism, The Theory of Double Affection* and *The Transcendental Turn*. He was awarded a Fulbright Fellowship in 1963.

PAUL GUYER is Associate Professor of Philosophy at the University of Illinois, Chicago Circle. He has also taught at the University of Pittsburgh and the University of Michigan. Among his publications are *Kant and the Claims of Taste, Essays in Kant's Aesthetics* (edited with Ted Cohen), and articles appearing in *Kant–Studien, Journal of Philosophy, The Journal of Aesthetics, American Philosophical Quarterly* and others. He was awarded an NEH Fellowship for research in Epistemology and Psychology in Kant's Theory of Knowledge.

JAAKKO HINTIKKA (Dr. Phil., University of Helsinki) is Professor of Philosophy at Florida State University. He has held or is currently holding appointments at Stanford University, University of Helsinki, and Academy of Finland. He has authored 13 books and monographs, which have appeared in six languages, and over 200 papers. He is a former President of the American Philosophical Association (Pacific Division), a former President of the International Union of History and Philosophy of Science (Division of LMPS), the John Locke Lecturer at Oxford in 1964, and the Editor–in–Chief of the International Journal *Synthese* in 1965–1976.

PHILIP KITCHER is Associate Professor of Philosophy at the University of Vermont. He has also held positions at Vassar College and the University of Michigan. His articles appear in *Philosophy of Science, Philosophical Quarterly, Journal of Philosophy, The Journal of Philosophical Logic, The Philosophical Review, Nous* and other journals. He has recently finished a book–length manuscript on mathematical knowledge.

CHARLES M. SHEROVER is Professor of Philosophy at Hunter College and a member of the Doctoral Faculty of the City University of New York. He has also been visiting professor at Duquesne University, SUNY–Stony Brook, and the Graduate Faculty of the New School. His publications include *Heidegger, Kant and Time, The Human Experience of Time*, and numerous articles on ethics, political philosophy and the philosophy of time.

Index

Adickes, E.: 53, 97n.
Affection: 52–53, 55, 58, 60–63, 65ff., 70, 74, 153n., 268
Allison, H. E.: 248n.
Ameriks, Karl: 196n.
Amphiboly (of the Reflection of Concepts): 77, 265–66
Analogies (of Experience): 58ff., 68, 114, 159, 190, 194, 245–46, 261, 277n.
Analytic/synthetic distinction: 107, 112, 201
Analyticity: 222–28, 231, 244, 247n.
Anticipations (of Perception): 36n., 114
Antinomy (of Pure Reason): 68, 93–94, 269, 272, 277n.
Appearance: 14–21, 24, 27–34, 34n., 36n., 37n., 39–40, 45, 51–52, 55–58, 60, 62–63, 67–68, 71, 74, 76, 85, 88, 91, 93, 97n., 98n., 109, 112, 131–34, 136, 149ff., 152n., 153n., 154n., 173, 176, 182, 185, 190, 193, 197n., 220–21, 232, 234, 236, 238, 240, 242ff., 254, 256–57, 259, 261–74, 277n.
Apperception: 64, 93, 112, 160–63, 172, 174, 179–86, 188–89, 191ff., 195, 196n., 197n., 198n., 199n., 157ff., 264, 277n.; see also self-consciousness; consciousness, unity of

Apprehension: 11ff., 15, 18–24, 28, 31, 33–34, 109, 146, 171, 182, 188, 255, 261–62
Aquila, Richard: 196n.
Aristotle: 203–204
Austin, John: 116–17, 126n.
Axioms (of Intuition): 36n., 114, 232–35, 237, 239–42, 244–45, 247, 248n.
Ayer, A. J.: 17, 36n.

Beck, L. W.: 160, 196n., 248n.
Bennett, Jonathan: 155n., 198n., 248n.
Berkeley: 12–13, 29, 32, 35n., 40, 46, 48, 67, 95n., 96n., 98n.
Bird, Graham: 159, 196n.
Brentano, Franz: 9–12, 16, 19–22, 33, 34n., 35n., 37n.
Brittan, Gordon G.: 308, 210, 213–14n., 215n.
Broad, C. D.: 151n., 153n.
Bübner, Rüdiger: 126n.

Cassirer, Ernst: 208, 210, 213–14, 215n.
Categories: 45, 52, 56ff., 65–66, 72, 75, 82, 89ff., 95n., 98n., 103–104, 110, 112, 123–24, 157, 160–66, 168ff., 189–90, 192–95, 198n., 236–37, 240, 256, 258ff., 262–63, 266, 270, 273, 277n.
Causality: 41, 51, 59–60, 68, 83, 89, 193–94, 271, 275
Cavell, Stanley: 101, 125n.

Cognition: 42, 44, 48ff., 52, 54, 58, 61, 63–64, 70, 73–74, 78, 85, 87, 97n., 111, 113, 122, 167, 171, 178, 183, 185, 190, 252, 254–57, 260, 262–63, 265, 267

Combination: 59, 122, 163ff., 172, 175–76, 178, 181, 186–87, 192, 197n., 198n., 237–38, 242; *see also* synthesis

Consciousness, Unity of: 160f., 168, 176, 190, 199n., 257ff.; *see also* apperception; self-consciousness

Crawford, Patricia: 126n., 155n.

Dedekind, R.: 249n.

Deduction: metaphysical, 103–104, 110, 121, 123–24, 177; transcendental, 42, 64, 87–88, 103ff., 114, 124, 157–63, 165ff., 171, 174, 176–80, 182ff., 190, 192ff., 196n., 197n., 198n., 199n., 232, 236–37, 239, 243–44, 248n., 255, 259, 263, 267, 276n.

Descartes, René: 14–15, 36n., 46, 48, 63, 95, 96n., 98n., 197n., 206

Eberhard, G.: 63, 228, 232, 246
Erdmann, Benno: 259
Euclid: 203ff., 211, 213, 215n.
Ewing, A. C.: 248n.

Feyerabend, Paul: 86
Firth, Roderick: 25, 37n.
Frege, Gottlob: 116, 241, 248n., 249n.

Geometry: 204ff., 209, 211–14, 215n., 234–35, 240–41, 243

Gram, M. S.: 105, 109, 125n., 126n.
Grice, Paul: 116–17

Habermas, Jürgen: 41, 47, 87
Heidegger, Martin: 41, 44, 47, 95n.
Henrich, Dieter: 159, 196n., 197n., 198n., 199n.
Herz, Marcus: 190
Hintikka, Jaakko: 152n., 214n.
Howell, Robert: 36n., 198n.
Hume, David: 13, 40, 46, 48, 60f., 67, 96n., 98n., 187
Husserl, Edmund: 9, 34n., 39, 43–44, 74, 76, 95n., 96n.

Idea, transcendental: 88ff., 92–93, 273
Ideal (of Pure Reason): 273–74
Imagination: 36n., 37n., 48, 54–55, 58, 65, 79, 97n., 98n., 144, 165, 173, 183, 192, 201, 207, 237, 248n.
Intuition: 9, 14, 22–25, 27–31, 34n., 35n., 37n., 50, 55–56, 58, 61–62, 64–65, 72, 74–75, 77, 90, 93, 109, 111ff., 115, 122, 134–35, 138, 145, 153n., 158–59, 164–65, 169–70, 177, 181–85, 188, 190, 192, 201–202, 204–207, 210–13, 214n., 217, 226, 234–43, 245–46, 254–55, 257ff., 263–66, 269f., 273, 276n., 277n.; formal, 56, 237–38; form of, 14, 23–24, 29, 50, 56, 110, 132–39, 164, 192, 199n., 235, 237; (*see also* space; time; sensibility); intellectual, 46, 48, 68ff.

Judgment: 15, 26, 31–32, 57, 121, 159–60, 162, 166–70, 174–78, 183, 189–90, 192–93, 195, 197n., 198n., 217, 219, 222, 229, 248n., 263; analytic, 209ff., 225, 228–29, 248n., 260; synthetic apriori, 71, 112–13, 123, 208, 210–11, 245–46, 248n., 253, 258, 260; of experience, 56, 169, 197n.; of perception, 55, 57, 169, 197n.

Katz, Jerrold J.: 117, 126n.
Kaulbach, F.: 214n.
Knowledge, synthetic apriori: 71, 85, 107, 113, 123, 158, 162, 170, 222, 231f., 246
Körner, Stephen: 125n.
Kripke, Saul: 247n.
Kuhn, Thomas: 86

Leibniz, Gottfried Wilhelm: 13, 40ff., 44ff., 48–49, 63, 67, 95n., 98n., 113, 209, 214n., 220, 265
Locke, John: 12, 48, 63, 95, 98n., 185

Mathematics: 202ff., 206, 209, 217–18, 232ff., 236, 238–39, 241, 244–45, 248n.; synthesis in, 205–209, 212–13, 234; and mathematical construction, 201–202, 205–206
Melnick, Arthur: 37n., 198n., 248n.
Mill, J. S.: 227, 247n.
Mittelstrass, Jürgen: 214n.
Moore, G.E.: 151n.

Newton, Sir Isaac: 80, 82, 95

Noumenon: 39, 46, 48, 53, 69, 73, 75–79, 263–64, 266ff., 272, 277n.

Object, transcendental: 44, 47–48, 50ff., 54, 62, 64–65, 67–70, 72, 77ff., 88–93, 96n., 251–58, 260ff., 264–76&n.
Ontology: 39ff., 43ff., 53, 58, 65–66, 73–74, 80, 82–85, 88, 91, 93, 95n., 96n.

Paralogisms (of Pure Reason): 131ff., 135ff., 141, 146, 149–50, 152n., 154n., 155n., 267–68
Parsons, C.: 214n.
Paton, H. J.: 248n.
Patzig, Günther: 98n.
Peirce, C. S.: 205, 214n.
Perception: 9–13, 15, 23, 25–26, 28, 30, 32, 34, 41–42, 48, 58, 64, 89, 131–32, 134–39, 144, 147–48, 152n., 154n., 155n., 159–60, 162, 167, 169, 175–76, 185, 192–93, 197n., 208, 236, 242, 244, 261, 270–71
Phenomenon: 33, 40, 48, 51, 56, 76, 80, 82, 138, 263, 265
Plato: 40, 273
Postulates (of Empirical Thought): 114, 140, 142ff., 146, 148ff.
Prauss, Gerald: 36n., 53, 97n., 197n.
Putnam, Hilary: 97n., 247n.

Quine, W. V. O.: 125n., 218, 222, 224–25, 227, 229, 247n., 248n.

Reason: 60, 71, 80, 82–83, 87, 89, 91–94, 217, 269, 272ff.; constitutive and regulative employment of, 85–86, 88, 92

Receptivity: 12–15, 59, 61, 64, 74, 255

Recognition, synthesis of: 171, 256, 267; *see also* synthesis; combination

Refutation of Idealism: 32, 104, 127, 135–38, 141–42, 146–48, 151, 190, 194, 277n.; *see also* Postulates (of Empirical Thought)

Representations: 17–18, 34n., 57–58, 63ff., 67, 110, 112, 121ff., 135, 139, 148ff., 159ff., 163–68, 170–78, 180–94, 197n., 198n., 199n., 201, 204, 206, 236ff., 240–43, 248n., 254–61, 264, 268–69, 271–72, 274–75, 277n.

Reproduction, synthesis of: 165, 172f.; *see also* synthesis; combination

Rorty, Richard: 100, 125n.

Rosenberg, Jay: 125n.

Russell, Bertrand: 115

Schematism/schematization/schemata: 45, 56, 65, 72, 90, 92, 110, 123, 194, 240, 260

Schultz, J.: 207, 228, 232, 248n.

Searle, John: 116–17

Self-consciousness: 112, 160–63, 174, 179–80, 182–85, 196n.; *see also* apperception; consciousness, unity of

Sensations/sense data: 9, 11–19, 22–25, 27, 30–31, 33, 34n., 35n., 36n., 37n., 40, 49, 52–53, 55, 57–58, 63, 65, 152n., 154n., 159, 175, 191, 201, 264ff., 275

Sensibility: 45, 47ff., 52, 54–55, 57–58, 61–70, 72–76, 78, 90, 97n., 98n., 122, 237–38, 254ff., 265–66, 269, 274–75, 277n.; *see also* intuition, forms of; space; time

Smith, Norman Kemp: 64, 151n., 152n., 159, 196n., 198n., 199n., 248n., 251, 276n.

Space: 28–29, 36n., 46ff., 55ff., 61–62, 66, 73, 89–90, 96n., 110, 132–35, 138–39, 141–42, 146, 149–50, 153n., 158, 165–66, 178, 193, 201–202, 205, 220, 233–38, 240–43, 245, 249n., 259, 262, 265, 268ff.; *see also* intuition, forms of; sensibility

Spinoza, Baruch: 13, 35n.

Spontaneity: 59, 164

Strawson, P. F.: 70–71, 98n., 104, 108, 115–16, 119, 155n., 159, 248n.

Stroud, Barry: 105, 125n., 126n.

Substance: 41, 46, 142–43, 145–46, 148, 193–94, 246–47, 268, 271, 275

Synthesis: 15–16, 26, 30, 56, 58–59, 65, 89, 93, 103, 109, 112, 122–23, 165, 170, 173, 175, 177, 181–84, 186–89, 191–92, 194–95, 198n., 218, 237, 242, 248n., 257–58, 263, 267; *see also* combination

Thing-in-itself: 29, 31, 33, 36n., 39, 46, 51ff., 60, 63–64, 67–70, 78–79, 90, 93, 97n., 98n., 112, 124, 127, 133–36, 138, 149ff., 151n., 153n., 193, 197n.

Thompson, Manley: 214n

Tieftrunk: 66

Time: 29, 46ff., 55ff., 61–62, 66, 73, 89–90, 96n., 110, 132–35, 138–44, 146–50, 153n., 164ff., 179, 191, 193, 201–202, 205, 220, 233–234, 236–37, 240, 242, 245, 259, 262, 265, 268, 270, 276n., 277n.; *see also* forms of intuition; sensibility

Transcendental aesthetic: 24–25, 135, 139, 150, 155n., 158, 197n., 202, 206ff., 217, 219, 221, 232–40, 243–44, 246, 248n., 249n., 254–55, 263, 267–68, 271

Transcendental analytic: 24, 217–218, 221, 245ff., 263, 265, 267

Transcendental argument: 71, 83, 99, 103–14, 120–25, 154n.

Transcendental dialectic: 80, 267, 272f.; *see also* paralogisms (of Pure Reason); Antinomy (of Pure Reason); ideal (of Pure Reason)

Transcendental illusion: 94; *see*

also transcendental dialectic

Transcendental logic: 50, 113, 255; *see also* transcendental analytic; transcendental dialectic

Transcendental reflection: 71–74; *see also* Amphiboly (of the Reflection of Concepts)

Understanding: 45–49, 52, 54–55, 57–58, 65, 68, 71, 73, 75, 78ff., 83, 87, 89–93, 97n., 98n., 103, 113, 115, 168–69, 176ff., 183, 191–92, 194, 238ff., 260, 263–66, 275

Vaihinger, Hans: 52, 151n., 211, 215n.

Walker, R.: 105, 125n., 248n.

Walsh, W. H.: 248n.

Wilkerson, T. E.: 126n., 152n.

Wittgenstein, Ludwig: 41, 74, 121

Wolff, C.: 209, 214n.

Wolff, R. P.: 97 n., 196n., 248n.